Hoops Ac Ocea

CW00530874

The rise and fall of the Irish basketball team

Conor Meany

Published: 2021

Copyright: Conor Meany

ISBN: 9798495813540

Imprint: Independently published

2

Foreword by Jarlath Regan, creator of the Irishman Abroad Podcast Series

Basketball came to prominence in Ireland and in my life at a very grey time. It was the antithesis of everything conservative, closed off and restrictive about the country. Part of that was the game itself. It couldn't be further from the sodden fields, nut hugger shorts and "don't get fancy" mantra of Gaelic Games at the time. Basketball was about freedom of expression, trickery, dexterity, colour and joy.

In many ways, it was the most American game on earth. America and the players that came here to play in our clubs were as much the attraction to me, my friends and the thousands of kids that took to the sport back then and embraced it and took it with them through their lives. Those players and this game spoke to an optimism and inclusivity that was rare in Ireland at that time. It wasn't about putting the ball in the goal. It was about self-expression and freedom of expression. It was exotic, it was bright and new. It was from another place in this world, where it felt like more was possible than just the county championship. I felt alone a lot of the time as a kid in that Ireland.

Basketball, and the community it gave me, was the first time I, and many others felt like one fit in or had found a group of like-minded people. My family certainly struggle to understand this. The author of this book Conor Meany has captured all of this. He has gone even deeper than I ever thought possible and uncovered what lay on the other side of the rectangular wooden stage I watched these American players play on. The lives and times, the impact of these people and this game on our country can only be understood through a book as beautiful as this.

Maybe you didn't get the basketball bug back then.

After reading this book you will.

Acknowledgements

This book wouldn't have been possible without both the support and contributions of so many people.

Firstly, I'd like to thank my amazing wife Lyndsey for all her love and support. This book became a project to occupy my mind during Covid and grew into something much bigger. Thank you for tolerating the constant late-night Zoom calls and for listening to all the stories as I discovered them.

To Arthur and George, thanks for reminding me throughout, that this wasn't the most important thing in the world, and that you both are.

To the whole Meany family. Basketball has been a big part of our lives and this book was something else that helped share that bond. Your enthusiasm when I sent through the first short stories that led to this book is the reason I kept going. Mum and Dad, thank you for everything you have done to make this possible too.

To Natalie Young, your help and support were incredible throughout. I knew nothing about writing or editing and you helped me more than I ever could have hoped for.

To Mary McGuire thank you for being one of the early guinea pigs with who I shared this. Your enthusiasm and support and early editing helped make this a reality.

To Adam Ingle, thank you for taking the time to create the cover image.

To Jarlath Regan, thank you for taking the chance on me and writing such a wonderful introduction.

Lastly, and most importantly, thank you to all of those contributors who let a novice interview them and put their stories together. I hope that I have been able to do your story some justice.

Dedication

This book is dedicated to my family and to all of the people around Ireland who have volunteered their time and helped basketball to survive and grow over the past 76 years.

Author's Note

The website www.hoopsacrosstheocean.com has been created as a supplementary resource to support this book.

On the site, you will get in-depth overviews of the careers of many of the Irish-American players that feature in this book. It's worth checking the site as you read through the book as it will give greater context to why some of these players sacrificed to play for Ireland.

Disclaimer

This book was written by Conor Meany and does not reflect or contain any views of Basketball Ireland.

Preface

I don't remember the first time I saw a basketball game. I was basically born with a basketball in my hand, as our family lived and breathed the sport throughout my childhood.

We still do today.

When I was eight years old, my dad was serving as the President of Irish Basketball. His work meant that we were often up in the National Basketball Arena, which had just been built the previous year in 1993. At the time, the Arena was the most incredible place I'd ever been, with actual bleachers surrounding the court, the cool varnished look inside and the bizarre roof on the outside.

I remember seeing the Irish team playing for the first time in the Arena back in 1994, and eight-year-old me was mesmerised. Not really by the team or the competition, but by Ireland's 6'10 big man, who at the time was dominating games and helping Ireland beat other countries. I had a new favourite player in the world, and his name was Alan Tomidy.

Honestly, I don't know if I knew Alan's name back in 1994, I just knew he was good, and he was huge. In my mind, he looked like

Max from Streets of Rage (a SEGA Mega Drive game we owned at the time) as he was bigger and stronger than everyone around him. The fact that I didn't know much about Alan was a problem and one that would plague Irish basketball for years. At the time, Ireland was bringing in Irish American players to play on the national team, and by and large, nobody outside of the team had a clue who they were.

Ireland was still coming down from the peak of the domestic game in the eighties, and basketball knowledge beyond our shores was limited (especially compared to today). People could see the NBA mainly on internet highlight-videos or the occasional live game on Channel 4. Basketball had exploded globally after the US Olympic 'Dream Team' in 1992, but the real effects were yet to be seen in Ireland. Outside of the NBA, people only knew major NCAA schools like North Carolina or Michigan State. Watching college games in Ireland wouldn't happen until around 2003, when the North American Sports Network arrived. Going beyond America, if you mentioned basketball alongside names like Olympiakos or Real Madrid, you would be looked at as if you had two heads, although that may still be the same today for most people.

In recent years, I started working for Basketball Ireland, and that same arena is now my office. Through my job I first met Pat Burke, who is pretty well-known in Ireland as the only Irish-born player ever to play in the NBA. Pat is as down to earth and personable as anyone you could meet, and has a genuine desire to help Irish basketball progress. When I chatted to him and started looking up more and more about his history as a player, I quickly realised that his NBA years are actually the least interesting years of a fantastic career. Pat got me thinking back to Alan Tomidy and many of the other players for Ireland I grew up watching. I started wondering who they were, what they had achieved, and why they wanted to play for the country.

What admittedly started as a curiosity about guys like Dan Callahan, ended up in hours of zoom calls with men and women worldwide with connections to Irish basketball. With each call, my appreciation for Irish American history grew, and I quickly started to see how important playing for Ireland was for these players and their families. The group includes former NBA players, EuroLeague and EuroCup veterans, journeymen pros and college stars. All of them were so obliging with their time. What unified them is that they all wanted to talk about Irish basketball because it left a significant mark on their lives. What struck me even more, was many of them are still in contact with each other, as they share a badge of honour, being one of the players who tried to help Ireland progress.

The men's journey was one that should be a simple good-news story for Ireland. They went from being minnows of Europe, not beating any continental opposition before 1977, to becoming a competitive team that vied against Germany and Croatia by 2002. That journey was made possible by the vision of several people involved in Irish basketball and high-level players' willingness to come over and further the Irish cause.

The positive memories of the era are tempered somewhat by the impact that the team's progression had on domestic players in Ireland at the time. From early on in the process, there were doubts about a national team's potential professionalism in a sport that was effectively fully amateur in Ireland at the time.

It raised the question; was it possible for a sport to raise its level and succeed against professional opposition without being fully professional?

In many ways, the rise and fall of the national team mirrored the Celtic Tiger, as the sport rose from poverty in the 1980s to unprecedented wealth by the early 2000s, before eventually crashing back down to earth by the end of the decade. Basketball's story and the decline of the national team is complicated by the fall from grace that the sport suffered in 2010 as the National Federation found itself in €1.2 million of debt.

My dad had the onerous task as a volunteer to keep Irish basketball afloat without much government support. As part of a significant reduction in costs, the national teams were pulled, in a move that proved hugely damaging, particularly to the women's programme that was becoming increasingly competitive at the time. It was a decision that wasn't made lightly, and those who know Paul's love and dedication to the sport, understand it was done as a very last resort.

The lack of external financial support meant that basketball was bailed out from within, which brought resentment from the basketball community who understandably wanted somebody to blame. The men's national team, filled with professional, American-born players, was a more obvious scapegoat than most other options. As a result, the Irish

American era of the national team has been perhaps unfairly tarnished, despite not being directly linked to the financial issues.

Looking back at the journey the team made, it's hard to blame anyone for trying to move Ireland forward in the way that they did. It's only looking back at the decisions with the perspective of hindsight that it's possible to make that judgement. I know there will be a criticism of my review on this, particularly due to Dad's involvement at different points in the journey, and my involvement working for Basketball Ireland. Despite that, I genuinely think that most of the decisions made sense when they were pursued.

In retrospect, what was sadly lost was a connection to the broader sport, once Ireland took a more professional approach around 2000. I'm probably a good example of this, playing in the Super League for many years and on underage national teams during the era. By and large, during that time I had no affinity towards the senior team outside of wanting to see some top-level professionals play in Ireland. My excitement as a young kid watching the team in 1994 was replaced a decade later by a sense of apathy at times.

I sometimes wonder if that feeling would be the same if the situation were happening today. Was the disconnect because I couldn't watch these guys compete professionally and, outside a couple of games in Dublin, I never saw them play? Or was it because I grew up watching the Irish leagues and, outside of a select few, I never saw those same players representing the country? Having learned so much more about the men and women who came to help Ireland compete, I only wish that knew more about them then and that the national team hadn't been allowed to operate in a vacuum by itself.

This book ultimately looks at the relationship between Irish basketball and America. Throughout our history are so many stories of people going in either direction and making a significant impact. Some of these are well known, like Susan Moran's journey to the WNBA or Pat Burke's impact for Ireland. Others are less known and will hopefully be enjoyable for readers.

At the heart of it all, are a group of people who genuinely tried to improve Ireland's basketball situation and did it on the most part for selfless reasons.

I've tried to keep my opinion out of this as much as possible and have allowed those involved to tell the story themselves either directly to me or through the Irish media at the Ftime.

My motivation was simple: I wanted to understand a little more about the players I grew up watching. On top of that, I wanted to add another chapter to the Irish basketball story. If nothing else, hopefully it inspires someone else to add another one of their own.

Contents

Chapter 1: The Standard is a Joke

'The international standard of men's basketball in this country is a joke. It sounds harsh but this is the reality' *'Sunday Independent*, 18 March 1990

In 1990, when Cliona Foley wrote that the Irish men's national team's standard was a joke, it would have been hard for many to argue with her. In truth, the Irish national team was an afterthought for many at the time, as it played second fiddle to a thriving domestic league. In many cases, the national team competed in tournaments never watched by the Irish public and without much success. The general feeling towards the team was 'out of sight, out of mind', as the rare opportunities to see Ireland play were either local Four Countries events or as a competitor in one of Ireland's many invitational club competitions.

Nobody knew at the time, but the national team was halfway through a journey in 1990. Thirteen years before the article was written, Ireland had never beaten any Continental European opposition in competition and were coming off a seventy-nine-point loss in the 1976 Olympic Pre-Qualifiers. And yet thirteen years after the article came out, Ireland found themselves playing in the semi-final round of the

European Championships while fielding a team filled with EuroLeague and NBA experience.

For those involved in the Irish teams at the beginning of the sport's ascension in the late 1970s and early 1980s, the changing nature of international basketball was becoming increasingly evident, and Ireland was struggling to keep up. Most countries were availing of players with dual passports, as the importation of American professional players exploded around the club game in Europe in the late 1960s. As a result, teams were amateur only in name in the Olympic Pre-Qualifiers.

For Ireland, the FIBA rules around eligibility presented an exciting opportunity due to our unique migration history with the USA. Ellis Island, the famous entry point to the United States in New York, was opened just one month after Dr James Naismith invented basketball in 1891. During the sixty-two years of Ellis Island being open, over 3.5 million Irish people passed through on their way to a new life in the USA. This meant a vast number of Americans with Irish parents or grandparents were eligible to come and play for Ireland. For many of these families, 'Irishness' was a critical part of their identity and representing Ireland was an honour unlike any other for them. Ireland just had to find a way to recruit the right players and integrate them into our national teams.

Although the opportunity existed for Irish basketball, those around the game in Ireland were not always convinced that it was the best route to take. The argument favouring the move was that Ireland wasn't producing big players, so couldn't compete against the size we faced in Europe. Those in favour of the strategy hoped that by adding some big Irish Americans, the national team could become more competitive. In turn, it would help the sport grow. The argument against the idea was based initially around the marginalisation of homegrown players. It later developed into questioning the American-born players' motivations and whether they played for Ireland to help the country or simply help themselves.

The uncomfortable truth at home was that many domestic players were already on the outside for personal reasons. For lots of players who thrived domestically in the eighties, international basketball was an afterthought as they focused on the glamour of the domestic game instead. It's hard to blame any of them; at home, guys played in front of packed houses in the league and occasionally on television. Internationally, things were different, as Ireland competed away from the spotlight, and often took heavy beatings.

The stature that the Irish team held during the eighties was not a secret either. Danny Fulton was the national-team coach for many years in the seventies and eighties, and he tells a story about driving from Belfast to the West of Ireland to scout a game. Despite the national-team coach driving over five hours with his family in the car, he could not get his family in with him to see the game. The home club's security turned Fulton's family away as the crowd was already too big that night. Danny was left with no other option than to put his family back in the car and drive straight home again.

Simply put, the national programme struggled for respect.

What was needed to move the international team forward was a hardliner. The ideal candidate would have an irreverence for the status quo and a thick enough skin to follow through on an ambitious vision for the national team.

That man was Enda Byrt.

Enda Byrt served as the international team manager in 1980 under Danny Fulton and then progressed to be a coach of two Irish Junior Men's teams in the mid-eighties. By 1989 he replaced Fulton for the Senior Men's job. His rise to the top position may have surprised some, as he wasn't coaching in the country's top league at the time. Despite any negative perceptions, Byrt's appointment proved to be the catalyst for a seismic shift in the national team's approach and success over the following twenty years.

In many ways, Byrt was a visionary who saw a future for the Irish squad beyond what it was capable of at the time. The fact that he came from a second-division club and wasn't caught up in domestic title challenges likely helped that vision. As a secondary school teacher from Ennistymon in County Clare, Byrt had the ideal combination to take basketball forward: an ambitious plan and a practical determination to make changes. Byrt, in many ways, was ahead of his time, and his ability to connect with Irish America and develop lasting relationships is often taken for granted.

Despite his positive traits, Byrt proved to be a dividing character that enraged parts of the basketball community as he followed his vision. Byrt's strength of thick skin could also be perceived as being bull-headed at times. This approach meant that it was often Byrt's way or the highway for both the IBA (Irish Basketball Association) and many established senior players at the time.

As Byrt took control in 1989, there was an automatic divide between the new coach and many of the top teams in the domestic league who enjoyed unparalleled success and attention. Byrt told the *Irish Independent* back in 1989, 'most people don't give a damn about the Irish team. They are too caught up with the rigours of running national league squads which takes up a lot of time'. [ii]

Enda's own domestic experience meant that he had a different perspective. He had been around the national teams for almost a decade, and he certainly gave a damn and wanted the team to progress. His vision centred on two core themes. One had been clear for many years; Ireland just didn't have the size to compete internationally. Although everyone around the national team knew it for a long time, it was brought home for Byrt in 1984 when away with the Junior Men's team. At the end of the Under 19's tournament, he met the FIBA President of Junior Men's basketball who had been acting as the commissioner, and the message was clear. 'He called me over, and he said, 'Coach I must say one thing to you. With your team here, you make the excellent technical basketball, but you *must* get the high player'.' Finding talented height had always been a significant challenge for Ireland. Yet it was a problem that Enda felt that Irish American recruitment could provide an instant solution to.

The second issue proved to be the more contentious one, and in many ways came to define the entire Irish American era from the early 1990s to long after Enda had gone. To be successful at international level, Ireland could not continue preparing in the same way they had in the past. A more professional approach was needed, even if the players themselves were amateur.

When Byrt took charge of the team, a fitness test of the top domestic players in the country found that they were far off the pace of international sport. Ireland had other disadvantages, but Enda wanted to ensure that the most controllable weakness was addressed. 'It will never be convenient again to be on an Irish team. You are going to have to go out of your way; you have to step out from the crowd. We're asking you to do things that are difficult. You have to do more work. You have to be an uncommon person, and some people have a problem with that. You have to be very hungry to do it.'.[iii]

To Enda, an aggressive full-court game fit with Ireland's mentality and physique. Yet, it was a strategy that required a lot more physical preparation. In 1989, as Byrt was set to lead his first US tour, he spoke to Liam Gorman: We want to gather together the hardcore people who are prepared to work over a three year period. What a player does with their club is not enough – we gave them a summer fitness programme, and during the season they must be prepared to do considerable work on their own. Those going to the US are the ones who handled the programme best. Others were not prepared to live with it all . . . players have to be honest . . . you can play National League and be in pretty good shape – but not in proper shape for international athletics . . . It is not my intention to put out an Irish American basketball team. But if our players are not ready to work at the right level, we are going to have to import players. We need the results.'[iv]

The response to this request from the new coach highlighted how far away from Byrt's vision the thinking on the ground was. In

Cliona Foley's *Sunday Independent* article in 1990, some of the player's thoughts on this new regime were made clear.

'In my opinion, filling out logbooks and doing weights has nothing to do with playing well' said one player. Another added, Enda Byrt is not responsible for the development of basketball in Ireland. His job is to use the best talents available. His present policy of dictatorship has brought the international side into disrepute and is patently short-sighted in the context of an amateur sport.'

This is illuminating, as it highlights the conflict between some of the country's top players and Byrt. Many players wanted to thrive in an amateur sport, yet Byrt was determined to implement a more professional approach to enable Ireland to compete. In '89, Enda announced a very young squad to go on a tour of the States; his first trip with the Irish team. He was instantly accused of ignoring players from some of the country's best teams in Cork, including Neptune. They are the country's most decorated club side and were the league runners-up at the time. Neptune's club chairman, Dave Cody, told the *Evening Echo* that he had no respect for the coaching administration of the Irish team. 'We have no faith in the coaching ability of the team coach or his assistant. The whole selection process is crazy as it stands. The coach insists that potential players attend a summer training programme at Ennistymon, but that's just not on for amateur players who have been playing competitively from the end of August to the beginning of April. The coach wants the players to go straight from a long hard National League and Cup scene into training for the national squad over the summer months on a weekend basis. That's just not on for amateur players. They would get no break at all from basketball if that's the case. It's just not a realistic idea. The coach's overall theory and set-up in relation to the preparation of the national team is wrong and he has to recognise that fact. There is no way he is going to get all the players he wants for a summer training schedule. All our players at Burgerland [Neptune] opted out of this summer again.' [v]

Cody's points around player welfare and management of top players are not without merit. Byrt's hard-line approach undoubtedly ruled out some of the top domestic talents throughout his tenure as head coach. Yet, this new approach to preparation was one that he believed was critical to developing a squad capable of competing internationally.

Not all players were against Byrt's new methodology as he started. One of his early disciples was also quoted in Cliona Foley's article stating, Enda says one star player who occasionally turns up won't turn the team around. Maybe he's right. It's probably better to have nine of us who'll bust our guts. He's not prepared to risk us nine for one or two stars.' Byrt had the advantage of already coaching many of the young players in the squad, so many knew him and his approach before now. He quickly found those players willing to bust their guts for the team and those players reaped the rewards of their commitment over a decade of increasing success.

As Ireland progressed throughout the nineties and beyond Byrt's era into the 2000s, the issue of professionalism continued to be a significant question for everyone involved in the programme and the sport in general. Byrt's initial approach was to create a professional system using unpaid amateur players. For Enda, professionalism was as much about attitude and approach as anything else. Not long after his time as head coach ended, FIBA rules changed, and the path to an actual professional team opened up. Suddenly, the question was whether Ireland could afford to carry domestic players with them rather than recruit in the best possible players to allow the country to compete. Unfortunately, there were very few Irish professionals playing at that time, so the team naturally moved to become increasingly Irish American. The approach led to unparalleled success, but it came at a cost. Incredibly, in 2004 Ireland competed in more than one game with no Irish-developed player on the squad. This issue was one that even those involved in the teams would understand. Former NBA player Pat Burke, who was born in Ireland but raised in the States, summed up the issue. I know that all of us from top to bottom on the roster knew how important it was to have the natural Irish player on the floor participating because there is more of a connection inside that. The first-time viewer on TV at that time, if they heard or were watching a natural Irish-born player, it would have meant more. So we knew that we wanted that to happen. Let's be honest, a lot of us are sitting here, and we are Americanised. We're never going to have that, and I don't care how many interviews you do, you're never going to have that space because you didn't grow up here.'

Despite any negatives that were perceived around the era, Ireland was unquestionably successful on the court during the period. A

Promotions Cup (Ireland's only ever Senior FIBA tournament win), two top-eight finishes in the World University Games, qualification to the European Championship's semi-final round, and an agonising playoff loss with promotion to Europe's A Division were all experienced during the era. Ireland came a long way from not having beaten any team outside of the British Isles by 1977.

In the final paragraph of Cliona Foley's 1990 article on the national team's questionable standard and the direction it was heading, she wrote: For now both sides are stalemated. It will be a long way down the line before Byrt is proven right or wrong.'

We are a long way down the line now. It is time reflect on Ireland's most successful international era and decide whether the ends justified the means.

Chapter 2: The Olympic Dream

Ireland has had limited team success at the Olympic Games. The men's hockey team were only the second Irish team ever to reach the finals when they went to Rio 2016. The first team did so almost seventy years earlier, when the Irish basketball team competed in the London 1948 Olympics.

Those Games were unusual in several ways, as the world tried to regain stability after the Second World War. Great Britain was looking to find a way to show both national strength and a return to business as usual. As a result, they bid to host the games both in 1944 and then again in 1948, winning the latter.

Due to the recent war, both Germany and Japan were not invited to compete, and the Soviet Union decided to send observers with the intention of returning to competition in 1952. Aside from some notable countries' absence, the London Games were also unusual in that no new infrastructure was built and no athletes village was made available. The Games would later be dubbed the 'Austerity Games', with the Americans even flying over food to bypass the food rationing.

Basketball had started to grow worldwide in the thirties. The 1936 Olympic basketball competition was the first appearance of the sport as an official Olympic medal event (there had been a demonstration game in St Louis in 1904), and the only ever outdoor contest. Unfortunately, the sand-based court did not stand up well to poor weather during the final and the basketball as a spectacle was ruined. Over the following twelve years, the game progressed significantly in both North and South America, while it stalled in Europe due to the war. As the Games began in London 1948, twenty-three teams assembled to compete in the first-ever indoor championships.

Ireland's entry to the Games came due to our proximity to London and nothing else. In fact, Ireland did not even have a team ready to compete. Basketball was in its early stages of development, and the idea of international competition was a world away. But with a neighbour hosting the Olympics came an unusual opportunity, and one the recently formed Amateur Basketball Association of Ireland were keen to capitalise on.

The ABAI was formed just three years earlier, with the goal of spreading basketball beyond the army bases around Ireland and out to the civilian population. Basketball had spread globally through different armies, navies and air forces, and Ireland's introduction to the game was no different. By the time the ABAI was invited to London, basketball had been played in Ireland for many years as a form of exercise in barracks. Still, the version played at international level was very different from the Irish game, which used both a heavier ball and emphasised more physicality. In many ways, Ireland played a form of indoor Gaelic football rather than the evolving basketball game. Not to be put off, though, the ABAI contacted the then Minister for Defence, Dr T. F. O'Higgins, and asked for the army's support in providing both players and training facilities. Twenty-two army officers were identified as potential Olympians, and the ABAI sought for them to be released from their military duties to follow an intensive training programme. The army's Chief of Staff rejected the request, saying that a team of army players wouldn't be of international standard and that they could not produce a performance of sufficiently high standard to bring credit to the country and army. Despite the initial set back, the

ABAI pushed on and were granted a second meeting to discuss the project. When it was made clear that the Olympic Council of Ireland would pay for the players' travel and accommodation, the army permitted them to go.

When it came time to select an Irish team, the group of potential players assembled in early July 1948, just weeks before they were due to compete. Six of the Western Command made the squad, led by Lt James Flynn and Sgt Bill Jackson. Four more players joined from the Eastern Command, and the army contingent was rounded out with two from the Curragh Command. In total, eleven of the twelve players had military backgrounds. The team's final space was reserved for the only civilian on the panel, Harry Boland.

Harry Boland came from one of the most recognisable families in the Irish Free State's young history. Born in Dublin in 1925, he was the son of Gerald Boland and nephew of Harry Boland. Both Harry Sr and Gerald had a major impact on the Easter 1916 Rising and the subsequent formation of the Irish Free State. Gerald was directly involved in the rising, and would later have a major impact on the growth of Sinn Féin and the subsequent formation of Fianna Fáil.

Harry grew up in the shadow of his father and his brother, Kevin (who would also become a government minister). With the added burden of sharing his uncle's famous name, Harry needed to write his own chapter in history. His opportunity came in an unusual way, and it was via perhaps the most influential man in early Irish basketball history. In the 1940s, Harry was studying in UCD and while there he met Fr Joe Horan. (Fr Joe would later be identified as perhaps the most central figure in moving the game of basketball to a more general civilian population.) Fr Joe introduced the game to Boland who was immediately taken by it. By the time the Olympic trials came about, Harry impressed enough to become the only civilian selected. (Boland's legacy continued long after he stopped playing the game, as he was heavily involved in UCD basketball for many years. He also ran an accountancy firm alongside Charlie Haughey, before Haughey went into politics and became Taoiseach. Years later, Haughey stepped up to help Irish Basketball fund its National Arena and the connection to Boland certainly didn't hurt.)

With the team picked, the next issue was what they would wear, as there was no such thing as an Irish jersey yet. Thankfully, the army donated a set of gear to them, and the team made their way to London to be part of the twenty-three-team tournament. Without an Olympic Village, the setting was already a bit unusual. It was even more so for basketball, as the venue was an indoor greyhound track that also hosted boxing and ice hockey. Ireland was drawn in Group D alongside France, Mexico, Cuba, and Iran. What was a monumental task to start with wasn't made any easier with the draw. Both France and Mexico would make it into the top four of the tournament, with France eventually winning a silver medal and Mexico coming fourth.

Ireland's first game was against Mexico, and their slim chances were further hindered when their bus got delayed, and they arrived twenty minutes late. Mexico started strongly, and Ireland had no answer to a level of basketball they had never seen before, as they lost out 71–9. Losses to Iran (49–22) and Cuba (88–25) followed, before the group stage wrapped up against the eventual silver medallists France (73–14). In the classification tournament, Ireland lost to Great Britain 46–21, and ultimately finished last as Switzerland beat them 55–12.

Despite the heavy defeats, it was hard to expect anything more from a team of relative novices assembled just a month previously.

Despite the defeats, the Association itself was only three years old and had already competed in the world's top basketball competition. There was hope that this could be a platform for Ireland to build and become a competitive basketball country.

Chapter 3: The Wilderness Years

Despite and hope that may have been held after the London Games, in Ireland's first decade after the Olympics, they managed only two victories, both of which came against fellow minnows, Wales. The first win was in 1953 with the second coming three years later. In 1958, as Ireland was set to play the Welsh for the third time, the squad announcement in the *Irish Independent* would have been familiar reading for Enda Byrt years later. While the team may be slightly on the short side for international basketball, they are all brilliant ball-handlers and court strategists, and fully capable of defeating Wales by a more impressive margin than they did in 1953.[vi']

More common than actual internationals at the time were games featuring US Navy and Air Force teams who played against Irish Army teams and select groups. These games happened everywhere from army barracks to Killarney Racecourse.

Outdoor racetracks and barracks weren't the only unusual venues for basketball in the early days either. Ireland faced England in a 'minor' international in 1960 in the dining hall of the mental hospital in Kilkenny, in what was billed as the first-ever international match in any sport in Kilkenny history. This wasn't the only mental hospital where games were played either. From the early 1960s onwards, Ireland regularly played in St Ita's Hospital in Portrane, one of the country's largest and most notorious mental health facilities.

As Ireland progressed and became more competitive with their local neighbours, an attempt was made to gain Olympic qualification again by entering the 1972 Olympic Pre-Qualifiers in the Netherlands. Dave Fitzsimons and Joe Palmer led the team, but in truth, they were entirely outmatched, losing two of their four games by more than sixty points. The qualifiers were an early indication of where international basketball was moving, as the Spanish team featured two naturalised Americans who were playing for Real Madrid at the time.

Four years later, Ireland would try the Pre-Olympic route again, this time in Edinburgh, Scotland. A seventy-nine-point loss to Italy and a sixty-two-point defeat against Belgium highlighted the gap that still existed. Yet, good performances against the British and French raised hopes going into the 1977 European Championship qualification the following year. By 1977, future Hall of Famer Paudie O'Connor was rounding into a top player, and as a 6'4 guard, he could compete with any of the best Ireland faced. The team were burdened by many of the same pressures that remain commonplace for Ireland. They only brought ten players despite being allowed to have twelve, due to several players pulling out due to injuries and work commitments. In the *Irish Press*, the preview of the tournament laid out the challenges the team faced: 'Realistically, the Irish team, which has been forced to overcome considerable financial handicaps this season has only a slim chance of qualifying. Apart from the off-court pressures of having to pay their own way to tournaments because the parent body just has not got the funds available, the lack of really tall players has proved a difficulty.'[vii]

In the tournament, things were looking up when Ireland pushed Iceland trailing by just two points with forty-four seconds to go. Still, the elusive first European win remained out of reach, despite head coach Danny Fulton crediting the team with their best display to date. In the final game of the qualifiers, Ireland played Portugal and caused a dramatic shock as they scored their first-ever win against continental opponents. Paudie O'Connor led the way with twenty-three points and was helped by sixteen apiece from Belfast's John Kennedy and Killester's Martin Grennell. Paudie O'Connor's display throughout the tournament was so impressive that he became the first Irish player to be selected for a tournament all-star team. The win and the performance overall under Fulton proved to be a turning point for Ireland. The team had now beaten continental opposition, and with O'Connor in particular, there was now a belief that Irish players could compete with their international counterparts.

In 1980, Ireland looked to build on the momentum of 1977 but were drawn in a daunting Pre-Olympic group with Italy, West Germany, Bulgaria and Holland. Ahead of the tournament, Ireland were already aware of how difficult it would be especially with the West Germans and Italians. The Dutch would also be a problem as they had six Dutch American players on their squad of twelve. When coach Danny Fulton was asked by the *Belfast Telegraph* about the competition, he said, I could do with a few 6 foot 10 Irish Americans that would give us a chance to at least compete on a level playing field with the rest of Europe. Every team seems to have an American in their side who holds a dual passport enabling him to play for his 'home' country.'[viii] Fulton faced other issues too, as a number of his squad had to withdraw due to work commitments. It turned out that neither issue got to impact Ireland, as the team withdrew from the Olympic Pre-Qualifiers, as part of a broader US-led boycott of the 1980 Moscow Games.

For basketball, the next opportunity to try and progress at the European level was the 1981 European Championship qualifiers. Ahead of the qualification process, Danny Fulton took his team down to Cork to play in an international tournament featuring Neptune and Blue Demons. The tournament would be a major spark for what was about to come both domestically and internationally over the next decade. Neptune had just returned to the top league in Ireland, and their American import, Pete Strickland, was acting as player-coach at the time. Pete was one of the key figures who helped ignite Irish domestic basketball's glory era by serving as a 'basketball missionary' around Cork city. In 1981, Neptune were looking to host an international tournament and looked to Pete for help. What resulted was a team called the Maryland All-Stars who were all-stars in name only. A solid group of players with connections to Strickland came to Ireland as the marquee attraction for the tournament, and they even made an appearance in Cork's St Patrick's Day parade. The American's lost to

Neptune's arch-rivals Blue Demons on a last-second shot in the group stage, in a moment that helped ignite a surge of interest in basketball in Cork city; people wanted more of what basketball had to offer. (Strickland himself would go down as a critical figure in the 1980s, and thirty-six years after he first arrived in Ireland, he came back as the national team coach.)

Lost in the footnotes of the Neptune tournament was the presence of the Irish national team. Crucially the team had some recruits, too, as the *Irish Press* reported: . . . for the Irish National Team hopes of qualifying for the European Championships will be boosted by the inclusion of two Americans in the squad. Both Leo Kane (Kingston) and Joe Maguire (FIAT) have Irish parents and should bring welcome height and skill to the Irish team.' [ix] Just two weeks later, Ireland headed to Scotland for a warm-up tournament and then on to Jersey for the European qualifiers. When Fulton announced the squad, there was no place for Kane who had picked up an injury, but Americans Craig Lynch and Joe Maguire who had both played in Cork made the team: 'The squad includes two Irish Americans in Lynch and Maguire, both of whom played in the recent Neptune International Tournament in

Cork. McGuire has been offered several lucrative contracts since the Neptune series last weekend. He was in superb form and averaged 36 points a game. Craig Lynch has family connections in Co. Cavan. Standing 6'8 he will be a great asset in the centre position.' [x]

In Scotland, the team looked promising as they beat Norway and Wales, but behind the scenes, issues were already mounting. Enda Byrt was Danny Fulton's team manager at the time, and he was in constant contact with FIBA about getting clearance for McGuire and Lynch to compete. Unfortunately, FIBA didn't clear either player, and as a result, Ireland headed into the Championship severely understrength. Already missing some key experienced contributors, Ireland were down to just eight eligible players for the tournament. A reflection shared in the *Irish Basketball Monthly* magazine highlighted the selection dilemma that Fulton faced. The preparation for this Euro Championship could hardly have been any worse, culminating in Ireland having eight players take the court in Jersey. National Team Coach Danny Fulton began with a panel of 22 and finally had 12 to select after defections for business and other reasons. A discouraging note was struck already when some established squad members did not have the courtesy to reply to invitations.' [xi] In the tournament, Ireland pushed the eventual group winners England, but went winless as they lost to Norway, who they had beaten with the Irish Americans' help only a week earlier.

Despite the disappointment of the qualifiers, the move towards Irish American players was cemented in the minds of Fulton and Byrt, who had seen what it could do in Scotland. Byrt wrote, the performance of the Senior Men's team in Scotland and Jersey raises new, but now realistic hopes for competitiveness at international level. Proper management and development of the Irish American connection could see Ireland ready to qualify for Europe at the next qualification round. The skill and total commitment displayed by the depleted squad in Jersey would gladden the heart of the most hardened sceptic! At senior level, the only deficiency lies in not having mobile big men in sufficient numbers. This is where the Irish American connection will augment the skilful and constructive aggression of our smaller players.'

Chapter 4: The Irish American Foundation

Away from the national team, the sport was progressing rapidly as the Amateur Basketball Association of Ireland was renamed the Irish Basketball Association (IBBA) in 1980 with Noel Keating at the helm. Keating was a pioneer for the sport who had an unrivalled eye for marketing and saw the potential of tapping into America to support basketball in Ireland. Through his work, Keating connected with a man named Dan Doyle, and the future of Irish basketball was about to change dramatically. Doyle was a college basketball coach at Trinity College in Connecticut at the time, but he also had experience in sports promotion having promoted Sugar Ray Leonard's professional boxing debut. Doyle arrived on to the scene in Ireland by chance, and yet he set about working with Keating to build a brighter future for the sport in Ireland. As part of their work, the new Irish American Foundation was established, with the initial goal of raising four million pounds in Irish American donations over four years. The purpose of the foundation was primarily to help build a new five-thousand- to eight-thousand-seat arena in Dublin, but it also had other intentions that included developing a new scholarship scheme for young Irish players to go the

States, an Irish American player-identification plan to help bring more eligible players over to Ireland, and finally, to help generate funds for Irish clubs through a franchising system that allowed them to register as businesses and sell a percentage of the control to American businesspeople.

One of the most prominent patrons of the franchise system was Larry O'Brien, a first-generation Irish American who would go on to become both the commissioner of the NBA and one of JFK's most trusted advisors. (O'Brien was at the heart of two major news stories in American history as he was in close proximity to JFK when he was assassinated, and later, his office was broken into during the infamous Watergate scandal. O'Brien also has the honour of having the NBA trophy named after him.)'

Doyle's goal of identifying eligible Irish American players fit with the plans that Enda Byrt and Danny Fulton already had in mind the previous year. The new venture was described as a scheme identifying 'young Americans of Irish parentage who would be willing to play for Ireland. The young Americans to be canvassed will be under-19-year-olds on the college circuit in the United States, and those identified and willing to play will be brought to this country immediately . . . a novel means of boosting the strength of the Irish Men's national squad . . . the scheme will, in time, lead to the establishment of dual nationals for the Irish squad – a situation that has pertained in England and Scotland for the past number of years . . . The ultimate aim is to bring between 25 and 30 young Americans to extensive Basketball clinics in the US in July.'[xii]

As part of the sport's fundraising initiatives, Ireland began going on tours to the US to play against some East Coast colleges. The trips allowed Ireland to compete against healthy competition while also raising money through guarantees from the colleges and fundraising events held around the games. In 1982, when Ireland were visiting Scranton in Pennsylvania there were some doubts in the local papers that couldn't be ignored: 'Because of a series of fundraisers several years ago, some of the yields were thought to be sent to the Northern Ireland rebel forces. The national and local sponsors of this basketball spectacular are careful and strong in their contention that their endeavour has no such overtones or undertones.'

'There is no rebel connection with this one,' Doyle said 'nothing political comes into this at all . . . Kids from Belfast and Cork. Protestants and Catholics alike will be the beneficiaries of any money raised.' The Scranton concerns highlighted a common adage at the time, that only three groups could fundraise in the States: the church, the GAA and the IRA. Despite any concerns, the combination of sponsorship from big companies like Budweiser in 1982 helped Ireland raise over eighty thousand pounds in just one year. Money that was unheard of compared to the support that was coming from the Irish government at the time.

1982 also saw the start of the scholarship scheme and it did have success particularly for female players in the 1980s. There were concerns about Doyle's intentions in the Irish American recruitment drive, as the try-outs seemed to be more of a money-making scheme than a genuine opportunity for young players.

More pressing for Irish basketball, however, was a power-grab move that had albeit been anticipated by some. In the announcement of the Foundation, it was mentioned that Doyle might look to get directly involved in coaching the national team. Doyle who has vast experience in basketball, could well be asked to coach the international sides and put them firmly on the map, and that could be very feasible with the American connection.' Later in the year, the IBBA's executive decided to replace head coach Danny Fulton with Dan Doyle. It was a decision that the former CEO Noel Keating told Kieran Shannon in his book *Hanging from the Rafters* that he regrets to this day: 'That's one of the regrets I have as the IBBA president, really and truly. It was an executive decision but I should have been strong enough to say to Dan, Look, we have this experienced, qualified national coach; if you want to become part of the coaching staff, that's fine. But Dan pitched it that it was an all-or-nothing package, so naively, we bowed.'[xiii]

The Irish American Basketball Foundation's impact was immediately evident as Doyle brought in two Irish Americans to help the senior team at the European Championship Qualifiers. As Noel Spillane wrote in the *Echo*, the announcement was framed as a development that could help the domestic game. The two Irish Americans – both under 19 – who have opted to play for the Irish squad are John Smyth from New York a 6'8 centre, and Gerard Corcoran 6'5 also from New York. Both these Irish Americans are likely to play in the National League and Cup in Ireland next year and should further the links of the Irish American Foundation[xiv].' This recruitment was a continuation of the attempted move by Fulton in 1981 to use Joe McGuire and Craig Lynch that ultimately had proven unsuccessful.

Despite his coaching pedigree at Trinity College in Connecticut, Doyle's time as national-team coach is considered farcical at best. In 1983, as Ireland faced Stonehill in the first game of their US tour, Peter O'Hehir described the ridiculousness of the pre-game situation: Due to the procedure used in choosing the squad, Doyle had to be introduced to some of the players.' [xv]Ireland ended up trailing by twenty at the half, and Doyle walked off the court with a mystery illness. It was his last act as the Irish coach, ending a strange two-year period for the team. Blue Demons and Cork legend, Seanie Murphy, took over for the remainder of the tour and the next qualification campaign. Murphy even managed to lead the team to some credible performances including a brilliant victory over Holy Cross 74–71.

Doyle's involvement in Irish basketball didn't end as quickly as his coaching reign did. He created a non-profit company called the Institute for International Sport – the charity's first programme included volunteers being sent to Ireland to help promote cross-cultural basketball in Belfast. The programme led Doyle to eventually create the World Scholar-Athlete Games in 1993, which saw athletes from 109 countries come together to play. The event was built off philanthropic funding, and by 2001 it had got so big that Bill Clinton delivered a keynote address at the Games. Doyle's work was so well respected at the time, that Senator George Mitchell stated that he knew of no organisation that does more to help young children on a worldwide basis than the Institute for International Sport'.

Unfortunately for Doyle, his empire unravelled years later when a grand jury investigation into the Institute's funding returned an eighteen-count indictment against him. The charges included a claim that he had embezzled money from the organisation. In total, it was alleged that he had taken over one million dollars for personal gain. Doyle maintained his innocence throughout, but in 2017 he was sentenced to seventeen years in prison, with seven to serve and the rest suspended. When he was charged, his lawyer issued a short statement saying, 'don't forget the good he has done'.Pete Strickland summed up Doyle's involvement in his own words: I could never fully figure out if

Doyle's involvement with [Irish basketball] was just to make money. I could never figure it out. Not in a bad way. He was pretty tunnel-visioned. But then you'd introduce him to someone; he'd have a fine way about him. Even though he had this vision, I'm not sure how much of it was about money, and how much of it was about seeing the sport grow here. But maybe there was more to it than I saw.[xvi]'

Despite the issues he had later on and the suspect motivations, Doyle's involvement in Irish basketball indeed did contribute to the start of many good ideas. His efforts did help kickstart the funding for the National Basketball Arena, although to credit him with that does a disservice to people like Noel Keating and Liam McGinn. They made huge personal sacrifices for Ireland to get their arena in 1993. The funding for clubs through the franchise scheme was patchy at best, as most clubs struggled to generate anything from the arrangement. Kieran Shannon highlighted the issue in *Hanging from the Rafters*: Dan Doyle's franchising scheme had not generated the funds envisaged, and in the case of most clubs had not been a success. Some clubs were operating in debt with little hope of raising the necessary funds, while others were spending next to nothing on underage teams and hadn't developed links with local schools.' The clubs' issues eventually led to problems in the league as the number of Americans in the competition was reduced, effectively ending a period of dominance that the sport experienced domestically in the 1980s.

Without a doubt, the scholarship scheme was the most successful of the ideas –from 1982 onwards, Ireland had an almost consistent presence at NCAA Division 1 level, a trend that continues today.

Chapter 5: The IIRM

Every year there are multiple Irish players playing NCAA Division I basketball in America. This wasn't the norm at the start of the 1980s. The first person that many Irish people remember following this path was Tony Gorman from St Declan's in Dublin, in 1981. Admittedly Tony's time playing in Seton Hall was short-lived. What many don't realise, though, is that there was a player from Cork, during the seventies, that competed at the highest level of NCAA basketball.

John O'Donnell was born in Cork to a famous family that included the founder of Barry's Tea and several TDs amongst them. John's uncle John Kerry O'Donnell is a well-known name in GAA circles, as the man who bought over Gaelic Park in New York as the GAA were about to lose control of the iconic venue. When John was just seven years old, his family moved to the States to help his uncle run Gaelic Park, and he even worked there himself, selling Irish newspapers to the crowd. While in school, John was introduced to basketball, and before long he blossomed into a 6'6 athlete, who was performing well in the elite New York Catholic-school leagues. He was so good, in fact, that he was recruited by the legendary Dean Smith from the University of North Carolina where he would play three years of varsity basketball and enjoy a trip to the 1972 NCAA Final Four.

After starting as a senior, O'Donnell also became the first and only Irish-born player ever to be drafted in the NBA, although he never played in the league. It was an honour that even surprised him. 'I didn't think I was good enough to play in the NBA, but Dean Smith said, "You're from New York, do you want to get drafted by the New York Knicks?" I said, sure! So, I was drafted by the Knicks in the tenth round, which was a courtesy round that they don't have now.' Despite not playing in the NBA, John did become Ireland's first professional player as he played a year in France before returning to North Carolina as a graduate assistant for Smith. His medical studies eventually got in the way and he ultimately had to give up his assistant role, filled by a future Hall of Famer Roy Williams.

O'Donnell was more of an anomaly than anything else, though, and a more strategic view on developing players was needed.

When the Irish American Foundation was set up in 1982, one of its goals was to help young Irish players go to college in America. That goal quickly became a reality, with women in particular able to make the transition successfully. Throughout the '90s and 2000s, both the Men's and Women's national teams benefitted from Irish-born players with NCAA experience, and it remains an integral part of the national teams today. Many players never returned to Ireland after college, though, and some never got to display their skills in the green jersey. The first two female players to break down the barriers to play in NCAA basketball did so without much fanfare in Ireland. Their journey turned out to be far more important to Irish Americans' lives, thanks to the relationships they developed across the pond.

Having played for Danny Thompson on the Irish U19 team, Una Geoghegan had aspirations to play in America in 1980 when she finished secondary school. That dream looked like it was set to be fleeting as she took a job working in St James's Hospital in Dublin. Despite having started her working life, Una played for the (amazingly named) Sardi's Disco Dodgers when Dan Doyle arrived in Ireland promoting the chance to go to America. Una set up a meeting with the American and quickly convinced him that she needed to be on the initial summer trip to Connecticut. That early camp was a great opportunity for young Irish players to experience basketball in the States.

Doyle had recruited a local Irish American fireman to help with the logistics, Jim Larkin. The son of two Irish emigrants and the husband to another Irish emigrant, when he was growing up, Jim would often come downstairs in the morning to find a stranger fresh off the boat from Ireland that his dad had met in the pub the night before. The Larkins always wanted to help accommodate Irish people, and the camp was a great way for Jim to do this. It didn't take long for him to question Dan Doyle's motives, though. As Jim's son Michael recalls, Doyle had sold them a story about poor Irish kids coming over, but then it turned out he was simultaneously charging the players: 'When you are inviting kids over, and you are asking people to set them up in their neighbour's houses, these kids don't have any money, that's why we're setting them up in the house. All of a sudden, there's a turnaround, and they need to pay for the camp! Since when? That's when my dad lost it with him. 'You never told me about that when you asked me for help.'

Despite issues away from the court, Una Geoghegan impressed on the court. The young guard became the only player offered a direct scholarship to university when Marist College came calling. The scholarship only became available at the last minute and had standard protocol been followed, Una may never have been able to accept it. 'The scholarship had been offered to another girl who decided at the last minute to go to Auburn instead. So, Sue Deer had this scholarship that if she didn't use it, she'd lose it.' Geoghegan was visiting friends in California and was able to arrange a quick detour to meet the coaches.

I stopped off in JFK and met the assistant coach in the airport and got the train to Poughkeepsie, New York. I couldn't believe how beautiful it was, not the concrete jungle I was imagining. I met the coach, and we played some three on three and five on five, and she offered me a scholarship. I flew home, and I had two weeks to quit my job and go to the embassy. They told me under no circumstances was I to get on a plane and go back to the United States because the paperwork alone would take about a year to process. So I called Jim Larkin, I told him the embassy said I can't go. He told me to hop on a plane and tell Customs when you're coming through that you're trying out for a scholarship, not that you have it, and then we'll take care of it once you get here. So, I hopped on a plane, I tell the guy at customs I'm trying out, and he wishes me good luck, and I go to Marist. That October I go down to INS in New York, and they tell me under no circumstances should I have been allowed back into the country. Still, they processed my paperwork, and I got to stay.'

Jim Larkin's intervention was the first of many by him. After a tough first year for Una in Marist, Jim came to Ireland to the famous Dungarvan basketball camp (Ireland's top residential basketball camp for many years) to help convince her to stay on the journey. 'I had a horrible first year. I didn't even want to finish it. I was miserable. The game they play there is different than the game I grew up with. The problem here and it's still the same, is that when you come on scholarship, they own you. In Ireland, you pay to play while here you're paid to play. They just own you. Everybody who comes in on scholarship have all been big fish in a little pond, and they all come in competing against each other as opposed to playing together. So that was devastating for me. I wasn't coming back after my first year. I met Pete Strickland and Danny Thompson with Jim Larkin in Dungarvan, and the three of them explained it would be foolish not to go back and it was an amazing opportunity, so I came back.' Not only did Una go back, but she progressed to being a team captain and played ninety-eight games between 1982–86, leading Marist in assists in both her sophomore and junior years.

One of the things that helped Una was the presence of another Irish player who followed her to Marist. Jennifer Gray was a 6'1 forward from Killester,Dublin, who landed on Sue Deer's radar by a quirk of fate. Debbie Doyle, a well-known coach and referee in Dublin, had been in the States in 1983 and met Sue Deer. Sue had just had a scholarship open up because a player had become academically ineligible, and Doyle recommended Gray. Jennifer had finished school and was working in the ESB at the iconic Poolbeg site in Dublin. Having been introduced to basketball at St Mary's secondary school in Killester through Imelda Grennell, Jennifer was playing in Beaumont at the time when an out-of-the-blue call took her by surprise.

'Debbie called me at work and said, would you be interested in going to America on a basketball scholarship? I said, are you kidding me? She said no, be home tonight at six o'clock, you're going to get a call from a woman called Sue Deer, who's the coach at Marist College in Poughkeepsie. That was the first I'd heard of Marist College'.

No trial was necessary, and things were lined up quickly for Jennifer to follow Una to New York. Before going, she went to Dungarvan where Jim Larkin was helping to convince Una to return. Jim came to Dungarvan, and that's where I met him. I really had no idea just how much work [he put in] and how much he pulled the strings in the background to help Una. When I first went over, we went straight to his home and then he drove us to campus. He was really like a second father, he took care of us, he called the coaches, he would check on us, he was just phenomenal.'

Jennifer's on-court experience was similar to Una's as she struggled to adjust to the business-like realities of basketball in America. Despite that, she played in one hundred and two career games for Marist. She was mostly a reserve in her first three seasons, but she started twenty-six games as a senior. That year (1986–87), she had career highs in points per game (4.8) and rebounds per game (5.1 – second on the team). Like Una, Jennifer quickly realised that there was going to be more to life than just basketball for her. 'By the end of my second year, I realised it couldn't all be about basketball, and Jim Larkin was a big part of that. He said I had to realise that at the end of four years that that piece of paper is worth more than basketball could ever give you in your life. Basketball opened the door, basketball got you over here, but it's the degree that's going to open the doors for you for the rest of your life.'

Jim's impact was as a fatherly figure for the two Dubliners, but he also helped bring others over to America, and even brought American coaches to Ireland to recruit. His hard work started a revolution on the women's side of the game that led to many more Irish players coming to the States including Karen Hennesy and Maggie Timoney in Iona, Teresa McDermott at Central Connecticut State and Ruth Halley in Marist, amongst others. His true impact, though, was away from basketball. Having seen Una and Jennifer's struggles after completing college, Larkin was determined to make a tangible change in America for Irish immigrants.

A 1960s bill, ironically supported by John F. Kennedy, negatively impacted the Irish immigration situation in the States. The legislation only helped people who already had families in America to get visas. As Ireland went through a period of prosperity in the sixties and seventies, emigration to the States had slowed. In the 1980s, as

Ireland faced harsh economic conditions again, Irish people struggled to legally enter the States without having a family established there. Larkin was already passionate about supporting Irish people and did a lot of work in his community. But with the arrival of Una and Jennifer into his family's life, he became more and more determined to lead change. Through his work, Jim met the founding members of the Irish Immigration Reform Movement and became a founding member of the Connecticut Chapter. Jennifer has no doubt that it was their arrival into his life that led to the work. I think he only got into the IIRM because of Una and me. I think he realised that the visa system wasn't helpful to anyone coming over from Ireland. He got engaged with the founders of the IIRM, and then he connected them with Senator Morrison in Connecticut.'

The IIRM was a lobbying group, whose hope was to tackle visa issues for Irish arriving into America and help the illegal Irish already in the States. The Mayo-based *Western People* paper wrote an article commending his excellent work : Mr and Mrs Jim Larkin of West Hartford Connecticut, are to be commended for the interest they are showing for the welfare of many Irish exiles in the Hartford area today.

For years, both have helped Irish girls get US basketball scholarships. So far he has helped bring nine Irish girls to US colleges. Jim and others have formed a Hartford chapter of a group named Irish Immigration Reform Movement, which are fighting successfully to change immigration laws. What was frustrating Larkin prior to getting involved in the new group was that many of the girls that came to the US college and graduated had to return home against their will as they did not qualify to stay in the US. Jim states, 'They are not here on welfare, they can get that at home. These are the people who built America. They are here to work. With unemployment at an all time low in the US, it's ludicrous to say there isn't room for them. [xvii]

As part of Larkin's campaign, he directly canvassed the Connecticut senator Bruce Morrison and set about influencing him to deliver change. The IIRM is largely credited with helping to deliver the 1990 Morrison Bill. The legislation gave amnesty to many illegal Irish Americans. It also opened up a new visa system with guaranteed allotments for Irish people. Of the annual 40,000 visas, Irish people were guaranteed 16,000 a year in the first three years, although they could get a more significant share if they had enough applicants. The system required a basic letter on behalf of the applicant, and people could submit more than one letter as part of the initial green card lottery. Larkin championed a letter-writing campaign that helped illegal Irish flood the lottery with applications, aiding countless Irish families to gain legal status. Not only that, but Larkin also coached families as they prepared for their interviews with immigration. As Una recalls, 'He was amazing, he was a mover and shaker, he just got things going. He was very passionate about giving opportunities to people in Ireland. To this day, I'll tell my kids about it because they won't believe that a letter-writing campaign could achieve so much in terms of getting the visas, but it really did. He was just so passionate about Ireland and could tell you anything about its history. He was very instrumental in that and helped mobilise that campaign.'

The timeline parallels cannot be ignored. As the first wave of Irish American players arrived in to help the Men's national team in the 1980s, female players heading to America were indirectly influencing the lives of countless Irish Americans at the same time. In a way, Irish basketball was giving back to the Irish American families trying to help them.

For Una Geoghegan, the experience as the first Irish-developed player to go and play four years for a Division I NCAA college wasn't necessarily the dream come true on the court. Still, it was a life-altering choice that she doesn't regret. 'I'm not a success story from a basketball standpoint. My dream was to get better, come home, bring skills home to play on the national team and bring skills home to coach. Basketball was my life. It was everything. I realised midway that basketball wouldn't pay the way, and I focused more on my education. I still played, and I played for four years, my best year was probably my junior year, and I was co-captain on the team. It was good, though, that it opened the doors for others coming through. There's no doubt about it, if I was enjoying the game on the court better, I wouldn't have walked away so disillusioned. I love the game, but it didn't turn out the way it was supposed to, but it was the stepping stone for the life I've had, there's no way I was going to be here without it.'

Despite not having the dream career, Geoghegan did break down the door for so many Irish women that followed her. Jennifer Gray was the first just one year later. Both players and so many who followed after them got much more from their basketball journey than basketball itself, and their impact on Jim Larkin also helped paved the way for better situations for countless Irish people in America today.

Chapter 6: The Junior Men

As Dan Doyle took over the Senior Men's team, Danny Fulton moved to take charge of the U19 team. The move showed Fulton's desire to help Irish basketball above all else and Ireland was set to benefit from the development of a new generation of internationals under his tutelage. The seeds of Ireland's international progression in the nineties were sewn in the Junior Men's programme between 1984 and 1990.

One factor impacting youth development was the increase in Irish players starting to take up scholarships in the US. In 1981, Tony Gorman became the first player since John O'Donnell to leave Ireland and play for an NCAA Division I school, briefly attending Seton Hall. Gorman's clubmate Karl Butler was one of the first men to follow this path. The 6'3 guard would become an instrumental part of the Irish set-up at both Junior and Senior levels. Butler's first big mark was as captain of the Irish U19 team as they headed to Finland for the 1984 European Championship qualifiers.

Ahead of the tournament, the team was billed as the most talented junior team Ireland had ever produced. The squad could have been even more gifted, but future Basketball Ireland Hall of Famer

Liam McHale was cut just days before the tournament due to missing training. (His absence was sadly a precursor for most of his career, as Ireland's most gifted natural talent never regularly played for Ireland, despite being arguably the country's best player ever.) Despite Liam's absence, the team still had Butler and a strong frontcourt in the Cork duo of Don O'Sullivan and Paul Fitzgerald. The only player on the squad under six foot was a young point guard from Corinthians, Mark Keenan. The 5'5 point guard was playing two years out of his age group but was already an incredible floor general and leader for the team. For coach Danny Fulton, Mark was critical to the team. Danny's faith in the young guard was rewarded with an explosive start to a legendary international career that has seen him captain and coach Ireland. From this point until 1997, Keenan was directly involved in everything Ireland achieved as he consistently dispelled any doubts that his height would limit him.

During the tournament, Ireland came agonisingly close to qualifying as they recorded their first-ever European Championship win at U19 level, beating Denmark behind twenty-six points from Butler. The team eventually missed out on progressing by just four points after a narrow loss to a Dutch team that included a very raw, future NBA star, 7'4 Rik Smits. The *Irish Press* revelled in Ireland's progress: 'Irish international basketball came of age in the European Junior Championship in Finland, though yesterday the Irish were most disappointed in losing to Holland 69–65, following their tremendous win over Denmark on Saturday night by 69–64 . . . Holland had beaten Spain, France and West Germany already in prep. Karl Butler (6'3) had 26 and Ireland led in the second half before losing out in the final minute . . . Ireland's first win in European Championship junior basketball came in magnificent style, as they came from 62–54 behind with four minutes to go, to leave Denmark in total disarray with a 69–65 victory. The Danes were outscored fourteen points to two in the final four minutes. Ireland went into an early ten to two points lead, but again the bigger Danish team caught up and were one point ahead at half-time. There was to be no denying the Irish victory, however, and combining spirit with intelligence they outhustled and outfought the Danes.' [xviii]

Ireland had acquitted themselves well with Karl Butler third in scoring, while Paul Fitzgerald finished fourth in scoring and was also

74

the third top rebounder of the tournament. For the crowd in Finland, there was a clear star of the future on show. The Finnish crowd reserved their most enthusiastic applause for the Irish team at the awards ceremony, with guard Mark Keenan, the tournament's smallest player, receiving a tremendous ovation.'

At the same time that the Junior Men were progressing under Fulton, Seanie Murphy was stewarding the senior team into the Olympic Pre-Qualifiers in France (after Dan Doyle's sudden resignation). Again, there would be Irish American representation as Gerry Corcoran from North Eastern University was drafted in to help on the boards. Ireland was drawn alongside Sweden, Finland and the mighty USSR, who had won the previous 1980 Moscow Games when the USA had boycotted. During the tournament, teams practice behind closed doors; the Irish were of so little threat to the Soviets that they were allowed to watch the team practice. The Irish watched in fascination as the Soviets stretched out their young 7'3 big man Avydas Sabonis, who was only eighteen. Sabonis was just coming into a period of dominance that saw him become one of the most decorated players of all time. Many consider him the best big man in the world during the late 1980s and early 1990s. Ireland lost to the Soviets as they struggled to deal with the size and athleticism of the opposition. Despite the loss, the Irish played well, and there was a moral victory for the boys in green, as former Irish captain and coach Timmy McCarthy put it. 'We lost 118–46, and we played exceptionally well! I remember being interviewed in the corridor afterwards and being asked about why [we came] . . . I pretended I didn't understand the question. Eventually, [the French journalist] said, "You have no chance of winning, why are you here?" I said we're here to represent our country. We all work full time at home and are part-time players, and this is a pride for us. If it's about just winning, they should just have the Soviets and the US play in the final every year. The Olympics is about qualification and playing. They wrote an article the next day in *L'Equippe* saying Ireland are the true bastions of the Olympic flame because we were amateurs. The Soviets back then were not amateurs.'

As Ireland tried to compete internationally, it was becoming increasingly clear that it was far from a level playing field. As early as 1980, seven of the twelve players on the English team had dual nationalities, and the same was true for many European countries.

Others were also almost exclusively professional, and despite the advancements of the Irish league, that remained a world away for us. The worrying question was, if Ireland ever wanted to compete internationally, could they do so without going to an entirely professional team? And likely a majority group of Irish American players?

Chapter 7: The First Wave

In 1985, Danny Fulton's time with the juniors ended, as he returned to the top job. Ahead of the Four Nations tournament in Cork, Peter O'Hehir examined the question that was already developing. Would Ireland focus purely on homegrown talent or would the country aim for short-term success to help build the country's international programme?'The national teams are the ultimate gauge of a country's worth, not a national league or tournament court when surrounded by Americans. Irish teams have, in recent years, regularly included an Irish American dimension. It is currently uncertain whether the Association will attempt to include such players in the squad for the Four [Nations] campaign. Clearly, it must be decided whether we want to become competitive in the short-term or to work for long-term improvement and development. Priorities will be tested.' [xix]

While Danny Fulton was back with the seniors, Enda Byrt stayed with the Junior Men and took over as head coach. Byrt was convinced that Irish Americans could help Ireland on the court, and having got to terms with the FIBA rules, he felt that young Irish Americans were the route to pursue. FIBA rules meant that any player who got their passport before the age of nineteen was automatically eligible for the senior team. Enda knew that finding players while they were still eligible for the Junior Men would create a continuity and possible platform for the Senior Men to develop moving forward.

Byrt also hoped that by exposing young Irish players to American college players might raise their standards. '[Out of] the deficiencies we saw at the time, number one was height. Every position on the floor, and particularly when you went out to small forward and power forward, were six inches smaller than [the European] guys.' The second issue he identified was that Irish players were not getting enough court time to develop as players. He saw the American players coming through a system that allowed them to develop daily and he wanted that work ethic to rub off on the Irish players. Over a period of time, this exposure had Byrt's intended effects.

Although Irish Americans had already represented Ireland at senior level, the real Irish American era started from 1986 onwards, as Byrt's recruitment began to reap rewards. Philip Reid of the *Irish Press* documented the first two Junior Men's recruits as an extension of a process that was happening amongst other sports in Ireland at the time:

Ireland's top U19 players have been joined by two Irish Americans –
John O'Hare and James O'Boyle – on this occasion for the qualifying
tournament. The trend of importing foreign players to aid Irish teams, it
seems, has extended to almost all sports! However, their inclusion
should boost Ireland's hopes of edging out Spain, Turkey, Holland and
Portugal for that final spot. O'Hare and O'Boyle, who both have strong
Irish connections are 6'5 and 6'7 respectively, and the pair should
improve Ireland's chances in the rebounding area, an area of the game
which has let Ireland down on a number of occasions.'[xx]

O'Boyle was a strong high-school player in New York's
Catholic school leagues, where he had a healthy rivalry with a young
big man called Marty Conlon. Enda Byrt found out about both players
and met with their families with ambitions of bringing them both to
Ireland. Conlon, who would go on to play in the NBA for many years,
was aware of the opportunity, and the idea of playing alongside a local
rival like O'Boyle interested him. Still, it wasn't to be; he had just
committed to playing for Rick Pitino at Providence, and he had to go to
summer school to get ready for his freshman season. As it turned out,
Marty had to wait almost twenty years before eventually getting the

opportunity to represent Ireland with the senior team. Despite Conlon missing out, O'Boyle was a tough-nosed forward, and it was hoped he could add some strength on the boards for Ireland.

O'Boyle's partner from America was 6'5 forward John O'Hare, born and raised just outside Philadelphia. O'Hare's father came from Castleblaney in Co. Monaghan, while his mother was from the Glenties in Donegal. The couple met in Ireland before visiting an uncle based in the States in 1963 and they never returned home. Enda knew the type of Irish families he was looking to reach all read the *Irish Echo* newspaper. He took out an ad asking Irish American players to come to a trial in Fordham University. For O'Hare, the commitment to play for Ireland, in a country that he hadn't been to before, with people he had only met once, was a massive leap of faith, especially for a seventeen-year-old. I had no idea what I was getting myself into. I had never talked to anyone who had done it before. My father came with me too, it was kind of neat, all the times I played in Ireland he took his vacation, and he came with me.'

After arriving in Ireland, John met Mark Keenan and stayed with his family as he tried to figure out what he had got himself into.

Fortunately for John, basketball proved a universal language, and he was quickly at home.

The Irish team headed to Andorra with hopes of pushing on from the first win in 1984. For Keenan and the other Irish players on the squad, the new additions gave them hope that they could compete internationally. It was definitely a good addition, and it was generally guys with a bit of size to help the team. We definitely lacked [it]; we couldn't compete on the size element for whatever reason. They definitely added that extra dimension.'

The impact was seen throughout the tournament as O'Hare excelled. Ireland managed to win another game as they beat Portugal 90–83 on the back of twenty-seven points from O'Hare and fourteen from Keenan. The individual highlight for O'Hare came in the group's final match as he scored an incredible forty-six points against the Netherlands. This record has never been topped by any male playing underage for Ireland. The accurate measure of how Irish O'Hare is, came in-between games, as he fell afoul of a problem facing any Irish team who play a tournament in a warm-weather country. A bunch of us took our mattresses out on the roof; it was so nice there. Half of us fell asleep, so by that night, we are wearing green, and I was purple, and we were getting hit all over. I looked like a lobster!'

The team finished on one win, but there was huge promise for the future. For O'Boyle, it was a one-time-only event as he returned to the States and eventually became a member of the New York Fire Department. For O'Hare, it was the start of a longer journey that included playing for the senior team in both the Olympic Pre-Qualifiers in 1988 and the 1990 Promotions Cup in Wales. After a standout career in Cabrini College in Pennsylvania, O'Hare played professional basketball briefly for the Washington Generals on their European tour, playing against the Harlem Globetrotters. By the time his basketball career ended, O'Hare started his second life as a police officer, which he remains to this day. Anytime John needs to remember his journey as a young man, he just has to walk into the den in his house where he only has one jersey hanging from the rafters, his Irish number 7.

O'Hare in particular was further confirmation for Byrt that the recruitment idea was something that could work. Not only had he found an excellent player straight away, but he had also found a high-character player and family. The combination was exactly what he was looking for. The evidence was enough to motivate him to continue with the plan as Ireland looked ahead to the 1988 Junior Men's qualifiers.

The 1988 team became a template for Enda Byrt's future squads as they embarked on an eighteen-month training programme that saw them as prepared as they could be for the qualifiers. In 1987, three new Irish American recruits were added to the domestic contingent that included Paschal Brennan from Limerick, Cormac O'Donoghue from Killarney and Gareth Maguire from Belfast.

Maguire, in particular, went on to become the embodiment of what it meant to represent Ireland. From 1987 until the early 2000s, he became one of the most important figures ever to represent the country. Gareth's love for basketball and representing his country stemmed from an upbringing in Belfast that was extremely challenging both at home and in the community. As he grew up, the city was struggling during the height of the Troubles in Northern Ireland: Basketball for me, it got me out from what was happening at home. When I went South, you left all that crap that was happening up there, the mayhem in Belfast. Basketball took me out of an environment that was vicious and dangerous. You couldn't walk down the street without being stopped by the police . . . If I was playing in Andersonstown Leisure Centre you would experience the centre being raided. That was our life.'

As a teenager, Maguire started to progress on the basketball court, and he was more than willing to put the extra work in off the court in the weight room – precisely what Byrt was looking for. In his local gym in Andersonstown, the guys working-out beside him were often former prisoners back in the Belfast community: When I was sixteen, those times in the weights room you learn a lot . . . I was asked to do some stuff at a young age; all my mates were involved, everybody was involved. It was a very difficult environment . . .We used to travel back and forth across the border on the train . . .I would never get asked or stopped [by the police]. So, I was basically asked to carry information [for the IRA] and was asked to be involved. I was then given a lecture by one of the senior Republicans, and he told me it was my job to play for Ireland and leave all the other shit to them. That was my green card to go and play.'

As the new wave of Americans arrived in to help, Maguire was excited by the opportunity but also a little embarrassed about what Ireland was presenting. Personally, as a player I loved it. I loved the challenge and the opportunity. I was embarrassed at times, being honest, because I knew where these guys came from. Even as a young kid at sixteen to seventeen, I was always strategically very aware of the surroundings around me. They were coming over here saying what the feck is this all about! They must have looked at us as if we were mad, but I loved it, and it made me better.' In 1987, the recruits included Brendan O'Sullivan and John Dormer from New York, and John Brennan from New Jersey. In particular, Dormer was a name that stood out within Irish sport, as his father Richard played inter-county football for Laois before emigrating to America in the 1960s. By 1988, for the actual tournament it was Dormer, John Brennan and Sean McDonagh from Boston on the team. McDonagh's cousin Norah was already a familiar face in Irish basketball as she played in the Irish league for Naomh Mhuire. Of these recruits, John Brennan became the key addition for a wide variety of reasons.

Brennan, like O'Hare two years earlier, saw an ad about trials in the *Irish Echo*. He went down and met Gerry Nihill (another instrumental figure in the Junior programmes alongside Byrt and Fulton) for the first time, and he soon committed to ten weeks in Ireland before he had ever finished high school: 'It was a big leap of faith. You're going for ten weeks at seventeen years old; you have no idea who is on the team and who Gerry or Enda are. I lived with Gerry or Enda for most of the summer. I spent time in Dublin and Belfast; you just spent time where you could between tournaments, there was no housing or apartment that you could stay at, it was really fly-by-the-seat-of-your-pants kind of stuff . . . I wouldn't say that we were pioneers, but we were doing something on the heels of John O'Hare– there was no path, there was no structure, you were figuring it out as you went along.' The Irish team deepened a strong bond between John and his dad, who had never been outside of America until he came to Ireland to watch his son play. The Brennans were instrumental for several years in generating enough money for the Irish dream to continue, especially as Ireland lacked any high-performance funding for the national team. A lot of the funding we got to play was from Irish Americans. Friends of my dad and uncle who saw this as an opportunity to expand where we could go and play.' For John at the time, the prospect of having a successful basketball career on the back of the Irish team wasn't even something that figured in his mind. He was more focused on ensuring they were able to continue it going for as long as possible: It was more a thing of pride. My grandmother is from Donegal, and my grandfather is from Tipperary. When I first came over in 87, I felt a real connection to where they came from and what they did, and it was a pride thing. We had to raise money to play; we had fundraisers, golf tournaments, and dinners.'

Brennan was an outstanding player who would go on to play for Lafayette. Despite his on-court achievements, his most significant impact was on the national team programme's Irish American culture. Brennan ended up living out the vision Enda originally had in 1980, as he played for the junior team, progressed up to the senior side and also came to Ireland and played. He would even work for the Federation as a young man looking to extend his time in Ireland as long as it was financially viable. John spent time working for the IBBA for Noel Keating and Pat Coffey and even played professionally for Frankie O'Loane in Dungannon. It was almost a vocation for John as he tried to spread the game in the same way that Pete Strickland had in Cork years earlier.

John's impact on his teammates was an important one too, with Gareth Maguire being the biggest beneficiary of a close bond with the Brennans. The Brennan family helped Gareth go to America and get away from Ireland occasionally, and the impact on Maguire couldn't be overstated. Thirty years later, Gareth runs a foundation called Sports Changes Life that brings American masters students into Ireland and helps them impact the community. As part of the foundation's work, they host a major NCAA tournament in Belfast each year which broadcasts Northern Ireland into millions of American homes on CBS. The Foundation idea's genesis came from Gareth and John's relationship as teenagers, and the two remain close today. For a foundation that requires links to America to keep it going, Maguire recognises how advanced Enda Byrt's approach was in the early eighties. 'Enda was way ahead of his time, strategically he was a genius. He was opening doors to America for business which nobody grasped hold of, but he was also raising the talent level. People have gone to America for a hundred years with their hand out looking for something in return. Enda went with a phenomenal opportunity to these

Irish American kids who are equally Irish because their families came from here.'

At the Junior Men's tournament that year in Spain, Ireland played some excellent basketball and were in good physical condition thanks to none other than future Irish rugby coach Eddie O'Sullivan, who was the team's strength and conditioning coach. Despite the progress, Ireland still struggled to make an impact on the boards.

While Byrt was starting to see the fruits of the Irish-American recruiting plan at underage level, Danny Fulton's time as Senior Men's coach was coming to an end. Danny's last stand saw him bring many of his Junior Men's team from 1984 to the Olympic Pre-Qualifiers in the Netherlands. Ireland overmatched again, but Fulton had provided the foundation for a new generation of Irish teams. He has deservedly become a Hall of Famer in Irish basketball, and his work in establishing the national team as a credible force can't be understated.

Chapter 8: The Disconnect

Paudie O'Connor led Ireland to its first-ever victory against continental opposition in 1977, but he wasn't satisfied with that. Ireland's talisman wanted to see the level of basketball in the country improve, and he was precisely the type of creative thinker that was needed to do it. O'Connor felt that Americans coming and playing in the domestic league would help raise the standard, so in 1979 he brought in the first professional Americans into Ireland. American players had been in the national league for several years, mainly through RCSI and other medical schools. This new move in Killarney was different though, as Paudie brought professional players in with the sole focus of playing basketball. The move was a seminal moment in Irish basketball that transformed the sport domestically, almost overnight.

The eighties are Ireland's most celebrated basketball decade, as the game broke the sporting barrier and became a pop culture phenomenon, particularly in Cork City. Basketball became the place to be seen, and everyone wanted a piece of the action, including sponsors who were willing to pump money into the sport. With the money, came import players of the highest standard that the country has ever recruited. Names like Jasper McElroy, Terry Strickland and Ray Smith would all become household names for their performances on the court.

As the era began, then President of the IBBA, Noel Keating, could sense the coming opportunity, but also saw the bigger picture worrying the organisation, as teams started to chop and change Americans regularly. Clubs were spending lots of money on players, but many were doing so without a strategy. In Keating's opinion, there needed to be a long-term vision for how these import players could help the game to develop. Noel felt there was a particular opportunity around exploring the Irish American linkage. He explained his perspective to the new *Irish Basketball Magazine* in 1980: We can be certain that there are many second and third generations Irish, who have played good basketball and who would love to come to Ireland and play basketball while seeing and living in the country of their ancestors. Clubs are recommended to research this idea and negotiate special educational courses of credit potential with universities and higher educational colleges with a view to making an attractive low-cost offer to visiting American players, coaches and, best of all, player coaches. The mere hiring of American players to win matches is of little benefit to Irish basketball. Clubs should involve their American players in local coaching clinics for schools and clubs. Clubs should pick Americans who are articulate, stimulating and genuinely interested in the development of Irish basketball. As our coaching in many areas needs improvement, clubs should choose American players with previous coaching and teaching experience – only then will the 'American link' pay off.'[xxi]

At the time, Keating's view married well with Enda Byrt's vision. Enda later admitted it was naive, but his initial idea was to find players who would help the Irish league and play for Ireland. Ultimately, this happened very rarely, as initially the players weren't what clubs were looking for and later the players were simply too good for the league.

As the professional Americans came in the early eighties, the main focus of Irish-born players was firmly on the home league. International competition tended to be club competitions like the Federations Cup, the Roy Curtis tournament and the Neptune tournament. Since the 1970s, Irish club teams were being heavily influenced by visiting teams like the Murray Metals from Scotland, and the competition level between Irish and British clubs was healthy. For players like Timmy McCarthy who captained Ireland and starred at home for Blue Demons, the club scene offered tremendous opportunities at the time. In 1983, Blue Demons went further than any Irish team had prior, when they beat Solent to win the Federations Cup. Demons played in a packed Parochial Hall and then travelled to play in Livingston in a seven-thousand-seat arena in the final of the competition. It was a far cry from Ireland's eight players playing in the European Championship only a year previously. For McCarthy, it was as if his club and national teams were operating in different worlds; The reality was that the clubs didn't really link to the National programme. We, as players who were selected, were very proud to play for our country. Blue Demons would never have honoured me for captaining my country – it wasn't in their DNA – and I'd say that was the same for most clubs. The clubs had no linkages with the international programme'.

With this disconnect as the backdrop, Danny Fulton and later Enda Byrt both struggled to get a regular commitment from all of their Irish stars. It was an issue that could be understood in many ways as

It's easy to save with Supe

What do members get?

1 Earn points & exchange for discounts off your shopping bill

100 points = €1 off your shopping. *

*Please refer to our Terms & Conditions for full details.

2 Use your points when YOU want

Unlike other schemes you don't have to wait for paper vouchers - use your points at any time you choose within 6 months of issue.

EUROSPAR

supereasy

Rewards

Start collecting points and avail of exclusive in-store prices today...

amateur players had to find a balance in their lives. Danny Fulton spoke with Tony McGee in the *Irish News* about the issue, and he was frustrated by the situation. Fulton has been criticised in the past for his selection of players. But he stands firm in his opinion that those he picks have fully earned their caps. He is not prepared, and who could blame him, to bother with players who will not show commitment. There are certain players for whom I have bent over backwards but they are not reliable. Why should I pick a player who I'm not certain of turning up at the airport? I have chosen players in the past who have rung me up the night before a game and told me they wouldn't be there. I have picked others who haven't even bothered to do that and haven't turned up. I have been criticised in the papers for not picking certain players and picking others. Those who have criticised me have not bothered to ask me why I make these choices. And to say that a player who hasn't played in the first division of the National League is not worthy of international selection is rubbish.' [xxii]

The one thing that the Irish team could offer was the opportunity to go to America, after Dan Doyle helped set up the US tours, starting in 1982. The trips served as fundraisers, but also gave players exposure to more top-level competition against US universities. From early on, American-born players were included with players like Kevin Greaney from St Vincent's making an early impact. The tours gave players like Deora Marsh, Dan Trant and Jerome Westbrooks opportunities to play for Ireland, but not all of the players who joined the Irish team were received positively by the Irish public or media. There were still questions around the national team and, in particular, the value of the US tours that had an over-reliance on American players.

Despite the tours' issues, Irish basketball was thriving, and any problems at international level barely made a blip on the radar of your average basketball fan. Crowds were flocking to games in away that transcended sport and became a cultural phenomenon at the time.

Throughout the decade, countless former NBA draft picks played in the league. The quality of American imports was at an all-time high, and crowds were willing to queue for hours to see them play. The strength of the era is illustrated by two players who made a brief appearance in Ireland. Mario Elie fleetingly played for Killester, winning the National Cup in 1987, before going on to reach the NBA, becoming a three time NBA champion. Less well known is Mike Smith, who played for Marian at that same time. After just one year in Dublin, Smith went on to play for Spanish giants like Joventut and Real Madrid, as he became the MVP of the ACB (Spain's top league), and he played all forty minutes of a Euroleague Championship game win for Real Madrid. Smith would even gain Spanish citizenship and represent Spain in the European Championships and Olympic Games.

As good as Smith and Elie were, their real impact on Irish basketball would pale in significance to some of the men who stayed longer in Ireland. That link between the Americans who arrived (and stayed) in the 1980s and the national team would progress in 1988.

Back in 1981, FIBA had decided to launch a new competition beginning in 1988 in Malta. The idea behind the competition was simple. Countries like Ireland who were being heavily beaten in European Championship qualification, needed another tournament with teams of a similar standard to develop. As Peter O'Hehir in the *Irish Press* put it, Irish Men's basketball teams seldom hold realistic hopes of victory at international level. But this new tournament catering for Europe's smaller nations provides Coach Fulton and his squad with competition at an apparently suitable level'[xxiii]. Initially, the tournament allowed an American guest player, and Kenny Perkins, the father of future NBA Champion Kendrick Perkins, was Ireland's. Perkins was not eligible for an Irish passport and was only allowed to play in this tournament because of this specific rule. His presence gave Danny Fulton's team greater size inside to compliment the Irish guards like Timmy McCarthy and the young Mark Keenan. Ireland instantly became a more rounded team. The rest of the squad was made up of domestically based talent, except for Karl Butler who was studying in the states at Vasser College in New York.

In the group stages, Ireland easily won against Gibraltar and narrowly beat Iceland by three, setting up a crunch game with San Marino. During that last group game, Timmy McCarthy, Ireland's captain and one of the team's most experienced players, picked up an ankle injury and was side-lined alongside Karl Butler and Cormac O'Donoghue. Ireland trailed at the half 42–35, but Kenny Perkins and Tom O'Sullivan galvanised the Irish with twenty-four points each to help Ireland win 79–74. The youth development was starting to be seen too, as Gareth Maguire, who had just turned eighteen before the tournament, put in an excellent performance. The win set up a semi-final matchup with Luxembourg, and despite the Irish injury concerns, the team narrowly won 91–87 to reach the first-ever Promotions Cup final.

Ireland would have a rematch against Iceland, who they had beaten already in the group stages. Despite a bright 14–5 start, Iceland was now familiar with Perkins and Paul Fitzgerald inside, and forced Ireland into poor turnovers that proved costly, causing them to lose 86–69. It was a disappointing end to a very promising tournament for the Irish. The loss of captain Timmy McCarthy proved insurmountable, as Ireland lacked enough experience at senior level to win a final without their best guard.

Despite the loss, there was a lot of reason for enthusiasm. The newly established Promotions Cup had given Ireland an opportunity to compete at a suitable level and the team were slowly gaining credibility as the eighties were drawing to an end.

Chapter 9: The Second Wave

Heading into 1990, Gerry Nihill was now in charge of the Junior Men as Enda moved up to head the Senior Men, but the underage recruitment policy remained the same. The inclusion of Irish Americans was close to being accepted as normal, as John Whelan articulated in the *Irish Independent*. His article, titled 'US Stars to knock Stripes off Opposition in Sheffield', stated, The Irish Junior men's team travel to Sheffield this weekend for the European Championships Qualification Tournament, and in the national squad will be two Irish Americans, Frank Powell and Tom Casey. The inclusion of the American power forwards is part of the Irish Basketball Association's policy of cultivating Stateside personnel for the Irish teams. The Jack Charlton-like tactics are an attempt to beef up the men's international panels who have difficulty at Junior and Senior level taking on top European sides like Italy, who number among their opposition at the Concord Sports Centre in Sheffield. The Irish Americans qualify to play for Ireland once they declare before their 19th birthday. The IBBA policy now is to discover young talented Americans and build up a pool of specialist players to complement the Irish members of the squad. Powell, at 6'7, from Holy Cross College, and Casey, at 6'8 out of Columbia University, are not displacing Irish players but rather filling a void, according to an IBBA spokesman. The Americans are not the tallest members of the panel to face Italy, Turkey, England and Wales. This distinction goes to John Burke of Newbridge and Mark Ellis of Belfast, both of whom measure 6'11, and are being groomed for the senior international team'.'[xxiv]

Indeed, two new top Americans were coming in, and Byrt had found height in two project players in John Burke and Mark Ellis. John Burke's journey into a senior international and a professional is scarcely believable, and yet it also reinforces what Enda Byrt could achieve when he believed in someone. Burke was a tall, gangly seventeen-year-old when first introduced to high-level basketball. The teenager hadn't grown into his body yet and was undoubtedly lacking in confidence. John played with a group of friends in the Dublin league without much success, but things would change when the group decided to go to the National Camp at Dungarvan. Enda Byrt was coaching, and his eyes turned to saucers when the big man walked in the door.

101

'How tall are you?' Enda asked.

'I'm 6'9,' replied John.

'No you're not, you're more than 6'9.'

'No, I'm not.'

'Yes, you are.'

So Byrt got out the measuring tape and found out that Burke was already almost 7 feet tall. 'Why do you say you're 6'9?'

John told him he hated being tall because of the social awkwardness that came with it, especially as he was a 'skinny young kid' as well. 'Whether it be basketball or anything else, when you're not good at something you're just another kid, but when you're not good, and you're tall, and everyone can see you, it can be quite horrific. I didn't want to be tall, which Enda found hilarious.'

Enda suddenly had a project, a young man that he could try and mould into one of the big players he knew they needed. Immediately Enda started to instil in Burke that America would be the place for him to develop. He convinced him to go to prep school in the States. 'I was a guy who was not comfortable with his height, who had no ideas or anything about playing basketball at any level . . . Enda was insistent that I go to the States, that with the potential I had, which I didn't see myself at that time, it was the only place for me to go where I could develop.' His time in prep school quickly got him on the radar of the former Lakers coach Butch Von Breda Kolff at Hofstra. 'So I could leave prep school early, I decided to sign with one of the schools who would take me, which was Hofstra. Enda was coming over with the Irish national team, and he met me at the airport and told me if I went to Hofstra I was off the Irish national team. I said, "Well, I'm going to Hofstra, I've made my decision." He told me, Butch Von Breda Kolff is seventy years old, is not into working and coaching and developing players. It's very lackadaisical and loose there; you're not going to develop and get better . . . I spent two years at Hofstra, by which point I knew I had to transfer to try and get better, so that tells you right there who was right or wrong when Enda told me I shouldn't go to Hofstra.'

Burke transferred to Southampton LIU a Division II school. But before he ever really progressed, his father became terminally ill with cancer and Burke returned home for a year to be closer to his family. Despite John focusing more on drinking and smoking than basketball at the time, Byrt wouldn't give up on Burke and the future he saw for him.

'A month or two before my father died, Enda came to visit the house; he spoke to my father alone, and my father said to Enda, no matter what happens, to make sure I go back to America, to get my education. So, when my father died, Enda came to the funeral and spoke to me after . . . I went back to America. My junior year at Southampton LIU I didn't do anything special, I was just ticking along. Very luckily for me going into my senior year, Southampton appointed Sidney Green as the head coach. Sidney had played ten years in the NBA and had been a big-time player with UNLV in the eighties. He turned me into a player, and I led Division II in blocks . . . From a purely selfish point of view, Enda was a godsend for me.'

Burke's development into an NCAA Division II All-Star, future professional and international is perhaps the best evidence of Byrt's hope that Irish players' standards could be raised by playing alongside Irish American teammates. Burke eventually went on to play professionally in Greece and Sweden amongst other countries. He even spent several games as the starting centre for Magic M7 in Sweden's top league. Incredibly, the team had Magic Johnson as one of their part owners, and the former Lakers and Dream Team star even suited up for some games that year.

The 1990 team also featured another critical figure in Irish basketball history in Befast's Adrian Fulton. The son of former Senior Men's head coach Danny, he was already a rising star in St Malachy's College. Adrian had been on the fringes of the 1988 team, and it was Irish American John Brennan's presence that meant Fulton was surplus to requirements. Despite the initial disappointment, it was a catalyst for Adrian to push on as a player:'There was a bit of disappointment and maybe a bit of resentment at the time of the process, but it didn't last for very long. I think I appreciated that things had to move on. He was twice as strong as I was and older than me. It was a wake-up call. If you want to play at this level, this is the level you have to get to.'

In the backcourt with Fulton was Stephen McCarthy from Cork, who became one of the Irish league's generational talents. Unfortunately, McCarthy and Byrt would never see eye to eye on the Irish senior team, and McCarthy's involvement ended up being very limited. As McCarthy looks back on the era, he does so without any regret. However, his absence at senior level was one that both could and should have been avoided, as finances became an issue between the team management and the player. 'I was young and only starting out in my career as such. I went to the States on a training week with the Irish team. After that, when we came home, we were going to Iceland for the European Championships. But I got a job and had to pull out of that trip. Whether it was the team manager, Enda or Basketball Ireland at the time, they were looking for me to refund them the money for the flights to go to the States for the training camp. That was the main reason I never played through that period, the fact that I had issues with the manager who was pushing for it at the time. As long as Enda was there, I wasn't playing on his side as well.'

The U19 competition in Sheffield was an important milestone, as Ireland won two games at a Junior Men's tournament for the first time, courtesy of defeats over Wales and England. McCarthy stole the show in the English game with 24 points as Ireland beat their neighbours for the first time at this level on a scoreline of 59–51.

In the Welsh game, Ireland won by 96 points, as Frank Powell became the second Irish American to break the forty-point mark for Ireland. Powell was to become one of the most important recruits ever unearthed by Byrt. The 6'7 forward was an incredible shooter and brought a level of confidence with him that no Irish player ever had before. As much as his Irish teammates were in awe of Powell's abilities early on, he also saw the opportunity to star for Ireland as an important step in his own evolution as a player: 'When I joined the team, they immediately looked at me as a primary scorer. [In] my college team, I was one of a handful of scorers, so there was an increased level of responsibility initially for that Junior team. That undoubtedly impacted on increased confidence level when I went back to Holy Cross.'

Tom Casey for his part averaged 7.3 points a game in the Ivy League for Columbia, including over 13 a game as a senior. The 6'9 forward was a key cog for Ireland as the team moved into the nineties and he also had a successful career in the UK. Significantly, Casey was one of the first recruits found through an Irish American resource that Enda Byrt had discovered. Enda's relationship with the St Thomas Aquinas head coach Dennis O'Donnell would lead to an introduction to one of America's most famous talent evaluators Tom Konchalski. Tom's family were from Tipperary, but he grew up in New York and developed into one of the top high-school analysts in America, becoming the author, editor and publisher of the *High School Basketball Illustrated* newsletter. Growing up in Queens, Tom's older brother Steve played for Archbishop Molloy High School, but Tom quickly found himself to be more of a writer and developed a niche analysing the game. When he retired in 2020 due to ill health, the top coaches in America all paid tribute to him. Dave Odom, who coached Tim Duncan at Wake Forrest, summed up the coach's feelings:'He is to basketball what Secretariat was to horse racing, what Sinatra and Streisand were to singing: just the best there ever was. When the Five-Star camp was at Honesdale [in Pennsylvania], all the coaches would go out to a place called Fireside after the night games. You had guys like Hubie Brown, Rick Pitino, Bob Knight and Chuck Daly — and plenty of others. We'd sit there and argue back and forth about players, coaches, everything basketball. Tom would sit quietly at the end of the table until finally we'd all turn to him and say, "What do you think?" Tom would then tell us everything — I mean *everything* — there was to know on the subject. And we all knew that everything he said was true.' Tom's relationship with Byrt would be a critical factor in unearthing some of the most talented Irish American players that played for Ireland in the early nineties. The Konchalski family's basketball connections to Ireland became even deeper when Tom's brother Steve was an assistant to the Canadian national team. The Canadians held a training camp in Dungarvan of all places in 1976 ahead of the Olympic Games. While in Ireland, they played an all-star team from Cork but as an article in the *Irish Examiner* outlined, they were more interested in training and a bit of team bonding: 'Up to then they had concentrated on training, their most ardent supporters some nuns who watched them train on Monday night and a group of Co. Waterford locals who joined them in a public house for a few refreshments following on training each evening.'

With Konchalski's help, Enda and Ireland were starting to have more success identifying players that could come in and make a significant impact for Ireland. The first of these was Casey, who attended the same high school that Konchalski had, and he had Irish heritage on his father's side from County Clare. Casey marched in the annual New York St Patrick's Day parade alongside his dad for many years, and the opportunity to represent Ireland opened up a new connection to the country. 'I considered myself very fortunate to do it because it did open up that pathway to not only learn my roots, but to see them.'

The recruitment of players like Casey and Powell by Byrt and Gerry Nihill opened up the possibility of improvements at Junior Men's level and a flow of eligible talent into the Senior set up. That impact at Senior level began in 1988 when John O'Hare was the first Irish American graduate from the Junior teams to appear in Olympic Pre-Qualifiers.

The real fruits of the Junior Men's programmes came later in 1992, as all but one player could trace their links back to those junior teams that Fulton, Byrt and Nihill had developed.

Despite some reservations about the way Enda Byrt was 'disregarding' experienced players, the youth policy was born out of progression at Junior Men's level and there was a growing confidence that Ireland were starting to go places. The change would really start to be seen at the start of the nineties, as a new culture was developing. Interestingly, one of the big drivers of that change would not come from young Irish Americans recruited in, but rather some of the established American import players who had come in during the

eighties and were now settled in Ireland.

Chapter 10: The Men Who Stayed

Kelvin Troy was as close to a superstar as Ireland would ever have. In reality, the country should never have benefitted from him playing here, especially for so long. During his college career at Rutgers, Kelvin was identified as one of the ten best defenders in America by *Sports Illustrated*. The 6'5 forward was a supreme athlete and averaged 12.3 points a game for Rutgers over 119 games. He helped his team reach the Sweet 16 as a sophomore, and in his junior year, he averaged 18.9 points while becoming an honourable mention All-American. His college career saw him inducted to the Rutgers Hall of Fame in 2000 and also saw him drafted by the Milwaukee Bucks in the fifth round of the 1981 NBA Draft. Like Elie years later, things didn't work out for Kelvin with the Bucks, and he had to start his career elsewhere. Fortunately, that elsewhere was Ireland.

Kelvin arrived into the country and instantly made an impact on several Irish club teams, most notably Killester. During their time together, Mario Elie lamented that Kelvin shouldn't be in Ireland because he was too good to be in the country. Kelvin, though, would be like many of the Irish players who came over in the eighties, finding a home that offered him more than just basketball. It was a decision that saw him discover happiness on and off the court. He got married, started a family, and became the first-ever American-born player to be inducted into the Basketball Ireland Hall of Fame. After some high-profile seasons in Ireland, Troy became one of Byrt's early American-born players as he brought Kelvin onto the Promotions Cup team in 1990. This was seen as a significant risk, as Kelvin had a larger-than-life personality and was notoriously temperamental. However, Byrt was willing to take a chance, and he was instantly rewarded in doing so. Kelvin's gratitude for the opportunity was evident from day one: 'It meant a lot to me. Enda Byrt was a great coach, and one thing he used to say to me was Americans just play for the money, but we (the Irish) play for the love of the game, and I never understood that. He made it clear to me that the reason was Americans were being paid to play, while we pay to play. That's true. I enjoyed playing for Ireland. I think it was the idea of playing for the country and playing for Enda.'

For Enda, having Troy was a major coup early in his time as Senior Men's coach, as it gave the team instant credibility. Troy not only provided a spark on the floor, but his presence gave legitimacy to

Byrt's programme at a time when both the team and Byrt needed public support most.

Sadly, Kelvin's time with the Irish team was limited by a long-term kidney issue that required a transplant. While Troy was in the hospital waiting for dialysis, Byrt stopped in to visit him. Sitting in the bed, Kelvin sat up in his usual animated way to greet his coach, wearing his green team polo. Troy told Enda that any time he required dialysis he insisted on having his Irish polo on, such was the significance of it to him.

It was moments like this that reaffirmed in Byrt's mind the vision he had for the Irish team was one worth following. People on the outside may have seen non-Irish-born players pulling on a jersey for selfish reasons, but when the real personalities and stories were explored, for some players, playing for Ireland seemingly meant so much. Reflecting years later on his time in the green jersey, Kelvin looked at what it meant to both his family at home in the States and Ireland. His brothers at home kept a close eye on him and were thrilled to see him add another chapter to his legacy in Ireland. The person most proud of Kelvin's international achievements was his wife Anne: 'My wife was so proud of me for anything to do with basketball, but to be a part of Irish basketball, she would brag about it all the time! We'd sit and have discussions about the game at all hours of the morning, and she was always so proud of me.'

As much as players like Kelin and Mario Elie were stars destined to make big names for themselves wherever they went, Jerome Westbrooks had to do more to carve out his place in history. Jerome arrived in Dublin from Chicago in 1981 and little did he know that he would still be playing basketball in the Dublin men's leagues almost forty years later. Aside from his longevity as a player, Westbrook's impact in Irish basketball as a player and a coach cannot be overstated and it is only a matter of time before he gets recognised in the Basketball Ireland Hall of Fame.

In truth, playing for Ireland wasn't on Jerome's radar when he first arrived in Ireland to teach, but an anniversary trip to Paris with his wife Lois would change the direction of his life forever. In 1988, on his way back into Ireland, Jerome was stopped at immigration and told that he faced a writ of deportation and would be sent back to the States. As it turned out, his new work permit had not yet been processed, and his existing one had expired, technically making him illegal in Ireland. Westbrooks was told that this writ of deportation could only be cleared by ministerial pardon and that his chances were slim. Fortunately, Jerome was able to turn to close friend, and Dublin football star, Brian Mullins, who pulled some strings to help get the situation resolved. While dealing with immigration, it was noticed that Jerome had been in the country long enough to be eligible for citizenship. If he took it, he would never have to deal with an issue like this again. Once he was assured that applying for Irish citizenship wouldn't affect his American citizenship, Jerome jumped at the opportunity. Around that same time, Westbrooks signed for Team Callahan Concrete in Trim, Co. Clare, where he would play regularly against Enda Byrt, who soon asked him to utilise the citizenship and play for Ireland. For Jerome, not only would it start a fascinating journey on the court with Ireland, but it would also help to solidify his own identity off it, especially as his own kids also grew up in Ireland. 'My involvement with the Irish team, that feeling of what established my Irishness, centred around all of the relationships that were part of the teams I was on. Enda was huge there; I can't say enough about Enda. I have so many stories that relate to

Enda and his passion. It was infectious. His passion for the Irish team and his ability to connect all of us . . . He was really able to establish that connection of who I was as a member of the Irish team and what Ireland was to me . . . The team itself, my connection through family that were born here, all of that became a part of the mix that began to combine the red, white and blue with the green, white and orange. The tricolour and the star-spangled banner definitely began to mix in that sense.'Jerome became a critical team member and calming influence as Enda established a new culture around the Irish squad.

Jerome's ultimate impact though was not on the court, but rather on the sidelines. Staying in Ireland as a teacher, he went on to have a major impact coaching in both St Fintan's College in Sutton and Holy Faith in Clontarf. The conveyor belt of talent he coached included numerous professional players (including his sons), countless internationals and multiple NCAA players. In one thirteen-year spell with St Fintan's, Jerome's teams won sixteen 'A' national titles. In many ways, he was the embodiment of what Noel Keating had hoped Irish American players could become in Ireland.

As much as Jerome and Kelvin would add to the Irish programme, they knew that their relationship with the team was slightly different from the rest of the players. On the American tours that visited Irish American hotspots on the East Coast of the States, they sometimes were questioned about their involvement and why they were there. As Jerome recounts, 'Even on the tour we probably had dealt with a number of situations there on the East Coast in very staunch Irish American communities, that were kind of going, Oh! Looking at us in the sense of, "you don't look too Irish".' For both men, they were used to race as an issue when they arrived in Ireland; many Irish people weren't used to seeing black people.

Both Jerome and Kelvin experienced looks and comments throughout their time with Ireland, even from opposing countries. Most were without malice, but there was always a note that they were different. Despite being looked at differently abroad, the basketball fans at home were happy to see them play and even separated the duo from the Irish American players that were starting to play for Ireland. 'There was no negativity, partly because of Enda's commitment to us. There was a perception within the Irish community in Ireland that perhaps we were more connected to the Irishness of the team than maybe others. You did hear that, "oh, well Jerome and Kelvin are here with us, they live with us. These other guys are blow-ins." We had lost a bit of our blow-in status because there were bigger blow-ins to deal with. In that sense, we were made to feel a part of the Irish team, and legitimately so.'

Chapter 11: The New Boss in Town

When Enda Byrt took over the national team, it wasn't met with enthusiasm in some quarters, and it only got worse when he picked his initial lineups for his first US tours. Byrt felt that an injection of youth and professionalism was needed. His initial squads for the tours were met with derision – it was thought that he was purposely ignoring the top players in the country. As we've seen already, that approach was borne out of successful Junior Men's campaigns, and yet Byrt was called out in the press by Roy Curtis for the two-tiered treatment of Irish and American players. 'Hypocrisy is alive and well in the upper echelons of Irish basketball. That is the only possible comment I can make after staring incredulously for several days at the recently announced Irish national team that will tour America later this month. Forget for a moment that this squad would do well to win the Carlow and District Under-19 B Championship. What really bugs me, and all the genuine basketball supporters is the double standards which Coach Enda Byrt seems to operate. Enda informed all and sundry that players like Liam McHale, Paul Fitzgerald and Tom O'Sullivan had been left out of the squad because of their inability to give a full-time commitment to a number of basketball camps over the summer. Fair enough. But then how in God's name, can he justify including a pair of American professionals who are about as Irish as Yorkshire pudding in his squad.'Others would also call out the new selection policy that Byrt and the IBBA were implementing: '. . . and the sensational selection of coach Enda Byrt, who has full control over team selection without interference from the IBBA, has been greeted with dismay by basketball fans all over the country . . . In April the IBBA devised a tough new policy which demanded an all-year-round commitment from players, including attendance at rigorous weekend training camps. Players of the calibre of Liam McHale and Tom O'Sullivan failed to make the panel, and with some notable exceptions, the side for the States is perceived by many as second rate.'[xxv]

The issue was primarily around the lack of Cork players; 'there are just five first division players named on a controversial Ireland basketball team to tour the East Coast of America next week and Cork's Burgerland/Neptune, runners up in NBL last year, and the North Monastery have been totally snubbed by Ireland coach Enda Byrt.' Despite the negative press, the Chief Executive of Irish basketball, Noel

Keating, publicly backed his coach's approach. 'It's part of current association policy and Enda is approaching it correctly.' [xxvi] Ireland was developing a clear policy for the national team, and the coach and federation were on the same page.

Byrt's youth injection to the team was instantly felt when the young duo of Adrian Fulton and Paschal Brennan from Limerick were brought into the squad for the 1990 Promotions Cup in Wales. Byrt was already getting negative press for his move away from the older guard, but his 1990 team gained more attention because it featured three American-born players. Unlike Perkins in 1988, the trio were not guests and were fully eligible internationals.

John O'Hare was part of the Junior Men's team and had shown himself to be a capable scorer at underage level, scoring 46 points in one game. His addition got less attention than the other two players, Jerome Westbrooks and Kelvin Troy. In particular, Troy's inclusion raised eyebrows as people weren't sure how he would fit into the team. The *Irish Press* wrote, 'Troy meanwhile hero and villain during his stay in Ireland is a potential match-winner. A late call-up to the squad, he should make a huge contribution if he fits into the team pattern.' [xxvii]Tro y was a star in every sense and one that required Byrt's full attention. Having never been selected to go on any of the US tours with the national team, the request to play for Ireland in 1990 was both a vindication and a great honour for Kelvin. 'I was always aware of the national team, but I was never asked back when I first came. When I was asked to play in 1990, I said, oh yeah I'll play. I always threw my nose up at it because I always felt that because I wasn't asked a long time ago, I was a bit jealous. But when I had the opportunity, I jumped at it, because I loved Ireland so much . . . I was just happy to be on the team. I was happy to be asked. At that time, I thought I was the best player, so I thought it was an honour for Ireland to have me and it was an honour for me as well.'

Ireland was keen to have Troy and Westbrooks, but other teams' feelings were pretty evident too. As the duo walked through the team hotel, their opponents noticed them. 'Kelvin and I are walking into the hotel in Cardiff, and Kelvin used to always say, "You hear that shit J, you hear that shit?" and what it was, in all these different languages, they were saying "Americanos". It was kind of funny for us because we definitely didn't feel like Americans playing on the Irish team. We just felt like we were members of the Irish team.' It wasn't only the opposition that noticed the two either, as Adrian Fulton remembers; 'It was the early days of drug testing. Jerome and Kelvin were two black guys, and it was pretty controversial. We were delighted to have them, but I know there was resentment from other teams. There was a random drugs test at the tournament, and the random tests for Ireland were Jerome and Kelvin. I still remember Kelvin turning to Jerome and saying, "random my ass, Jerome!"' Unsurprisingly, John O'Hare did not get the same 'American' attention from the others at the tournament.

On the court, Ireland destroyed Gibraltar by 73 in their first game but then worryingly struggled against San Marino in the second game. Kelvin Troy led the scoring with 23, and John O'Hare added 15. Still, it was two threes and 19 points from Paschal Brennan that gave Ireland a narrow two-point win 79–77. (Brennan was another young project of Enda's that would blossom into a player capable of going to America for college.)

Behind 20 points from Jerome Westbrooks and 19 from John O'Hare, Ireland then beat Luxembourg in the final group game to top the group and set up a semi-final with Cyprus. In a tense match, Ireland lost by a point as the game came down to the last possession. On the play, Kelvin felt he had the position to get the ball from Mark Keenan, but the ball didn't come inside. The play is something Kelvin reminds Keenan of at every opportunity, but others on the team could understand Keenan's decision. Troy was well known to both their opposition and the referees at the later stages of the tournament, and any hopes of Ireland getting a late call were slim. Kelvin knew he wasn't likely to get a call, in what would be a common theme for Americans over the fifteen years that followed. 'Refs just allowed them to bump me and grab me and all kinds of stuff. It was terrible . . . A lot of times because I was American, referees didn't allow me to play the way I was capable of playing.'

The loss was a bitter disappointment for Ireland, who felt they had the strength and squad to win, but instead, it was to serve as another battle scar on the road to better days.

Any hopes of the team's improvement leading to a change in heart from some of Ireland's domestic stars from the south were put to bed quickly the following year. The *Irish Basketball Magazine* was used as a mouthpiece to counteract some of the negative publicity the team had received in the previous years. The then team manager wrote, 'Following a fourth-placed finish in the Promotions Cup in December, coach Byrt again extended invitations to many players to his spring practice sessions. Despite Tom O'Sullivan and Seamus Woods declining for personal reasons, Stephen McCarthy and Colin O'Sullivan not replying to invitations and Paul Kelly and Don O'Sullivan confirming their availability, but then failing to attend the team practices, Coach Enda Byrt was able to name one of the strongest sides ever to represent Ireland for the "Belfast 1991" tournament.' Publicly naming and shaming players was something the management team felt necessary at the time, but it likely shut the door on any remote chances of the players reconsidering their options of playing for Enda. The disconnect between Cork players and the national team predated Enda's time with the squad. Yet, it will also forever be associated with his time as coach, too.

As it turned out, 1991 would be a crucial year for Byrt and his Irish squads both at home and abroad. Firstly, in July of 1991, Ireland took part in the World University Games for the first time. In July

1990, officials from the Colleges and Universities Sports Association of Ireland (CUSAI) met with the IBBA to discuss the possibility of sending a team to the 16th World University Games in Sheffield the following year. It was immediately recognised that this was a fantastic opportunity for basketball to develop, and the timing couldn't have been better. Byrt saw a unique opening, as the games allowed for an extended training camp and preparation stage that wouldn't traditionally be possible with the senior team.

The Sheffield team featured names like Pat Moran, Kevin Healy, Aidan Donnelly, Eamonn McCotter and Adrian Fulton. Alongside the names based in Ireland and the UK were five American based players who gave the squad more depth and height. The Brennan cousins John and Michael were there, with John in Lafayette and Michael playing at Princeton. Tom Casey from Columbia University, Brendan O'Sullivan from Dartmouth and Frank Powell from Holy Cross all joined the team to add scoring power.

The size and scale of the opportunity were clear from the outset, as the team joined 5,500 other athletes from 110 nations in the opening ceremony in front of 25,000 people at the Don Valley Stadium.

Ireland's first game was against Finland, and despite trailing by five after the first quarter, Ireland surged ahead thanks to Frank Powell and Tom Casey on the way to an opening win. The second group game provided an opportunity for Ireland that few would ever have expected, as the team went head to head with the United States of America. The USA team featured Duke All-American Bobby Hurley who had just won the National Championship the previous March, 7'2 Luther Wright from Seton Hall, future thirteen-year NBA professional Calbert Cheaney from Indiana, and his teammate Eric Anderson who was fresh off a first-team All-Big Ten Season. The match-up provided enough local media intrigue that Sky TV promoted the game as David vs Goliath and produced a unique documentary following the Irish team as they prepared for the game. The US team flexed early as they started the game on a 14–0 run, but Ireland settled down and had the score back to 21–13 behind seven early points from John Brennan. At the time, John struggled to get court-time in college for Lafayette, yet here he was going toe to toe with the best players in the country as he wore the green jersey. Ireland ultimately were outmatched, but the team's scrappiness forced 26 US turnovers, and the quality of Frank Powell with 17 points and Tom Casey with 11 did shine through. Sky's Clive Tyesley summed up the respect Ireland had earned: 'The result to the United States, but a night when Ireland gained the respect of the basketball public and their peers.' [xxviii] It was clear to anyone that Ireland was starting to make significant strides towards a more competitive national team. Ireland finished the tournament in tenth position as they narrowly missed out on a quarter-final spot.

Byrt was coming off the high of the first World University Games as Ireland took part in the annual Roy Curtis Invitational in 1991. The tournament was significant for Byrt's reign for several reasons. Firstly, it was the shining moment for one of the most beloved Americans ever to come to Ireland, Javan Dupree. Dupree was a 6'5 forward who had a standout career in North Texas before settling in Belfast. While playing for Danny Fulton in Star, he significantly impacted Irish internationals Adrian Fulton and Gareth Maguire and continues to impact players today as a coach. Away from the club game, Dupree was eligible for citizenship and came close to playing a similar role for Ireland as Jerome Westbrooks would. Javan never went on to play in a European Qualifiers or Promotions Cup tournament, but he did put on a dominant performance for Enda in the '91 Roy Curtis Tournament.

Secondly, it was one of the few occasions that one of Ireland's greatest domestic players lined out for the national team. Liam McHale was a Gaelic-football star as well as possibly Ireland's greatest ever basketball player. Sadly, he would never really get to play internationally in European competition due to his football commitments.

Lastly and most importantly, Ireland won the Roy Curtis, the country's most prestigious invitational tournament, which was a major early boost for Byrt's tenure as Irish coach. The win was made more incredible as it came after a six-overtime game against St Vincent's in the semi-final. The game held the record as the longest game in European basketball for many years. McHale shone with 31 points, while Dupree scored an Irish record of 57 points, in one of the most classic games in Irish history. Dupree would also perform well in the final, giving Enda his first silverware and the Irish team some much-needed credibility at home. The change in perception was seen in Cliona Foley's round-up of the tournament which referred to the team as 'Byrt's aces'. It was a long way from the 'joke standard' that had been referred to just a year earlier.

The tournament served as a tipping point for the Irish team as it started to gain more credibility. At the same time, the domestic league began to struggle after controversial new rules reduced Americans from two to just one per team. The move was made to protect some of the clubs who were struggling to stay afloat financially. It also aimed to increase Irish players on-court involvement.

Sadly, many of the top stars of that eighties era didn't follow Byrt into the new age of the Irish team, something that with the benefit of hindsight is a shame. The appetite for a new approach wasn't there for some players. Gareth Maguire felt that the US tours and some of the other tournaments were almost a break from their real basketball, 'The problem was those guys valued winning cups and leagues more than anything else. They enjoyed playing for Ireland, they enjoyed playing in Four Countries or Promotions Cup, but it was a huge change for Enda to come and try and change that mindset.' Stephen McCarthy was amongst the Neptune teams that were perhaps maligned. He recognised a difference in approach. 'I don't know if Enda had a problem with guys from Cork or Neptune as well. I think I was the only guy in the reckoning, even though we were still winning leagues and cups and stuff. I don't know whether that was a case of the older lads I was playing with didn't fancy playing for him, or he didn't fancy them playing for him. At the time, there was a culture where he was trying to bring in a more professional approach and bringing in more training outside of it. Those lads didn't have any interest in that. I was younger, and I had been with Enda, through Gerry Nihill and the U19 squad, so I was getting into that side of it as well. Whereas I was playing with Neptune, we trained hard during the week, and that was it, no one did gym or did extra stuff. That difference was possibly there between Enda's regime and the Cork players.'

Despite the ongoing differences between the national team and the country's top clubs, the balance of power seemed to be changing as Ireland entered the nineties. At the start of the eighties, the domestic league was set to explode with American players coming in to redefine the league. A decade later and it was now going to be the turn of the national team to progress.

As Ireland headed into 1992, there was growing confidence that the national team was ready to take a big step forward.

Chapter 12: The Women's Path

By the 1960s, men's basketball had gone well beyond the army barracks around the country and was now a popular national sport. Men's teams had already competed in the Olympics and European Club Championships in the short history of the game in Ireland. Although it has now grown into a 50/50 gender-balanced sport, women's basketball was much slower taking off in Ireland. Both the Dublin and Belfast Celtics had even competed in Europe before the women's game ever took hold. One of the critical early moments was a letter in the *Evening Herald* in October 1965 by Clem Keyes, seeking out female competitors interested in playing some organised basketball. The letter received over 600 responses, and the growth of women's basketball began.

Women's basketball wasn't hosted at the Olympics until 1976. Ireland did have the opportunity to qualify for these inaugural games, but expense got in the way of them ever competing. Initially, only six teams qualified to participate in women's basketball, unlike the twelve that took part on the men's side. The lower numbers and the slower development of the game in Europe meant that qualification was a worldwide event, rather than just European. In 1976, Ireland would have had to travel to Canada if they wanted to compete. At the time, the cost was prohibitive, and the team sat out.

Despite a later start internationally, the Irish women became competitive faster than their male counterparts. By 1976 they had already beaten Scotland and England, as well as Britain twice. Britain competed in the '76 qualifiers, and Ireland's control over their neighbours only increased the frustration that they couldn't compete at the top level beside them. The team's first taste of competition was in 1978 when they competed in the European Championships and beat Scotland.

The first attempt at Olympic qualification came in May 1980, ahead of the second-ever Women's Olympic tournament. Ireland, coached by Paudie O'Connor who was still playing on the men's team at the time, were overmatched in those early games, with the worst of the results being a ninety-nine-point loss to Czechoslovakia. Mary Baneham (one of the sport's most important early administrators and the Association's first female president) summed up the Czech match in the *Irish Basketball Magazine*: '(the game) demonstrated the inability of the Irish players to cope with a team which is professional in all but name. The dismal final score 26 to Ireland 125 to Czechoslovakia tells its own tale. Under pressure from the Czechs the Irish players seemed to lose all their ball-handling skills, while because of the height advantage, scores close-in were almost impossible.'[xxix]

Ireland struggled against elite opposition in part because of skill deficiencies, but just like the men, they also lacked size. In 1981, Liam Hartigan outlined similar issues to those Enda Byrt faced, as he proposed an idea to recruit and find tall players capable of making an impact for Ireland: 'A national scouting program for tall young girls is an urgent necessity. These could be brought together for special coaching in Dungarvan Clinic. With hard work, a number of these may be developed to national team potential.' [xxx] In essence, this is how Enda Byrt found John Burke and that success story validated Hartigan's vision.

As the eighties started, the women's game followed the men's game in other areas, including bringing in American players. The influx of Americans was very different from the men's though, and none of the female players created the same legacy as Kelvin Troy and Jerome Westbrooks.

Irish teams also took part in the Federations Cup, and in 1984 and 1985 Dublin's Naomh Mhuire followed in Belfast and Dublin Celtics' footsteps by playing in Europe. Although they were heavily beaten in both years, the club's ambition showed a belief that their domestic players (like the Grennell sisters) could compete beyond Ireland's shores.

Dan Doyle's arrival and the creation of the Irish American Foundation also impacted the women's game, albeit in a different way than the men's game. One of the Foundation's big focus areas was the creation of scholarship opportunities in the US, and it was on the women's side that this was truly capitalised. After the first summer trip in 1982, Sinead Daly from Blarney went to prep school, while Una Geoghegan from Dublin became the first Irish women to earn a Division I scholarship. Geoghegan didn't have the dream experience in college, but she broke down the door for others who followed soon after her. In 1984, hot on Geoghegan's heels at Marist, Dubliner Karen Hennessy signed for Iona College in New York. Hennessey had an excellent career, scoring 809 points for the Gaels, before coming home to Ireland and starring for both Meteors and the Irish team for many years. Karen's journey was one that many would see as the ideal for an Irish player. She went to America and did well and then returned to the domestic game and thrived for many years.

But as well as Karen Hennessy did in the States, it was her teammate Maggie Timoney that was the first to really become a star in America. Coming from the west of Ireland, Timoney was a tenacious guard who had been introduced to the game by the legendary Danny Thompson. Timoney had already benefitted by playing alongside the first female import player American Deborah Stancil for the Ballina Pacers, and she had also played for the Women's national team before arriving in college. At Iona, Maggie went on to have a Hall of Fame career, becoming Iona's leading scorer, a record which she held for many years. Timoney remains third all-time in Iona scoring history, has the second-best scoring average ever at the school, and also led the school in scoring each season she was there. In 2001, Maggie was inducted into Iona's Hall of Fame. (Later, she broke more glass ceilings as she became the first CEO of a major beer company in America when she took over Heineken USA.)

Timoney did also help the national team but did so mainly from a younger age. In 1984,when Timoney was just eighteen years of age, Ireland returned to the Olympic Qualifiers, and did so with an almost impossible trip to Cuba The tournament included Italy who finished fifth in the previous European Championships and South Korea who finished fourth in the last World Championships. Not only were Ireland facing top opposition, but a trip to Cuba was going to prove costly both for the organisation and the individuals. Coach Liam Hartigan pointed out the issue shortly after his squad won the 1982 Four Countries: 'Our girls will each contribute £200 of their own money to make the Cuban trip. Some of them will probably take out bank loans to raise the cash. Meanwhile, the heavily financed English players will be jetting to Miami to acclimatise for the Cuban tournament. This highlights the gulf our girls have managed to cross.' [xxxi] Acclimatisation turned out to be a major issue. The team arrived the day before the tournament and were obliterated by hosts Cuba the next day by 95 points. Despite the worst possible start, Ireland performed very well for the rest of the qualifiers, pushing both Mexico and South Korea. In fact, Ireland led both at half-time before losing. The scale of the achievement is best summed up by the fact that the South Korean's were in camp together for six months before the tournament and eventually went on to win the silver medal at the Olympics. Ireland wasn't losing to mid-tier European teams. The format was forcing them to play some of the world's top teams. Unfortunately, without sufficient experience, height or finance, they were struggling. The 1984 games did introduce Maggie Timoney, but also showed that domestic talents could contribute at the top table, with Marian Walsh in particular doing very well in Cuba.

As the disappointment in the early qualifiers mounted, a new competition arrived on the scene. The Promotions Cup had been a strong stepping-stone to international competitiveness for the men's team, and the women aimed to utilise it in the same way. Things looked promising as, in the first-ever tournament in 1989, Ireland found themselves leading 52–4 at half-time of their first game against Gibraltar, before winning by 84. Things did get more competitive, yet Ireland still reached the final before losing 63–57 to Austria in Luxembourg. The team were unlucky not to win the Promotions Cup as they made the final three times between '89 and '93, losing to Austria twice and Turkey once. What Turkey, a country of over 50 million people, was doing in the lower tier competition for smaller nations is another question.

During the Promotions Cup run, the Women's team stayed in European qualifiers. They hosted an unsuccessful campaign in Tralee that saw the team lose to group leaders Sweden and Finland and our local neighbours in England and Scotland. Ireland lost again to England in 1987 when we hosted Qualifiers in Neptune Stadium, after a late-game collapse. It was becoming a concern that as Ireland developed, others who we had been able to beat in the past were developing at a similar rate. The other avenue for development that the Women's team did look at was the 1991 World University Games in Sheffield where Jillian Hayes and Michelle Maguire led the team. Like their male counterparts, they got to compete against the Americans who were led by future Hall of Famers Lisa Leslie and Dawn Stayley. The only non-domestically-based players for the women were based in the UK, and the difference in approach between the men and women was starting to be noticeable. The men finished eighth while the women only won one game, beating Guam in their final match. In 1993 when the Men's team went to Buffalo in a turning point for Irish basketball, the Women's team did not go.

By 1994, the men were utilising their Irish American connections. They had found players to join both the Junior Men's teams and Senior team and had increased their competitiveness as a result. The Women's team did not have that same luxury, and finding American-born talent proved very difficult for Hartigan or any of the other coaches of the women's teams. This was in part to the simple fact that the women's professional game was less developed and less American players were coming to Europe to play. This fact only became more evident in the mid-nineties, when the Bosman ruling came into effect. Hartigan did try to bring one American-born player into his team in 1991. Just like Byrt he was attacked for doing so, although this was more due to the player in question rather than a philosophical issue as Peter O'Hehir wrote in the *Irish Press*: 'Coach Liam Hartigan has baffled all followers of women's basketball with his choice of an Irish squad to compete in an International Tournament in Luxembourg . . . included in the squad of ten is American Nora

McDonagh formerly of Naomh Mhuire and Corrib, but who has failed to hold down a regular spot in any national league team this season . . . McDonagh's inclusion as one of the "big players" means there is no room for former internationals such as Bernice Dowling, Sarah McCloskey, Mary O'Mahony or Martina Curry.'[xxxii]

Whether the Women's team could progress without Irish American help would be the question, especially as their male counterparts went headfirst into recruitment.

Chapter 13: The Battle Scars

As Ireland arrived in Cyprus for the 1992 Promotions Cup, the talk before the tournament was once again surrounding who wasn't there, as Liam McHale was a late removal from the squad. McHale was a crucial cog in the 1991 Roy Curtis win, but his availability was so limited that it effectively ruled him out of the team in '92. What got less fanfare at the time, though, was the influx of young Irish American talent into the Senior team. The vision that Danny Fulton and Enda Byrt had in the early 1980s was coming to fruition. Tom Casey, Frank Powell, Sean McDonagh, John Brennan and his cousin Michael were all included in the squad, with most of the group having already played for Byrt at the Junior Men's level. This time though, Ireland was without Jerome Westbrooks and Kelvin Troy. Westbrooks had returned to America for the summer, and Troy was sadly dealing with kidney issues that required a career-ending transplant.

Unlike in 1990, Ireland had little trouble disposing of San Marino as they led by almost 30 at half-time of their first game. A comfortable win over Malta in the group then set up a rematch from 1990 with Cyprus, who were now playing at home. The game proved to be a defining moment for Ireland, as the young group got to experience their first truly hostile environment against a very experienced Cypriot team. Frank Powell recalled that the game was 'as intense an environment as you can imagine. It was a gym with 2,500 seats on a Mediterranean island with 95 degrees outside. It was hot in the middle of June and the tension . . . they played with a different level of passion, they played like it was war and it carried over to the stands too. It was so hostile, I loved it, but there was an element that we had to watch our back here. Once the game was over, I remember Enda saying no showers, get on the bus and let's get out of here. I vividly remember the coins being thrown down [on us] . . . We were young kids between 18–23 and they had some grown men in their thirties who had been through some battles'. Despite the hostile environment, Ireland went into the final minute still in contention. Cyprus missed a jump shot in the last play but grabbed an offensive rebound and scored to win the game 90–89. Gareth Maguire's man was the one to score. He remonstrated with the referee about it being a push in the back, but as the team learned, that's not the type of call you are going to get in a hostile environment. 'The ref basically said to me if we didn't give him that basket we were all dead. He was probably right because at half-time I went to the toilet and I met some guy who was making a throat-cutting gesture to me!'. Ireland ended up losing the semi-final to Austria, as they could not find a way to bounce back from the Cypriot experience. Still, it was an event that the team recognised as a turning point for Ireland; the talented young group got a harsh life lesson in European basketball.

Ireland went on to play in the Pre-Olympic Tournament later that summer in Bilbao. The qualifiers highlighted that there were more lessons to be learnt and considerable room to go to catch Europe's next tier. The gulf in class could be partially linked to finances as Sweden's national team budget was said to be £350,000 compared to Ireland's £30,000. Despite losses to some of Europe's powers, Ireland were making progress, and in Frank Powell in particular, they had a growing star as he averaged 15.6 points a game. With ten of the twelve under twenty-four years of age, the prospect of the team improving dramatically over the next two to three years was very realistic.

Despite the positive progress on the floor, not everything was straightforward with the Irish American contingent. During the Promotions Cup in Cyprus, Michael Brennan joined the team to play alongside his cousin John. Michael was the higher quality player of the two and played for Pete Carrill at Princeton. Brennan played over 100 games in his career for Carrill, and in 1992 he was coming off his sophomore year in college. The Brennan family had been very supportive of the programme, helping to lead a lot of the fundraising in the States. Byrt was suddenly faced with a dilemma, as he knew he needed to bring John Burke to the qualifiers for Ireland's long-term benefit. Michael was the one to lose out. Byrt felt they needed height and Michael was competing against two of Ireland's developing guard talents in Adrian Fulton and Mark Keenan. Sadly, it would end Michael's involvement with Ireland. Although he played professionally for a couple of seasons in Europe before becoming an NCAA head coach, he never returned to the Irish setup.

The selection issue highlighted a complex dynamic for Byrt, particularly when families in America were putting in colossal work fundraising to ensure the team could exist. At times Byrt was having to coach the team and keep it going with his tireless work in America. Michael Brennan and Stephen McCarthy were two warnings that this balancing act might be an issue moving forward.

Ireland was now a decade removed from Dan Doyle's power move to take over the Senior national team in 1982. Although it was a moment of regret for everyone involved at the time, it led to a resurgence in youth development as Danny Fulton, Enda Byrt and Gerry Nihill focused on the Junior Men's team. The Irish and American-born players who came through those teams had laid a foundation for a promising future.

The team that went to Bilbao for that Olympic Pre-Qualifier in 1992 featured Karl Butler, Frank Powell, Tom Casey, Sean McDonagh, John Brennan, John Burke, Mark Ellis, Gareth Maguire, Adrian Fulton, Mark Keenan, Paschal Brennan and Ken Sullivan. Sullivan was the only player not to have come through those early Junior Men's squads. The four Americans on the squad were Ireland's top four scorers at the tournament. Although the team struggled, the tournament pointed at the possibility of a future where Irish Americans could help lead Ireland to a brighter future.

As John Brennan pointed out, 'The glory of it all came later in the nineties'. It was a leap of faith for these early Irish American players that they felt was worth taking because of a strong sense of commitment to Ireland. For people like John Brennan, they were just glad to find people along the way that were willing to support them. 'Without the Irish team I wouldn't have been the same player and for sure I wouldn't be where I am today. The impact of having that experience with Enda, Gerry, Noel [Keating], Pat [Coffey] and all those people who took the time to help me figure things out and even Frankie O'Loane in Dungannon.'

Many of these early players arrived in before opportunities to professionally benefit from having an Irish passport existed. The only time they got to talk about the experience was at job interviews or business meetings when they were asked to tell the panel something interesting about themselves. Although they didn't benefit from their involvement professionally, Ireland was set to go to a new level thanks to the foundation this initial wave of Irish American players helped to lay.

That next level would come quickly, as Ireland was about to unearth a new generation of Irish American talent.

Chapter 14: The Class of '93

Byrt's players were developing a comfort level in competing internationally both at World University Games level and with the Senior national team. The Promotions Cup in 1992 left a sour taste in their mouths, and yet it was also a coming of age for them in a way, as Cyprus taught the young Irish team some tough lessons. Now heading into 1993, Enda Byrt needed to find new Irish American talent to work alongside his current crop. Ahead of an Easter camp in New York, Byrt took out another ad in the *Irish Echo* simply calling out for Irish American basketball talent eligible for the national team to come to New York for the trials. This time he also had the help of Tom Konchalski, who was alerting him to potential targets.

At the 1993 trial were four players who were about to change the entire trajectory of what Ireland could aim to achieve. Amongst the group was a trio of big men in Alan Tomidy, Dan Callahan and Pat Burke. Alan Tomidy was a 6'10 big man from Marist College; Dan Callahan a 6'8 workhorse, who was already one of the best rebounders in the Big Ten Conference; last but not least was 6'10 Pat Burke, who was born in Ireland but had left at an early age and was now playing at

Auburn University. Enda had hit the jackpot, and guys like Frank Powell knew that things were about to change. What had been an ad hoc collection of Irish- and American-born players being brought together, now had the chance to be something even more, because of the new talent available: 'In '93 we have a couple of guys who are clearly going to have post-collegiate careers and are 6'10/7 feet . . . I loved that '92 team [in Bilbao], but I used to think about what it would have been like to have the '93 team in those games. If we had that '93 team, I think we potentially could have fared better.'

Not only was there confidence that the recruits had talent but, critically for Byrt, the characters were right too. Guys like John O'Connell and Dan Callahan arrived in and had the utmost respect for what playing for Ireland could mean. O'Connell was still developing as a player in St Anselms, a Division II school, but he was sent to the team with strict instructions from his college coach to copy everything Callahan and Frank Powell did. For O'Connell, being around the group became a stepping-stone for his career. He would also go on to distinguish himself as a professional playing in several of Europe's top leagues.

Critically, the players were from families who valued the idea of playing for Ireland above everything else. The meaning of representing Ireland was summed up by O'Connell: 'Nobody had more pride to put the Irish uniform on than a third-generation kid like me, whose parents grew up here in America but their family is in Ireland. For my mum and dad to see me put on an Irish uniform, that was the most amazing thing. When I first jogged out in Buffalo [at the World University Games] in that Irish kit, my dad cried, he couldn't believe I was representing Ireland. I'm not saying it means more to an American kid's parents, but it was one of the most remarkable things in our family's history that I jogged out in an Irish uniform. And I know that was the same for guys like Dan Callahan, Frank Powell . . . we grew up in an Irish American home, and you *idolise* everything Irish. It was the most important thing in the world to us.'

Having earned their respect in 1991, Ireland scrimmaged against the US team ahead of the tournament and played them competitively despite being outgunned again. Ireland had promise, and one of the key players heading into the tournament was the 6'10 Burke who had the physical attributes to become a high-level professional. For Burke, the opportunity to represent his country of birth came at an ideal time. He struggled to transition from an ice-hockey player into a big-time basketball player, and the Irish team presented an exciting opportunity for him. 'I got to reinvent myself. My story of having that growth sport later in life, changing sports from ice hockey over to basketball, I wouldn't say I mastered any skillset, I was just somebody who was going to give you 110 per cent. When I went off to college that first year, my collegiate team was less than supportive. It was almost like, when you get here, you better be ready; well, I was not ready. I had the frame, but I was nowhere near an understanding of the game or what was necessary, and I hadn't put the work in like they did. So, there was a lot of snide remarks in the locker room, people saying things under their breath, inside jokes that I didn't know about. So when I left, that was one of the nice things with the Irish team, none of them knew any of the commentary that was coming from the university, so I got there, and I got to pull my superman cape out, you know? . . . There was a lot of positive praise going around with everybody saying "good job". I was probably more guarded at that point because of my experience at the university, so when I got there, I got to reinvent myself.'

153

Ireland had a lot of talent at their disposal and had high hopes for reaching the top eight. For Byrt, the challenge was getting the team up to speed quickly. As became the norm over subsequent years, preparation time and finances were significant barriers to the team moving forward. In his post-event report to CUSAI, Byrt outlined the issues: 'Because of financial constraints we had to confine our preparation to a one-week residential camp at Nazareth College, New York. While this was excellent in every way, it still proved inadequate, particularly in the area of quality scrimmage games . . . if a men's basketball team travels in 1995, then a three-week training camp would be a prerequisite.' [xxxiii]

Ireland's goals were also not helped by the late withdrawal of Mexico from their three-team group. Rather than a good test from Mexico, Ireland played Hong Kong twice and beat them by over 80 points both times. The group stage was a great opportunity for new Irish talent to shine through, as 6'11 John Burke made his mark. Paschal Brennan also played well, showing his development from now playing in the States at St Thomas Aquinas. Long-time St Vincent's stalwarts Stephen McGuirk and Karl Donnelly both showed excellent promise and the critical Belfast duo of Adrian Fulton and Gareth Maguire provided leadership. American-born players also included John Joe Farragher who played at Marquette, but whose time with Ireland was limited. The reward for the easy group wins was a quarter-final clash with the USA on American soil.

This American team featured an incredibly talented unit that included a backcourt of future stars Michael Finley and Damon Stoudemire, while they also had future NBA players Eric Piatkowski and UCLA star Ed O'Bannon. A measure of the moment's importance to the American-born Irish players was seeing some of their parents crying in the stands as the Irish anthem played. It was a special moment that only the World University Games could provide Ireland.

Ireland used a mix of defences and stayed in the game for long periods, trailing by just 15 with ten minutes left before losing 93–64. Richard Scott from Kansas led the USA with 21 points while Ireland was led by one of its eight NCAA-based players Frank Powell. Having already played against the States in 1991, Powell was comfortable on this stage. In this game, he scored in the high twenties, and his performance made a huge impact on the team around him. John

O'Connell's eyes were opened to what a professional really looked like as he sought to develop his own game: 'Frank Powell didn't care who was on that USA team. He didn't change his game at all, and he shot the lights out, he wasn't the slightest bit intimidated, and I remember being very impressed that he didn't care. It was cool to see it wasn't fake, Frank was the coolest guy you could see, and I admired that. That was one of the first times I saw and played with someone that I perceived to be a professional.'

Adrian Fulton played for Ireland for almost twenty years. That performance by Powell stands out above the rest for him. 'Frankie Powell put in one of the best performances I've seen in an Irish jersey from any player. He scored 32 against them; they couldn't guard him. He was Larry Bird at our level, the perfect Larry Bird shot, slow guy, couldn't jump, but wow, could he shoot it. They were going nuts because they couldn't stop Frankie.'

Ireland made an impression on the Americans again, but it wasn't enough and they lost. They had to play more challenging games against several top teams in the seeding games, including Croatia. The Croatians featured Gordon Giricek who went on to play a big role in the

NBA, while also becoming a thorn in Ireland's side almost a decade later in the European Championships. (Giricek also has a famous footnote in basketball history while part of the Phoenix Suns: ahead of a game, Giricek trash-talked his teammate Shaquille O'Neal. Shaq decided enough was enough and put the Croatian in a sleeper hold, leaving him unconscious on the locker room floor!)

For Ireland, the tournament was a significant development as almost overnight the calibre of player available to Enda Byrt had dramatically improved. Having had the opportunity to compete in the States, players like Dan Callahan were sold on the idea of playing for Ireland. 'When we played in the World Games in Buffalo in '93, my dad literally rented an apartment for the entire three weeks. He thought it was the greatest thing in the world that I played for Ireland. We had a lot of good memories up there. My whole extended family were ecstatic that I got to wear Ireland on my jersey considering that my grandparents came from Ireland; it was really special.'

Interestingly, the issue of Irish-born players vs US-born players was a discussion point at the time, as Byrt included in his technical report for CUSAI: 'Final selection comprised four home-based college players, seven Irish-born players, while the remaining five were eligible Irish Americans. I would reiterate our policy of selection here by stating that we feel a responsibility to the players, to the Irish Basketball Association and to CUSAI to place the best possible team in competition. It is very difficult for a coaching staff to do otherwise or to pick a team on a political basis.' The report was a classic example of Byrt sticking to his guns and focusing on what he believed to be the best use of the University Games. This wouldn't be the last time that Byrt and CUSAI would clash over selection policies.

Chapter 15: The Bittersweet Silverware

The Irish team were growing in confidence each year as they added in new talent. The core of young Irish players who had become believers in Enda Byrt's system were now battle-hardened after some close calls in Europe. The 1993 World University Games trip showed that Ireland was getting closer to being competitive, and the new Irish American recruits had the potential to be game-changers. Add in the fact that Ireland was heading home to play in the brand-new National Basketball Arena in Dublin, and Ireland's rise from the Promotions Cup level seemed like a certainty.

Little did anyone know, but the team's biggest obstacle was not the previous winners Iceland or regular foes Cyprus, but rather an internal disagreement that would almost derail Ireland's progress.

Enda Byrt was willing to put himself out there for what he believed in, even if likely lead to personal repercussions. That was clear when he took over as national coach and he was questioned about his selection policy and overall approach to the Irish team. Byrt's vision demanded an increase in effort from the players who were involved. He also wanted the same from the organisation behind them. If things were going to be done, they should be done right, and it would likely come at a cost for the organisation.

Suddenly Ireland was faced with the magnification of a problem that had always been there. The Irish team was never well-financed, and now that they had a genuinely talented young group looking to push on in Europe, the question of money was back on the agenda. The IBA had to consider how much financial support could be placed into the national team to enable them to compete internationally.

With little or no high-performance funding available, sports are often reliant on commercial revenue to fund national teams. The challenge in sports like basketball is that ticketing and TV revenue are not strong enough to financially support a major international programme. The sport's dilemma is whether to invest more money into the national squad, hoping that a team's rising tide raises all boats within the game, or to focus reinvestment back into the grassroots game to ensure that more people are playing and more future stars developed.

For his part, Byrt wanted to give the team the best chance of success. At the time, the *Irish Independent* reported that he had asked for £20,500 in November of 1993 to do just that. The same report did indicate Enda was willing to dial things back and was reportedly happy with £14,500. After meeting with the IBA's Chief Executive Noel Keating, there was an understanding that financial support would be there. Months later though, as the Promotions Cup approached, the budget allocated was just £3,000.

Byrt was so outraged by the disrespect being shown to the programme that he resigned as head coach just weeks before the tournament. For a man who had spent years building a team to this point, it was a dramatic move to make, but one that he felt was necessary if Ireland were ever going to progress. The challenge that faced Keating and the governing body was evident in his quote to the *Independent* in the same May 25th article, 'there was a misunderstanding about the allocation of finance available to them. Efforts were made to bridge the gap but were unfortunately unsuccessful. The Association tried to find extra money for the team from the international programme, and we raised our grant to £7000,' Keating added. 'We accept the management's resignation with great regret but to have agreed to the level of funding requested would have left our extensive other programmes in disarray.' [xxxiv] The other challenge facing the Irish Basketball Association was the financial cost of the National Basketball Arena. Although it opened in 1993, some additional work had to be completed due to protests from local residents.

With his head coach now gone, Noel Keating had to appoint someone quickly. He needed an independent candidate who could step into the breach without stepping on any other Irish coaches' toes. He was fortunate to have an option already working for the IBA at the time, in the National Coaching Officer, Richard Conover. Richard was a native of Connecticut and had played for Syracuse University before coaching at both high school and NCAA level. In an interview with Yvonne Judge in the *Irish Press*, the American outlined issues he was having in his first year in the coaching officer job: 'Let's say the last year has been something of an enlightening for me. There are really more cultural differences than I ever imagined. The way we deal with everyday things is quite different and again it's just a matter of adjusting and getting used to things.' xxxv In his new role as the Senior Men's interim head coach, there was no time for getting used to things as the Promotions Cup was only a couple of days away.

The first issue was whether or not there would even be a team to coach. There was a genuine possibility of a strike on the cards. Players struggled with the decision particularly out of loyalty for Enda. John Burke had come home from the States to be with his dying father at the time. He knew that an opportunity to play on live television in front of his dad was one he couldn't pass up. 'I wasn't going to play because of my loyalty to Enda. But then I thought about it, my father was in the hospice at the time, and I thought for better or worse. I'll play because I'll have an opportunity for my father to see my play on television before he dies.' For John O'Connell, who was still in college, the situation was strange as he arrived in Ireland to play for the senior team for the first time. O'Connell ended up sitting upstairs in the National Basketball Arena, calling home to America to explain what was happening. His father made it clear that striking wasn't an option for John, although, in reality, it was never likely to get that far. 'All along I think we knew we were going to play. I think we were just trying to be as supportive as we could to Enda; that was the instruction from the senior guys on the team, be loyal to Enda. He's the one who brought us all together; he's the reason we're all here. I think that was apparent from the very beginning, that we're Enda's guys, and I hope the memory is that we did that, that we supported Enda.'

Byrt met with his senior players and reassured them that playing was the right thing to do. As Jerome Westbrooks put it, 'For Enda, the country was always bigger than the person'. It took senior players like Jerome and Mark Keenan to ensure that the camp was happy. The abiding memory for most of the players was that they didn't go wanting during the tournament, as the IBA tried to keep everything sweet during what was a tense time for everybody involved. Conover himself felt that the best was made of the situation, 'I must say that the players were really quite reasonable and cooperative with me and we all had a commitment to keep the peace, so to speak; things never really got uncomfortable'. Undoubtedly, part of the reason for that peace was Joey Boylan's presence on the bench. Boylan was a very familiar face for the players, many of whom played for him in St Vincent's, and his relationship with the players helped calm any tensions.

Ireland's objectives were clear to the home crowd as they kicked off the tournament destroying Malta by 41. The new additions of John O'Connell and Alan Tomidy were working well with established

Irish Americans Frank Powell and Tom Casey, while Jerome Westbrooks added extra leadership. In the second game, a forty-four-point win over Wales kept momentum building before the most formidable challenge of the group, Luxembourg. Gareth Maguire scored 14 first-half points and put in a fantastic overall performance to help Ireland race into a 51–38 lead. Alan Tomidy dominated inside with 20, and Frank Powell added 17 (including three three-pointers) to give Ireland a comfortable 87–69 win to book their place in the semi-finals.

Despite the work by everyone involved, the whole incident with Enda had impacted the team, and Ireland felt they had to overcome that to try and make history for the first time. As Westbrooks outlined; 'Enda came on board and put us all on a positive platform. Enda was there to help us get through that knock. Then you're in the tournament and the tournament's going well, it's hard not to still reflect on who you feel deserves to be a part of that. So, you're constantly dealing with these battles in making this the most enjoyable experience possible given some of the difficulties involved with it'.

In reality, there was only ever going to be two teams that could challenge Ireland at the tournament: Iceland and Cyprus. Iceland lost in the group stages to Cyprus so were now waiting for Ireland at the semi-final stage. In the previous three Promotions Cup events, Iceland had only been present at two, in 1988 and 1990. On both occasions they won the tournament, including beating Ireland in the 1988 final by 17. Fittingly, what had always been Ireland's Achilles heel was now their strength, as their size and power inside was overwhelming for an up-tempo Icelandic team. Byrt had identified the weakness and gone out and found players capable of plugging the gap for Ireland, who were now paying dividends. Ireland went inside early and often putting Iceland into foul trouble throughout. Alan Tomidy showed precisely the force that he could be as he dominated inside on the way to 24 points, 12 rebounds and three blocks. Fellow Irish American Tom Casey added 23 points and 16 boards while Frank Powell had 13. Sixty points and over 28 rebounds from three players.

As per his 1984 advice from the FIBA Junior Men's commissioner, Enda Byrt had clearly got his 'high player'. It was unfortunate he wasn't there to see it come to fruition, as Ireland marched on to the final for a rematch with their old foes Cyprus.

For many on the team, the memories of the hostile loss to Cyprus in 1992 motivated them to show that they weren't young kids anymore. It was now Ireland's turn to be at home and although the Irish fans were unlikely to be throwing coins or offering death threats to the opposing players, home comfort alone was likely to play a big role.

Initially, home court advantage looked like the only factor as Ireland hit seven threes in the first thirteen minutes, as they raced into a commanding seventeen-point lead. It wasn't going to be that simple for them, though, as Cyprus led a strong comeback as the Irish stiffened up heading towards history. Alan Tomidy drew lots of attention on his way to 15 points, but Frank Powell's shooting led the way as he scored 20, while Gareth Maguire added 17. What could have been one-way traffic was made more difficult by Ireland missing 18 free throws, and the game remained close into the dying minutes. Sharpshooter Karl Donnelly was having a tough night, but he stepped up to the mark to hit a critical three late in the game to give Ireland a platform to win. The Cypriot guard Christos Styllianides matched Donnelly's heroics as he hit a late three with thirteen seconds to go, to leave just a basket between the teams. Fittingly, the Irish captain Mark Keenan, one of the key figures for Danny Fulton's Junior Men ten years earlier, stepped up and closed the game out with a crucial free throw. Ireland had done it and won their first ever FIBA trophy at senior level.

The scenes in the National Basketball Arena saw Mark Keenan hoisted on to Alan Conlon and Jerome Westbrooks's shoulders in a fitting image that summed up the Irish journey to that point. Conlon was one of the first exports from Ireland to America (playing at Plymouth State), while Westbrooks had come to Ireland during its basketball boom and was now helping Ireland to thrive. The fact that they were lifting Mark Keenan, who had been part of those early Junior Men's squads only made it better. Asked by Cliona Foley after the game how it felt, Keenan summed up the player's thoughts succinctly: 'We did it for Enda. He's the one who brought this team together over the past six years.'[xxxvi]

Despite the moment of achievement for Ireland, all was still not entirely right for the team, as Richard Conover outlined in an interview after the tournament. 'As a person who is now part of Ireland, I feel a loyalty here, if that is the right word to use. I am kind of surprised as to how many people here just accept it, but I suppose you're more used to it than I am. The option of declaring for Ireland is obviously attractive to a college player in the States because it means that he will get to play at another level. My only question is though, is it an Irish team? I don't see many other European countries doing it when they could, so I wonder sometimes. I have gone out on a limb before to say that I thought Ireland could have won the Promotions Cup with all Irish players. In that, incidentally, I include people like Jerome Westbrooks, because I believe he has proven himself as Irish, he lives here and has citizenship.' It raised questions that a small minority of Irish people continued to ask for the remained of the Irish American era. But whether it was simply a continuation of bad blood after the nature of Byrt's exit or not, it's hard to tell. For a number of the Promotions Cup squad, Conover's contribution to the win was mostly negative. Some even pointed to Joey Boylan as the crucial figure on the bench. As John Burke put it, 'Rich Connover had no clue what he was doing and was in way over his head. It was a team that basically played and coached itself. In terms of a glory moment, that was Enda's crowning achievement, and he wasn't there for it . . . I think anyone who knows anything about that time, knows that winning Promotions Cup team was all because of him . . . Joey Boylan, not only is he a fantastic guy but he's a great basketball mind. He has a real intuition and high basketball IQ. He was shrewd too; he knew that Connover was the head coach, but he played and worked him so that he didn't hurt us too much. If Joey wasn't there, we wouldn't have won'.

Defenders of the overall recruitment policy would argue that you only need to look at the semi-final game against Iceland to see the impact that these Irish American players were having. One month after the Promotions Cup win, the Irish football team played in the World Cup at USA '94, and again, defenders of the Irish American approach asked whether or not the basketball team were any less Irish than the footballers who had fifteen of their twenty-two players born outside of Ireland.

After the dust settled on Ireland's famous Promotions Cup win, relationships had to be mended. Seven months after the tournament, an enquiry into the incident that led to Byrt's resignation was completed. The *Irish Examiner* reported, '. . . yesterday the IBA, in a statement, said the "genesis of the crisis lay in November 1993 when ambiguous communication about the monies that would be available to the coach and management team, together with a lack of precise minutes about the outcome of a meeting of the International Committee and the management of the international teams, led to a serious misunderstanding about the financial allocation to the Senior Men's team. The Chief Executive of the Association, Noel Keating, has taken full responsibility for the preparation of the ambiguous document".' According to the statement, which also said that the lessons from last May having been learned, the Association will now move to appoint a coach to the Senior Men's team.' [xxxvii]

It was a testament to both Keating and Byrt that Enda was reinstated in 1995, and the goal for European competitiveness was firmly on track again.

Overall, the Promotions Cup served a purpose for Ireland, but now the team was looking to move forward to new goals. As they did so, the Irish American psyche was also starting to show through. Frank Powell, who had portrayed himself to be unflappable on the court both in 1993 and during the Promotions Cup, had much bigger ambitions for Ireland. Years later, he summed up the key milestone for Ireland perfectly: 'I would characterise that '94 tournament as Ireland having had arrived, or at least, at a minimum, having had graduated from the Promotions Cup level teams to more middle-tier European countries from a competitive level. No more were we going to be worrying about trying to beat Luxembourg or Austria or Cyprus. That's so far in the rear-view mirror; Ireland should be playing with Spain, Germany, Italy, given its ability to recruit from America too. I look at it as a nice milestone, and I give Enda Byrt a lot of credit for assembling the pieces and helping move the programme along to the point where we could get past that Promotions Cup level.'

Chapter 16: The Next Step Up

As Frank Powell put it, Ireland graduated from Promotions Cup level in 1994, and the team's sights were now set on European Championship qualification. Enda Byrt was back in the hot seat after a review of the issues that preceded the tournament in Dublin. He was ready to try and deliver on the vision that he had been building towards for over fifteen years.

Domestically, the game was starting to fade from the heights of the late 1980s, as limits on American recruitment impacted the league. As Ireland entered the new qualification campaign, they were bolstered by a strong St Vincent's contingent. The Dubliners had taken up the mantle as Ireland's club representatives in Europe. Irish clubs' history competing in Europe is a short one, with Dublin Celtics paving the way in 1961 as they faced Antwerp in Dublin. The Belfast Celtics followed suit in 1962 and '63, but there was a break until the mid-1980's, when Naomh Mhuire's women's team competed against Agon 08 from Dusseldorf and Den Bosch from the Netherlands. In 1985, Neptune pushed Austria's Klosterneuberg over two legs. The Cork crowd was silenced in the first leg as the home team lost 99–84, but away from home Neptune beat the Austrians 94–83 and could have won the tie (they lost on aggregate 182–178). Legend has it that Neptune couldn't afford to make it to the next round so eased up at the end to avoid the financial repercussions if they did win.

In 1993, St Vincent's had a strong core from the Irish team including Mark Keenan, Jerome Westbrooks and Karl Donnelly. They were the first and only Irish club team to win a tie in European competition as they beat Iceland's Ungmennafélagið Snæfell in the first round of the European Cup. Vincent's played the home tie in the National Basketball Arena and won 78–75, courtesy of a last-second John Fitzgerald three. With their small lead, they went to Iceland and found themselves trailing by eight with a minute to go. Terry Strickland scored and drew a foul to earn a free throw, and on the missed bonus shot, Aidan Nutley grabbed the board and got a three-point play of his own. Vincent's ended up losing by two on the night, but in doing so secured themselves a famous one-point aggregate win. Their prize was a tie with Den Helder from the Netherlands in the second round (which they eventually lost out 174–127). Vincent's also went on to beat Real Madrid in the 1995 Roy Curtis; admittedly this was the second team for the Spanish giants but still a significant scalp for the Dubliners. Their progress showed that Ireland had talent and could compete internationally. With more of the World University Games team of 1993 also graduating through to the senior team, it was clear that the Promotions Cup win wasn't just a lucky home-court victory. Ireland was ready for a new challenge and a step up in competition.

The first qualifying campaign in 1995 saw the team head to Macedonia to compete. The fact that Ireland wasn't playing in the cosy confines of home or on the protected Promotions Cup circuit was evident straight away before they ever played a game. The Former Yugoslav Republic of Macedonia was struggling economically at the time. Some of the Irish players had previously been on US tours in the eighties, where they stayed in nice hotels and were treated like kings. As the team arrived in their new destination, it was a wake-up call to the new world they were playing in. Enda Byrt, always the teacher, saw the player's bemusement at their accommodation and used the moment to build the character and culture he was adamant about. Jerome Westbrooks remembers the moment they arrived vividly: 'I'm looking at some of these houses and things along the road, and I'm thinking, whoa, this is a low-income poverty-stricken scenario that we're in. But I was thinking once we get to the hotel, it will be OK. I had been on some of the tours with the team in America, and some of the hotels we stayed in were some of the nicest hotels you could have imagined . . . Up to then, anytime we stayed anywhere it was a nice hotel . . . We arrived at the hotel in Macedonia, and not only myself, but every player who was there, their mouths dropped . . .. Enda calmly stood up and turned to the whole group and said, "Gentlemen, we are in a very, very poor country and we need not do anything to remind them of it.'"

The shock was to continue on the court too, as the step-up in the competition was evident from the first game, as Ireland went head to head with Belarus. Ireland had a similar team to 1994 with Frank Powell, Alan Tomidy and John O'Connell representing the Irish Americans, while Westbrooks was the only naturalised player. Tomidy had been the dominant inside presence during the Promotions Cup the previous year, but now the competition was much more formidable. He struggled against Alexander Koul, the seven-foot big man (who was playing at George Washington University), scoring just five points in

14 minutes. Ireland trailed by 28 at the half and lost by 46, making people wonder if the national team had come very far at all.

Tomidy was better than his first performance showed, and he bounced back with 20 points in the second game, but Ireland still lost heavily to the hosts Macedonia. Any chance of qualification required a win against the Netherlands in their third game. A tough first half offensively saw Ireland trail by ten, 36–26. Despite being within one in the second half, it wasn't to be for Ireland as they moved to 0–3 in the group, with two games remaining. Tomidy had impressed again with 20 and had pulled down seven boards despite being only twenty-one years old. The American-born duo of Frank Powell and John O'Connell both chipped in 13. Still, Ireland needed something extra to start winning games.

On the 27 May 1995, Ireland won their first game after returning to European qualification level as they used a huge second half to blitz Albania and win by 17 points. John O'Connell was brilliant with 22 points and 13 rebounds, while Tomidy and Powell both added 16, with Powell hitting five threes. With one game left to go, Ireland was growing in confidence that they could win at this level, and they showed it by dismantling Norway 86–65. Powell top-scored with 23 points (including six threes) and Tomidy backed him up with 19. After winning the last two games, it turned out that a win against the Netherlands in their third game would have been enough to send them through to the semi-final round. It wasn't to be, though, and truthfully, Ireland weren't ready yet.

Ireland were building, however, and not only on the court. A bond was being developed within the group. There was also a growing appreciation that the players were ambassadors for Ireland, regardless of where they were born. The emphasis on culture was something that Enda not only preached, but he also practised. He drove that point home with a gesture at the end of the tournament that Westbrooks marvelled at: 'Enda is a bit of a linguist, he speaks French and Irish. We're in Macedonia, and the team liaison is there, and Enda is constantly on the guy asking him for this word and that word. We are like, "Enda, give the guy a break." At the end of the tournament, the banquet is on, and there's a presentation of gifts to the host nation. Every country goes up with their liaison who interprets your message and translates it. They called Ireland, and Enda went up, but . . . he's going up by himself.

Enda gave his whole speech and his gift presentation in Macedonian. He had every one of us jumping on the tables going crazy! It was so impressive. He was always encouraging us in the sense of that cultural experience. Here he was giving this insight into what was important about what we're involved in here. Whether it was who these people are and what we can be to them, or where we are and how we can maximise the experience.'

Suddenly the vision of a competitive Irish team didn't seem so farfetched, as Ireland geared up for the next qualification group in 1996. Before those qualifiers, there was one more stop to be made as Ireland was entered into the 1995 World University Games in Japan. Any hopes that the issues Byrt had faced in 1994 were finished and that the tournament would be drama free were put to bed in the team's annual technical report for 1995. 'It was evident to the management that very little finance would be coming from the Irish Basketball Association for two reasons. Firstly, because of the soured relationship which had resulted from the Promotions Cup dispute, and secondly, from the poor financial situation the Irish Basketball Association found itself in, particularly relating to its need to develop its National Arena.'

The financial backdrop was a big issue; the team's focus in the months leading up to the tournament was on raising funds rather than performance, and that created problems, according to Byrt. 'We fully accept that we created a situation where the players could not play to their full potential [by] accepting our lack of sufficient finance in an effort to achieve our goal of attending these games. It should be said at this point, that when a coach has to spend much of his time dealing with financial contributions from players, their colleges and families, that it creates an unusual situation between player and coach and one that is not conducive to achieving the highest level of performance.' xxxviii

Although issues in preparation affected Ireland, they were still a talented team. (Hopes of an improved finish were dealt a severe blow when Pat Burke, who had blossomed into a star at Auburn, never made it to the full tournament. During a scrimmage beforehand, Burke was frustrated and took his anger out on the basket support, injuring his hand in the process.) Before the tournament, Ireland played a warm-up game against the USA, and it created some of the most memorable moments of any of the World University Games trips. As Ireland took the floor, John O'Connell and one of the Irish-born players had a quick conversation, one that O'Connell laughs remembering.

Teammate: Tell me about this fella?

John: It's Allen Iverson.

Teammate: I'll probably pressure him.

John: Don't pressure him.

Teammate: Should I force him left, or right?

John: Either way he's going to go by you, it doesn't matter what you do, Fulty.

Teammate: Who's that guy?

John: It's Kerry Kittles, one of the best shooters in the country.

Teammate: What about that guy?

John: That's Tim Duncan – these are the best players in the world, we're going to get killed!

'. . . It was just funny walking out there.'

The Americans featured Ray Allen, Tim Duncan, Allen Iverson, Kerry Kittles and lots more NBA talent. Not all of these stars were familiar with their Irish opponents either. O'Connell recalls one surreal moment; 'I think it was Allen Iverson, said to one of us, "Do you guys speak English?" [The Irish player] was like, "This guy!? Are you f-ing kidding me!?"' Despite being overmatched, Ireland started perfectly and opened up a four-point lead after just three minutes. What happened next is infamous within the group. Adrian Fulton was dribbling down the court, and he almost did a double-take as he looked to the sideline. 'We led for the first three minutes, and I still remember coming over the halfway line and glanced at Enda to see what he was going to say, what he wanted to run. He had his camera out and was taking a photo of the scoreboard. And they went on a 22–0 run. We went from leading by 4 to down 20 quickly!'. Enda's smile quickly disappeared during that run, with John Burke drawing the ire of his coach. 'During that explosion after the timeout, [the Americans] got a steal at half-court, and I think Kerry Kittles pulled up for a three. It hit the back of the ring, and the ball caromed up, so me and John O'Connell went to get position to get ready for the rebound. Next thing, Allen Iverson's balls are over my head and his legs are spread out like Jordan. He gets the ball, cocks it back and goes "aaaaagh" as he bangs it. There were no fans in there because it was a scrimmage, so it was just dead silence. John O'Connell turned to me and just goes . . . "God damn!" The two of us are running back up the court laughing, and Enda is on the sideline shouting expletives at us!'

Ireland headed into the actual tournament with high hopes, despite the loss of Burke and the other off-court challenges that they faced. The group was open for Ireland as they beat Korea, Finland and Mexico before losing comprehensively to Canada. The Canadian loss meant that Ireland faced Japan in the quarter-final. After the group stages, Ireland was weary, and were beaten well by Japan, before further defeats in the classification stages led to another 8th place finish.

In the post-event report, finance was the main issue highlighted. CUSAI were also clearly still unhappy with the composition of the team. Byrt addressed the problem directly in his typical shoot-from-the-hip-manner. 'I realise that CUSAI have a fundamental difficulty in recognising the Irish American player and to some extent the Irish player based at the American College. This is an area of policy that has to be crystal clear before embarking on any further Student Games. It is a cloudy area of policy and causes no end of embarrassment and heartache to both players and their families who support them in this endeavour. I realise that CUSAI is concerned about the relationship between the World Games and the development of university sports here in Ireland. This is something that requires thorough debate. To initiate the debate, I would like to know how we could evaluate the success of Sonia O'Sullivan and relate this to any impact on university sport in Ireland.' xxxix

Despite issues that were there, what was evident at the time was that the University Games was an accelerator for Byrt's vision for the national teams. Ireland had found talent that they could never have dreamt of before. They had also developed some of the young Irish talents into capable international players with a lot of experience. The issue now for Irish basketball was not one of talent. Instead, it was one of resources. Byrt wanted to push the boat out and find a way to make a breakthrough, whether the rest of the sport shared his vision or not was the question.

Chapter 17: The Bosman Rule

As Ireland were unearthing more and more talented Irish-American players, the attractiveness of what the country could offer was about to change dramatically, courtesy of a Belgian footballer.

Jean-Marc Bosman was a Belgian footballer who had represented his country at underage level and played professionally in the Belgian league. Before moving on to RFC Liège on a two-year deal, he initially started with Standard Liège and played eighty-three times in midfield. It was at RFC Liège where his troubles began. After just three appearances in two seasons (1988–90), Bosman was surplus to requirements, and he wanted to move on with his career. Dunkerque, a French club, tried to sign him and Bosman was happy to go. At the time, football rules stated that when a player's contract ended, he could only move if the club released him on a free transfer or sold him. RFC Liège had no use for Bosman on the field, but they still felt he was valuable, especially aged just twenty-five, and they placed a £500,000 transfer price on him. Dunkerque refused, and the deal was dead. After the agreement died, Liège cut Bosman's wages by 75 per cent, to just £500 per month. The move infuriated Bosman, and he decided to take his case against the Belgian FA and UEFA to the European Court in 1995. He accused the club of refusing to sell him after his contract expired, which violated his rights under the Treaty of Rome (1957).

One of the guiding cases for the argument was Irish American Larry O'Brien's creation of free agency in the NBA, which he had established as a way to deal with player movement issues after the NBA and ABA merger. The very same principles applied here; players should be able to choose their destination once their contract expires. Under the Treaty of Rome, members of the European Community (now the EU), were allowed freedom of movement within Europe.

The ruling from the court was in favour of Bosman, and the court deemed two critical factors.

1. Players should be free to move when their contract expires

2. EU clubs could hire any number of EU players

The impact of the ruling was astronomical, as it gave a higher degree of power to players. They could now force clubs' hands as their contracts were coming to an end. Clubs would have to agree to transfer demands or potentially get nothing in return for their player when his contract ended. Players could also use the free transfer as a way to demand significant signing bonuses. It's argued that the Bosman ruling helped limit smaller clubs and further separated European's rich elite teams within football. The presence of the same core teams in the Champions League is a testament to that argument.

For Irish basketball, the ruling was significant in two main ways. Firstly, domestically it opened the potential for EU citizens to play in the National League. In the club world, many teams looked to utilise this in the late 1990s and early 2000s with Americans holding European passports commonplace across Ireland. Eventually, the league implemented rules to limit this, and a new ruling that players had to be developed in FIBA Europe countries came into place.

The second impact was more immediate and, in the short term, much more influential for the national programme specifically. Suddenly a window of opportunity had opened for players with Irish passports. This directly led to opportunities for players like Alan Conlon and John Burke to go and play abroad, but it more critically opened the door to Europe for Americans with Irish ancestry. Getting an Irish passport suddenly became incredibly valuable, as the number of opportunities to play in the top European leagues increased. Most leagues had limits on American players, so an American player who could classify as Irish instantly became more valuable to the top teams in Europe. What quickly happened was that agents and players realised that utilising Irish heritage would open the door to greater professional opportunities and the ability to earn more money in Europe. This inevitably led to Irish Americans lending their talent to the Irish national team, where they otherwise wouldn't have. Whether or not this sort of reason for playing for Ireland was what had been originally hoped for when Enda started recruiting Irish Americans is something that would be come an ongoing debate for the next fifteen years.

The issue was a thorny one within European basketball too, and remains so even today. Many countries have been accused of having professional players with no connection to their country.

Ireland's link with Irish America was perceived internationally as being different. Henrik Dettman, Germany's coach in the early 2000s when they played Ireland, stated, 'Of course you have a different history, and your history gave you this opportunity which you used well. If I'm going to complain about something going on in European basketball, it's how many countries are recruiting a player where they are missing a key position. I didn't see Ireland doing this, it was natural, I didn't see it as a misuse of the rules. Some other countries don't need this and should do a better job with their own people, that's another story.'

As the Bosman rule came into effect in December 1995, Ireland was about to find a surge in interest in Irish passports amongst good American players. At the time, there was a rule requiring people to have their passport for a number of years before they were eligible to play for the national team, but even that would soon change. Thanks to the existing base of American-born players already playing for Ireland, the country was set up to take maximum advantage of the new rules.

Chapter 18: The Near Miss

Having learned lessons both on and off the floor in Macedonia, the team got back together one year later in 1996 and headed to Reykjavik in Iceland for the preliminary group of the 1999 European Championships. Ireland was drawn with old Promotions Cup foes in Iceland, Cyprus and Luxembourg as well as Denmark and Albania (who they had beaten the previous year). The top two teams from the group automatically qualified to the semi-final round of the European Championships. The team who came third went into the next qualifying round and still had a chance to proceed to the semi-finals.

The Irish team looked similar to the team that had attempted qualification in Macedonia with many familiar faces back. Alan Tomidy was the focal point of the offence again inside, and John O'Connell was back to provide his do-it-all energy from the wing. Crucially, despite having entered semi-retirement after starting law school in America, Frank Powell was back in action. He was expected to provide scoring that Ireland badly needed. In the previous campaign, Ireland had struggled against the better teams inside. It was hoped that seven-foot Naas man John Burke could take some of the pressure off Tomidy.

There were three more Irish Americans in the squad too. Dan Callahan made his European Championship debut, and was everything Ireland needed and more. He was a tough, hard-nosed big man who had a way of dominating on the boards. Despite being only 6'8, he was one of the NCAA's leading rebounders in college. He was an ideal partner for Tomidy inside. The American-born Joseph Intermann who had played at the World University Games also featured on the squad but had a limited impact. The final Irish American was a wildcard for Byrt, Ken Lacey. As the team arrived in Iceland to play the first game, Ken Lacey was only seventeen years old.

For the homegrown contingent, there were the ever-present Adrian Fulton and Mark Keenan, while the exciting prospect Niall Phelan made his Championship debut. Phelan was at California College and would later play at Robert Morris University, but was just twenty years old for this campaign. He was a late call-up to the squad as veteran Stephen McCarthy had to withdraw due to work commitments.

(The issue around work commitments reflected the wider imbalances between homegrown amateur players and Irish American players who were either professional or playing in the NCAA. Byrt was well used to top domestic players not playing; still, the work-commitment issue was something that bothered him, as he told Kieran Shannon in the *Irish Examiner*. 'You must respect the decision of his employers and you can hardly expect a player to dump his job, but it does reflect the current labour market. It would mean that representing your country doesn't mean anything anymore. It really does raise the wider issue of there being no policy in Ireland for amateur players getting access to play for their country. You have a situation at the moment that players are afraid to say at interviews that they play on an Irish team because employers think they'll be going away so often.' [xl] This issue still remains for the Irish team today. Interestingly, players from Northern Ireland did get additional time off for representing their country. Gareth Maguire and Adrian Fulton received time away from teaching, but their southern counterparts could not.)

With the combination of scoring, size and experience, Ireland expected a lot from the group, especially as they were facing off against teams that they had played before. In the first game, it was the old nemesis of Cyprus in the way for Ireland. Despite leading at the half by three, the second half saw Ireland's offence collapse as they fell 84–73 to the Cypriots. John Burke led the way with 22 points, but no other player had more than 11 in a frustrating night for the Irish. The absence of Dan Callahan didn't help things. He wouldn't play in the group's first three games as airline issues delayed his arrival into Iceland. Things also weren't helped by some shocking incompetence from the table officials in Iceland, as the *Irish Independent* reported: 'Ireland led 36–33 at half-time. But six minutes into the second half the team discovered that two fouls that should have been attributed to the Cypriot Lucas Antonius had been incorrectly attributed to an Irish player. The match commissioner accepted that the fouls were not Ireland's but amazingly did not return them to Lucas. If they had, he would have fouled out with five fouls at that stage, but he stayed on the court for the remaining 14 minutes and scored 14 points from therein, a major factor in the result.' [xli]

Ireland had to bounce back from the disappointment and Albania provided the second challenge of the campaign. Ireland easily dispatched of the Albanians again for the second straight year as they coasted to a 96–77 win. Frank Powell and Alan Tomidy led the scoring, and Adrian Fulton ran the show with six assists. The win set up a crucial game against the hosts, Iceland. Having lost to Cyprus already, a loss to the hosts would remove any chance of automatic progression to the semi-final stage, as both Iceland and Denmark were so far unbeaten. Unfortunately for Ireland, they went down early by 14 points, and despite getting it back level at the half, they again fell behind in the second half and lost 89–74. With two games to go, Ireland faced the group favourites, Denmark, who had won their first three games by an average of 34 points. Tied at 39 at the half, the second half provided lots of drama. Dan Callahan showed his worth as he fought inside, scoring 12 points and helping relieve the pressure on Ireland as Alan Tomidy battled foul trouble. John O'Connell played very well, scoring 16, but Frank Powell yet again led Ireland's hopes. Ireland trailed Denmark by one with 11.5 seconds to go, but a last-second three by the Holy Cross big man Powell secured Ireland's most famous win in qualification to date. Powell shot the ball amazingly all night, and the buzzer-beater was his seventh three of the evening as he finished with 27 points. All this while being semi-retired and in law school!

In the final game of the group, Ireland faced Luxembourg and destroyed the minnows 115–81. The game was most notable because Enda gave Ken Lacey his first big opportunity in the green jersey. The youngest member of the team, having turned eighteen on the second day of the tournament, Lacey was still very raw, but he scored 20 against Luxembourg. He did enough to catch the eye of professional scouts at the tournament, who immediately offered him a five year deal in Italy. It was a sign of things to come not only for Lacey but for the Irish Americans in general. The Bosman rule was starting to impact the European leagues and teams were figuring out that there were valuable players amongst the Irish squad that they could sign. For Ireland, this proved to be both a blessing and a curse in many ways. There was high-level talent coming to represent Ireland, but holding on to these players and dealing with their professional clubs was set to become a lot more complicated.

As the dust settled in Iceland, it was the start of a series of what-ifs for Ireland. A win in the opening game against Cyprus would have given them a major shot at the elusive semi-final round. What if the table officials had recorded the fouls on the right player? What if Dan Callahan had been able to join the squad from the beginning? What if Stephen McCarthy, a veteran domestic guard, had been able to get away from work to play? Unfortunately, it was the start of an ongoing trend for Ireland, where the margins between success and failure were small.

Despite the disappointment of Iceland in May of 1996, Ireland's hopes of progressing to the next round were not dead yet as they went on to play in a four-team qualification group. Irish hopes were further bolstered by the fact that the tournament was to be held in the National Basketball Arena in Tallaght. As Ireland came together in 1997 for the qualifiers, they had their big star Alan Tomidy back in the middle to lead the way. This time, Dan Callahan would be available from the start. Callahan's professional career had begun to take off after an initial false start straight out of college. He played the 1996/97 season in Belgium, so he was particularly excited to now face the Belgians in Dublin. Ken Lacey had turned down the pro contract offer after discussing the opportunity with his parents and had instead just finished his freshman year at Rider University. Lacey was now projected to be a contributor to the team, while the always reliable John O'Connell had also returned. Crucially, Frank Powell wasn't available, and Ireland was likely to miss his scoring ability, although domestic guards Gareth Maguire and Karl Donnelly would hopefully provide some scoring punch. The group included Belgium, Norway and the Netherlands, with the Dutch favoured to go through as group winners. Two teams would progress to the next stage, so Ireland targeted a win against Norway and a massive battle with Belgium for the second spot.

Belgium was the first game in the Arena, and it was a classic. Ireland raced out to an early lead with Tomidy, Callahan and O'Connell all doing damage as Ireland led by 11. Belgium battled back to tie the game before Karl Donnelly hit three threes to give Ireland a 50–44 lead at the half. Things were going well for Ireland, with Dan Callahan already scoring 15 points and grabbing nine boards after just twenty-three minutes of the game. Then disaster struck. On an innocuous play, Alan Tomidy and Dan Callahan collided, injuring Callahan and ruling him out for the rest of the game and the tournament.

It was a devastating blow for Callahan as he was finally getting to make his mark for Ireland and his parents were over from America to see him play. 'My parents flew over for the tournament, and Alan kneed me in the quad, and I had a contusion. My whole leg ended up turning purple for that summer. It was awful. I was excited for my parents to be there. After the tournament, my parents rented a car, and we drove down to our family farm, where my grandfather lived. I was so tall and had to have my foot straight, so I sat in the backseat with my leg between my parents in the front for four days as we drove around Ireland.' The disappointment for Callahan was compounded by how close he knew Ireland was getting to making the breakthrough they wanted; something that would play out in front of his eyes over the rest of the tournament. 'We had a lot of talent and had some chemistry developing between all the guys because we were used to playing together. Myself, Alan and Ken. We knew we were right there and ready to play through.'

The injury shocked Ireland, and they didn't score for eight minutes at the start of the second half. Belgium took advantage and pushed out a lead of eight with just three minutes on the clock. Through

Lacey and Tomidy, Ireland dragged themselves back into the game, and it was all to play for in the final minute before missed free throws from Ireland and some cool nerves from Belgium sealed a dramatic win 82–79. The fact that Ireland had come so far from losing to Belgium by 62 twenty years earlier, was scant consolation and the players were despondent at what was a missed opportunity. The Irish would rue the free-throw battle as they shot just 64 per cent from the line, while also giving Belgium thirty-five chances from the charity stripe.

Outside of the loss, an area for concern for Ireland was that Karl Donnelly was the only homegrown player to score more than one point in the game.

Ireland faced Norway in the second game and just like two years earlier they beat them again, this time 78–65. A much more balanced effort offensively saw the Star duo of Adrian Fulton and Gareth Maguire combine for 23, while Karl Donnelly added another 9. Alan Tomidy again led the way with 22 points and 9 rebounds. The win set up a crunch decider with the Netherlands. The Netherlands had already beaten Belgium by six, so if Ireland could win by four or more points, they would reach the semi-final stage. Things were made trickier by the presence of a seven-foot LSU big man who had been drafted in the NBA during the early 1990s. No, not Shaquille O'Neal. Gerrit Hammink was Shaq's teammate at LSU, a year behind the phenom. Hammink played very little while Shaq was on campus at LSU, but when Shaq left, he stepped up and averaged 15 points and 10 rebounds earning him a first-round pick. Knee issues limited him, and although he was around the NBA for several years, his production was limited to just eight total games and twenty-seven minutes. Despite his lack of NBA success, he was still a strong big man and was reportedly earning over a million pounds in Europe at the time. Hammink caused Ireland major issues with 23 points and 10 rebounds, as the Dutch again forced Ireland to foul, earning sixteen more free-throw attempts than the home team in a 78–69 win.

The disappointment for the team was palpable as a significant opportunity had slipped through their hands. Adrian Fulton recalls their frustration: 'I remember being absolutely devastated that we lost. I genuinely thought that we had a really good chance. At that stage, we really wanted to get to the next level, and we had been trying for a number of years without much success. We had been knocking on the door.'

Byrt told the *Examiner*, 'The players were totally despondent afterwards. If we had made three less mistakes in both the Belgium and Holland games, we'd probably have qualified. If we had qualified, we might not have troubled three of the six other teams in the pool, but we certainly would have the other three. The loss of Dan Callahan after Friday night's game was a big loss. I'm not offering it as an excuse because we still had enough talent, but maybe we wouldn't have had to demand so much from others if he was there.'[xlii]

These were the margins that Ireland faced. They couldn't afford to lose any player, especially when they were still struggling to get all of their players together. Pat Burke was the elusive target that Ireland sought out but hadn't been successful in recruiting. Byrt in his usual candid way opened up to Kieran Shannon in the media about the same frustrations that he had noticed thirteen years earlier. 'We were up against a lot of money in the paint [other teams had highly paid centres], but I was very pleased with the level of our inside play. But we were 7–24 from three-point range against Holland. If we had made

201

even 9–24 it would have made a big difference. Our perimeter shooting as a nation needs to improve and should be a coaching focus. When I got involved with Irish teams in 1984, we came up with four areas in which we needed to develop – superior conditioning, excellent outside shooters, identify taller players and combine these three into a full-court game to express our national emotional style. Last weekend proved we're still somewhat short in those first two areas.'

Outside the performance on the court, wider issues were coming to a head too. Byrt told Kieran Shannon that he had not decided yet whether he would seek re-appointment to the job. He was clearly unhappy with conversations happening behind the scenes. Ireland had a new Chief Executive in American-born Scott McCarthy, who had been in Ireland for several years while playing in Sligo during the eighties. McCarthy had Irish American heritage and was part of the first national team tours to the US, although he wasn't eligible to play in regular competition. Where Byrt stood with McCarthy was unclear. What was clear was that conversations were happening around the approach of the national team. Ireland wasn't going to the 1997 World University Games. There was uncertainty around the future of Irish American players, and Byrt called for clarity on the issue: 'I wouldn't be in favour of the IBA to decide to go solely with home-based players. But if they did, fine. We have a good junior squad at the moment. It would take a long-term approach, maybe six or eight years, for us to compete like we did at the weekend, but it would reduce cost. As long as people know where they stand. It shouldn't be up to a team or a coach to decide whether to fundraise to bring foreign-based players back.'

As Ireland dusted themselves off after their best effort at qualification to the semi-final round, one thing was clear: progress was being made on the court, but off-court issues were developing for Enda again.

Chapter 19: The Last Stand

In February of 1998, Enda Byrt was reappointed as the head coach of the Senior Men's squad as they headed into another qualification campaign. The preliminary group was held in Helsinki in Finland and Ireland had a tough group with Switzerland, Cyprus, Norway, Austria, Luxembourg and Finland. Aside from anything else, six games in seven days would be a challenge. Still, things would be a lot tougher for Ireland as they faced the group without one of their primary offensive talents. Alan Tomidy had decided to focus on his professional career in Europe and didn't want to risk injury playing for the national team. This was an understandable decision for a player with a short window to make as much money as possible professionally. Still, it highlighted a major issue that underpinned Enda's recruitment strategy. If Ireland were going to get Irish American players, there had to be an acceptance that some of their professional careers would take them beyond Ireland's reach and the country would lose them. FIBA's rules were in Ireland's favour: any player that was called up for the national team and didn't report would be suspended from their club team. The rule was there to protect national teams, but realistically for Ireland the soft power required to convince players and teams that this would happen was beyond the association's scope at the time.

The good news for the squad was that Dan Callahan was back, and Byrt was hopeful Dan could have his first full qualification campaign. John O'Connell, Frankie Powell and Ken Lacey had also returned. On the domestic side, there were many new faces, including Kieran Quinn and Neville Charles, who were both based in college in the States. Allan Conlan, who had extensive pro experience, was back too, as was Niall Phelan who was now at Robert Morris University. Mick Richardson made his debut, while John Teahan from Kerry was finally able to appear after a battle with FIBA over his eligibility (he was born in the UK, but lived in Ireland for most of his life).

The campaign started with a bang as Ireland beat the Swiss 88–80 behind a huge second-half performance that saw them go from two down to win by eight. Dan Callahan led the way with 23 points and 9 rebounds. The win set Ireland up for their next game, which was against old foes Cyprus. The fear for Ireland with Cyprus was that the Cypriot's experience would enable them to make any game into a dogfight, and that is precisely what happened. Ireland's offence ground to a halt and despite 22 points from Frank Powell, they lost by a single point 57–56. Ken Lacey was labouring with just 3 points in each of the first two games as Ireland struggled to find a way to replace Alan Tomidy's presence in the key.

Qualification hopes were gone by the third game as another familiar foe, Norway, got one back on Ireland. Mick Richardson scored 25 points in one of the best scoring outbursts by any domestic player for many years. Still, it wasn't enough, as Ireland lost by three 69–66. Norway had keyed in on Powell, limiting him to just 6 points, and without another big scoring option, Ireland were left wondering what could have been. A comfortable win over Luxembourg opened the group back up, but Austria and Portugal both comfortably beat Ireland in the final two games to end the hopes of automatic qualification. Poor outside shooting was still a problem as the team averaged just 27 per cent from deep. Without a dominant inside scorer, Ireland were now found wanting in the close games against teams they were used to beating.

The following year, Ireland entered the qualification round with hopes of making a breakthrough, but they were doing so without any momentum. Things were made more difficult with the loss of one of the senior players. Frank Powell had been ever-present since the Junior Men's days of the late 1980s but was now fully retired and focusing on his law degree and career outside of basketball. He had been an incredible servant to Irish basketball even after his professional basketball career ended. Still, it wasn't sustainable for him to keep coming to Ireland's aid.

Ireland started the group in Switzerland by dominating Denmark in a twenty-five-point win which bode well for a good week in Fribourg. Dan Callahan was fully settled into his role for Ireland, and his sixteen-point sixteen-rebound performance showed just what he was capable of. The other American's also chipped in in double figures while Adrian Fulton led the domestic contingent with 9.

Coming into the tournament, Georgia and Switzerland were identified as possible targets to beat as the other two teams, Portugal and Belgium, looked very strong. Georgia was Ireland's second group game. The match was balanced throughout as the teams were tied at half-time. Dan Callahan again led the way for Ireland, with Mick Richardson and Gareth Maguire's support, but Georgia ultimately prevailed 80–78. Again, the ability to close out tight games escaped Ireland, and nine missed free throws in such a close game left the team with a familiar feeling of having missed an opportunity.

Without much time to bounce back and with qualification still possible, Ireland faced Switzerland. Dan Callahan and Ken Lacey would again be the focal point of Ireland's attack as the big duo combined for 41 points and 19 rebounds. Ireland was the more aggressive team getting to the basket and the foul line, scoring 15 out of 18 free throws compared to the Swiss only scoring 3 for 7. The difference in the teams came in the European style though, as Switzerland moved the ball and shot well from the perimeter as they hit 12 threes (53 per cent from three) compared to Ireland hitting just three. Ireland again came up just short as they lost 69–68, effectively ending their qualification hopes. In the final two games, they lost to Belgium by 9 and then to Portugal by 15 as Dan Callahan sat out.

It turned out that Ireland needed to beat both Georgia and Switzerland to qualify, but three total points in just over twenty-four hours separated Ireland from the breakthrough they desired. Frustration was starting to build. Ireland was now not merely overmatched by teams they couldn't compete with, instead they were getting opportunities against teams of similar ability and weren't winning tight games. The most worrying part was that players like Frank Powell and Alan Tomidy were now gone and hadn't been replaced yet. Dan Callahan, John O'Connell and Ken Lacey were all giving significant contributions to the team, but something new was needed. For Byrt, this is where the lack of World University Games experience in 1997 hit the team. Instead of finding new talent, Ireland was relying on a small group, and as they had found out already, the margin for error was too small to continue like that.

Ireland was close to qualifying, but those frustrating factors were keeping success just out of reach. What the group didn't know was that the next time they got together to attempt qualification, they would do so without Enda.

Chapter 20: The End of an Era

Looking to bounce back from the disappointment of Switzerland in May of 1998, Ireland was set to re-enter the World University Games in July. The tool that had helped unearth players like Dan Callahan and John O'Connell was back for Ireland. Yet, instead of being a major positive for Ireland, it became a significant distraction point and drove another wedge between Enda and the Irish Basketball Association.

In 1995, Enda outlined to the college sports organising body CUSAI that American-based players had to be eligible. In Enda's opinion, this was a crucial non-negotiable fact for Ireland moving forward. Heading into the Games in Mallorca in 1999, it was a fight that he wasn't winning. Byrt wanted all but two players to be based in the States and couldn't understand the logic of blocking players who were eligible to represent Ireland. He told the *Irish Independent* ,'You can't pick teams by committee or by imposing quotas. If someone said you have to pick so many black or white players, they'd be accused of unfair bias, so why do it in this case? If you're eligible to play on an Irish team, then you should get a fair shot, and ruling out players who are pushing out the frontiers of the Irish game by pursuing their careers abroad doesn't seem fair.'[xliii]

CUSAI's opinion in many ways summed up a particular cohort of the basketball community when it came to the Irish American question in general, not only for the World Games. Their chairman Dave Mahedy simply said, 'How do you develop athletes at home if you don't give them opportunities to play at the top level?' For an organisation that represents university sport in Ireland, they had little interest in what the best Irish team could be, but rather what were the best opportunities they could give Irish athletes.

The issue caused a stalemate that brought into question Ireland's recruiting policy. Back in the early 1980s, Ireland was looking for a way to help the teams compete at the international level and in particular to find big men capable of helping out. It was initially intended as somewhat of a stop-gap initiative while Ireland developed more talent. In 1999, the Junior Men's team had just qualified to the semi-final round for the first time, courtesy of Michael Bree, Paddy Kelly and Gary Dredge amongst others. Some of the talents, like Dredge and Bree, were attending college in America. Others, though, weren't heading away, and Ireland was yet to discover how to develop players at home to create a deeper national squad. Byrt was eager for an U22 National League to help to do this. The question was, wouldn't a competition like the World Games be an ideal training ground for some of that domestic talent? Just like it had been for the likes of Adrian Fulton back in the early 1990s.

Byrt decided that he would not coach the team as CUSAI wanted it assembled, and for the second time in five years, Ireland had to compete at a tournament without Enda as the head coach.

At the Games, Ireland did have American-born talent in Ken Kavanagh who would later play for the senior team. They also had Michael Bree, who was now at Davidson. There were opportunities for domestic players like dual-sport star Trevor Smullen, Gary Edge from Marian and Joey McGuirk from St Vincent's. The team came twentieth, considerably away from the top -eight finishes of 1993 and 1995. Yet the tournament also had the potential to serve a bigger purpose. The fallout from the disagreement with CUSAI wasn't over yet, though.

There was little surprise for those around the game and Byrt himself the following November, when the IBA decided to sack their head coach with sixteen months left on his contract. The reason given seemed to be two-fold, although only one was shared publicly. Cliona Foley of the *Independent* outlined some issues; 'In preparing the team for their European qualifying tournament in Switzerland last May, Byrt's management team overspent the team budget by £5,800. While budget debts were regularly carried over into the next season in the past, national team coaches now have a clause in their contract which disallows this. And the NEC have decided to enforce it strictly on Byrt, despite the fact that he sought a meeting with them twenty-four hours beforehand to stress that the team were fully prepared to fundraise to pay off the debt themselves. However, Byrt's policy of using a high percentage of Irish American professionals and US-based college players in his squads also seems to have been a factor'. The IBA statement claimed that they 'felt a change was necessary to focus more attention on the linkage between the cadet, junior and senior programmes'.[xliv]

Byrt responded at the time defending his position. 'When we're looking for short-term results to qualify, we had to go with the best players we could find. We certainly weren't aware we rejected anyone; players who weren't in the team generally didn't make themselves available. As far as I was informed, I am out because of the budget issue but this statement implies other things my management team and I simply do not accept.'

Both areas discussed were points of friction during Enda's reign, both directly with the organisation and indirectly with the basketball community. Finances were an issue for Byrt throughout his time coaching with Ireland. His player-first approach always tried to push the envelope and attempt to drive Ireland forward. Many feel that he should be commended for this, especially as the progress Ireland made from an afterthought to a competitive European team was so profound. The reference to the development of junior players seemingly pointed to the World University Games incident directly. In the beginning of his time as coach, Enda had been linked in with the Junior Men, and later into the nineties had given opportunities to several young players including Niall Phelan and Mick Richardson. Whether there was pressure from the wider community to have more domestic players included in the squads was unclear.

Going back to 1997 and Byrt's reaction to losing to Belgium, narrowly missing qualification, Byrt had acknowledged talk of a need to integrate young Irish-developed players more and a desire to control costs.''

Ultimately the final straw that ended his tenure was this exact idea. The team tried to achieve qualification and had overspent their budget. Previously Byrt had lamented a lack of central decision-making and had said that decisions around finances shouldn't be up to the coach. Now this exact issue had come up and cost him his job.

It was a sour ending to what should be seen as one of the most positive periods of Irish basketball development. When Byrt first took over, Ireland could not always get the top players to play for the national team, and it was an afterthought for many others. By the time he was leaving, there were many people upset that they couldn't be a part of it.

Enda was a man of absolute principles and wouldn't waver from them at all. For the players he picked, this showed how much he cared about them, ensuring everything was right to create a proper culture within the programme. The fact that he made the programme about more than just basketball was critical for the Irish Americans he helped bring in. It also made the team into something beyond a simple win-loss record. Many of those initial recruits credit Enda with the careers they had in Europe and those domestic players who bought into his vision are unwavering in their support of him.

On the other hand, that player focus and those strict principles led to constant issues with the Irish Basketball Association, who were trying to find a way to have a competitive national team while growing the sport in other areas.

When the CEO Scott McCarthy took up his position, one of his first meetings was at a Cork County Board meeting, where he was interrupted during his opening remarks to be asked how much he was being paid and how much it cost him to be there. In another meeting the necessity of association itself was challenged, with the overall feeling being that the leagues could be run without it. For a sport that was trying to grow without many resources, the IBA were continually seeking the balance between the elite international game and the wider domestic and grassroots game. That balance still challenges the sport today.

The issues around Enda's departure were ones that hit home for a lot of the players he brought through the system. John O'Connell was one of Enda's most loyal players. As an Irish American, he always felt that the vision was one to help the future: 'What's your goal? Are we helping to advance the game in Ireland? That ultimately should be the goal whatever we are doing . . . raising interest in the game back home. I thought that was always Enda's point – we are going to use you stallions here to make kids see how exciting the game could be for them. I think Enda's view was always a temporary goal . . . to use the guys to try and bring some excitement into the game and then get Irish kids interested.'

Gareth Maguire saw the issues and yet also saw what Enda was trying to achieve on a higher level. 'I don't think the IBA took it seriously enough. We were a problem in that we were competing on that international scale, but we weren't winning enough.'

The issue of integrating younger players into the senior squad was mentioned in Enda's dismissal. As the nineties ended, it looked like Ireland were set to reinvest in their young players with a hope of developing a talented homegrown group.

But that plan would fly out the window less than eighteen months later as further rule changes at FIBA level opened the door to even more Irish American players.

Any future developments would be done without Enda, though, who had provided immense service to his country for over twenty years. When Enda took over the head coaching job, Cliona Foley wrote that only time would tell if Enda's approach would pay off. Nine years later as he left the role, the same journalist wrote, 'Few can argue that Byrt's policies got results. Ireland won the Promotions Cup in 1994 and only a three-point defeat by Belgium in 97 cost them their place in the European Semi-Final round.'

Regardless of where you stood on any of the other issues, Cliona has it right; few can argue that Byrt's policies got results.

Chapter 21: The Unexpected Chance

While the men's team progressed and were fighting to make a breakthrough, the women's squad were on their journey without Irish Americans. Having just come up short in the Promotions Cup in 1993, Ireland chose to re-enter the European Championships in 1995.

On 22 May their return got off to the perfect start as Ireland beat their Promotions Cup nemesis Austria in the first game of the qualifiers. The win was just the fourth in European qualification for the women (Scotland '78, Switzerland '83 and Denmark '87). Denise Scally, who had played for Lamar University, led the team with 24 points while Karen Hennessey added 17 as Ireland won by 13 points. A second win almost came the next day, but Ireland lost out narrowly to the Swiss by just five points, 67–62. Like previous campaigns, there were some heavy beatings the remainder of the way as Ireland had to deal with top European powers like Greece and a gruelling seven-games-in-seven-days schedule. The early victories were evidence that Ireland could compete and win internationally with homegrown players with NCAA experience like Hennessey, Scally and Kathy Reid. The blueprint was there for Ireland, and although it was a route that looked quite different to the men's game, it looked both promising and sustainable.

Even with the new Bosman rule coming into effect in '95, the impact on the women's team in the 1990s was much less pronounced. The women's professional game simply wasn't as developed as the men's at the time. Opportunities for Irish American basketball players to take advantage of their passports were less available. Regina Grennan is Irish American, and she played at Arizona before recruiting and coaching Susan Moran at St Joe's. She summed up what remains an issue thirty years later: 'For women, it wasn't that big of a deal . . . I'm going to get a job and start my career, maybe play in the YMCA league if I want to keep playing . . . I think it was a reality thing too, the money the guys are making in Europe is a lot more than the women are making, and the money they are hoping to make if they get another contract is so much more. Most women who go – and maybe it's a little bit different now with the WNBA – but most women who went were thinking, "let's take a year and have a good time somewhere, see the world a little bit and then get a job".' Gerry Fitzpatrick, who coached the women's team for the latter part of the nineties, echoes that same point: 'We just didn't know; we couldn't locate or access people who were eligible to play for Ireland, who were playing at a high level in Europe. Your best chance was finding a player in college who could declare, but even at that it was really difficult because it wasn't seen as a pathway for women as it was for men'.

For the women's team, the lack of Irish Americans wasn't a major issue at the time. The domestic league had many talented players, and there was enough talent coming back from the NCAA to help build a strong squad. Despite that returning talent, the 1990s were mostly frustrating for the Irish team as they had yet to make a significant breakthrough either qualifying to the semi-finals or winning a Promotions Cup.

By the time Ireland got together in 1997 for the qualifiers, major changes had taken place. Gerry Fitzpatrick, the dominant Waterford Wildcats coach, had taken over the national coaching job in 1996. With him, he brought back Jillian Hayes who had temporarily retired years earlier. Alongside Hayes, Fitzpatrick also added Michelle Maguire and Caitriona White from the Wildcats team that won the League in both 1997–98 and 1998–99. Some exciting NCAA talent also joined in the form of the Fordham duo of Emer Howard and Suzanne Maguire making their qualifiers debut. Howard was a guard heading into her senior season while Maguire had just finished her sophomore season, in which she had won All-Patriot League first team honours while leading the Fordham Rams to the conference title and an NCAA berth. Maguire would go on to have one of the most distinguished careers in Irish history. At Fordham she became a Hall of Famer, as she ended up fourth on the all-time scoring list, fifth in rebounding, fifth in steals, third in threes made, and led the Rams in scoring and rebounding for her final two years. After her Fordham career ended, she also had a significant impact both the in the domestic league and internationally. This debut in 1997 was noteworthy as it was the start of an international journey that wouldn't end until twenty years later at the European Olympic Games in Baku playing 3x3. The other addition to the squad was a seventeen-year-old prodigy from Tullamore who had just had a hugely impressive Junior Women's campaign only months earlier. Susan Moran was on the path to superstardom, and this tournament showed glimpses of that future.

Ireland faced tough opposition in Madeira and ultimately struggled throughout the group, losing all of their games. The Wildcats contingent led the team in scoring, but against the top opposition Ireland found it difficult to compete. The closest the team came to a win was a repeat fixture with the Swiss, who Ireland had lost to two years previously. Twenty-four turnovers (compared to the Swiss's fifteen) ultimately doomed the team as they lost 61–57. Of note, though, was the young duo of Maguire and Moran who led Ireland that day. Maguire top scored with 12 points while Moran chipped in 10. It was the sign of hope for the future – if the duo could develop together, Ireland might have something very positive to build on.

With some tough lessons learnt over the decade and some strong domestic talent added, Ireland returned to the European Qualifiers again in 1999 with renewed hope of making a breakthrough to the semi-final round. Greece was the destination this time for a five-team group that saw Ireland face Greece, Moldova, Slovenia and Denmark. Ireland's roster leaned heavily on the top two domestic teams with Wildcats and Tolka Rovers both well represented. Excitingly, Michelle Aspelle made her qualifiers debut in what would be a distinguished European career.

Susan Moran fresh off some NCAA-tournament experience was back in the line-up, and she was joined by Denise Walsh who played alongside her on their Junior Women's team. Unfortunately, Suzanne Maguire and Denise Scally wouldn't feature for this campaign.

In the opening game, Ireland struggled against the hosts in a mismatch losing 83–44. Ireland expected this loss, but the poor shooting display (27 per cent from the field) was a concern. In the second game, Ireland faced Moldova and again struggled from the field, particularly around the basket. Trailing by just one at half-time, the second half was disappointing as Ireland ended up losing by 16 (41–26). Susan Moran was coming into her own though, transitioning from a young player into a star as she scored 23 points and added 11 boards.

Ireland was running out of opportunities as they faced Slovenia in the second last game. Slovenia had already beaten Moldova and lost to Denmark, so they knew they would go through if they beat Ireland. They couldn't afford to lose, as they faced Greece in their last match, so a loss would put them under significant pressure.

In the first half things were going well for Slovenia as they led 39–34. However, an incredible second-half performance from the Irish reversed the score as Ireland stormed back to win 79–72. It was one of the biggest wins the country had ever recorded. Rachel Kelly led the scoring with 18, Michelle Maguire added 17, and Denise Walsh (who had scored just two points in the opening two games combined) exploded for 14, hitting eleven of twelve free throws. The famous Irish win set up a huge showdown with Denmark in the final match, with both teams knowing that a win would see either of them through to the semi-final stages.

The game was tight throughout with Ireland holding a narrow one-point lead at the break, 30–29. The second half was the same with both teams tied in almost every statistical category. Caitriona White hit four threes for the Irish and Michelle Maguire was causing problems inside on her way to a team-high 19 points. Susan Moran again chipped in a double-double, but Ireland's competitive inexperience ultimately cost them as they lost out by just one point 63–62. It was an agonisingly close effort from Ireland that came down to the final minute. Gerry Fitzpatrick remembers the game: 'It was a one-point game. It was your typical end of the game scenario, and we came out on the wrong side, unfortunately. We would have qualified if we won that game and that really was what sparked the thought of how could we bridge that gap [with Irish Americans] the next time. But it's like everything else, it depends on who you're playing and the situation you're in, and everything changes so quickly at international level. I don't think we went into that '99 tournament with expectations of qualifying, just expectations of trying to reach another level, but then we found ourselves in that situation.'

As Fitzpatrick outlined, there was a move to consider outside help to push the women's team over the top for their next campaign. Regardless of any external help, the what-ifs that existed in so many cases for the men were there for the women. The biggest problem for a fully amateur team was trying to get as many of the top players together for each tournament, which wasn't always possible for amateurs. In the men's game, FIBA rules could put pressure on players to come. The same wasn't true for the women as Fitzpatrick lamented,

'Internationally its such a small window, sometimes people just aren't available, whether it's through work or they've done their time and aren't moving on. You always tried to go with the best players available, but it's unlike a club team, and you just don't know who that's going to be next year. You can't plan in '99 for 2000, you just don't know. And they are not contracted, that's the big difference when you went with the men's team because they were professional players so if they were selected for their country they had to play. You didn't have that for the women, so it was a totally different scenario in the women's game, it was a player's choice if they were available or not. They were two incomparable situations.'

As Ireland finished out the nineties, the women's team had come closest to breaking through to the next round of the European championships and had done so in arguably more challenging conditions. Ireland had struggled for the most part, yet they had almost achieved their goal and had come within a basket of doing so. The hope was now that with Susan Moran, Ireland had a genuine star developing and lots of complimentary talent to go around her. With the obvious comparisons already there with the men's team, it looked like Ireland's women were about to begin recruiting more strenuously with the hope of finding just one player that could help lift them over the top.

Whether the women's professional game could facilitate this or not would remain the question heading into the 2000s.

Chapter 22: The Journey to the WNBA

As Ireland's men were searching for a transformational star from America that could help bring Ireland to the next level, Ireland's women had a homegrown star looking to do the same thing. Susan Moran is without question the greatest Irish-developed export the game has ever seen, rising from relative obscurity to a dominant NCAA star and eventual WNBA-roster member. Susan's rise in some ways was impossible to predict, yet in others, it was a continuation of the work that Maggie Timoney and Suzanne Maguire had done before her. Susan's journey is one of hope, yet it is also tinted with a feeling of regret. The regret doesn't come from her performance on the court, but rather the macro-environment she tried to thrive in. Ireland struggled to get Irish American women for so long because professional opportunities were few and far between for women in the 1990s and early 2000s. Our greatest ever export would end up being a perfect example of that environment, as her professional career ended up lasting just three seasons despite one of them being in the WNBA.

That WNBA experience would end on the bench of the New York Liberty during the 2002 WNBA Finals. The women's league was only six years old, and Nikki Teasley would give the league an early defining moment as she hit a championship-clinching shot with 2.7 seconds left on the clock. The game-winner helped seal the championship for the LA Sparks and their star Lisa Leslie, who won her second straight Finals MVP. Such an iconic moment in WNBA history is one that will forever be Teasley's moment. Still, it also has other significance, as sitting on the far end of the court sharing the defeat with players like Theresa Wetherspoon and Becky Hammon was Tullamore native, Susan Moran. This was the end of Moran's rookie season in the WNBA and, as it eventually turned out, her last moment in the league. As remarkable an achievement as it was for Susan to be there at the pinnacle of the sport, what makes the story even more impressive is just how unlikely her journey was.

Just over ten years before that WNBA Finals game in LA, Susan Moran and a group of friends decided to try something new. The group of twelve-year-olds had just started in Sacred Heart secondary school in Tullamore. One of their teachers, Ann Ganley, had decided that she would start up a basketball team. Susan was already an accomplished tennis player with excellent co-ordination, but it was the team element that got her interested in what Ms Ganley was offering. By her own admission, Ann was a relative newcomer to the sport herself, and her goal was to stay one step ahead of the girls she was coaching. Her work was making an impact though, as Susan began to quickly make huge strides. An international tennis player at U14 level, basketball started to come to the fore by the time she was fifteen. For most schools players in Ireland, the schools finals are the big goal. Sacred Heart reached both the U16b and U19b final in 1996. In the finals, Moran served the country notice about what was ahead, by having the most dominant single-day display anyone has ever produced in the Arena. St Joseph's Castlebar were first up in the U16 final and Susan scored 60 in the game. She wasn't done though. Later that day, as Moran played up in the U19 final, she added another 48 to take her total to 108 for the day!

Things continued to develop as Susan made Irish teams and put in impressive performances in the green jersey. Things escalated in 1997 as her contributions for Ireland went to another level. In April of that year, Ireland headed to Ponte De Lima in Portugal to attempt to get by the first qualification round of the Junior Women's European Championships. The Irish team were strong with future stars like

Siobhan Kilkenny and Denise Walsh playing alongside Moran. Still, it was clear from the outset who the star of the show was. Ireland agonisingly lost their first two games as the Netherlands beat them by three and Portugal beat them by just one. Susan had 26 points and 13 rebounds against the Dutch, and she went even further against Portugal with 28 points and 19 rebounds. Unfortunately, a loss to Belgium knocked them out of contention, and they only had a game against international powerhouse France left to play. Despite the massive underdog status, Ireland beat France in what could be considered the greatest win an Irish underage programme ever enjoyed. Moran had her fourth double-double in as many games (14 points, 11 rebounds) as Ireland claimed the famous victory. The French team still qualified and eventually finished tenth in Europe at that age group. The win was incredible for Ireland, but it also made them further rue the early two losses. A win in either game would have seen them qualify as the first Irish team to reach the semi-final round.

Without any time to pat herself on the back for a good campaign, Moran was drafted into the Senior Women's squad for their European Championship qualifiers in Madeira. At the time, Ireland's senior team was made up of former NCAA players like Karen Hennessy (Iona), Denise Scally (Lamar) and the Fordham duo of Emer Howard and Suzanne Maguire. Despite that spread of NCAA talent, it was domestic players Jillian Hayes and Michelle Maguire that statistically led the group.

Ireland lost all five games, but progress was being made, and Susan was a big part of that. In the opening games, Moran saw the court very little, getting just eight minutes. In a blowout loss to Croatia, Susan played twenty-one minutes and started to show her capabilities with 6 points and 7 rebounds. Ireland's match against the Swiss was Moran's last of the campaign and her best, as she scored 10 and added 4 rebounds in twenty-five minutes of action. The tenacious seventeen-year-old power forward proved that she could compete at senior level while showing people that lots more was on the way.

In an unusual turn of events, Moran's international season in 1997 wasn't yet over, as Ireland were also entered in the Junior Women's Promotions Cup for 1997. Ireland played Gibraltar, Malta, Armenia, Scotland and England at the tournament in Malta. Susan wound up having more points than minutes played in a dominant display as Ireland romped to gold. Moran played just twenty-four minutes a game yet averaged 27 points and 8 rebounds. Those averages were hurt by huge wins over Gibraltar and Malta, in which Susan played less than twenty minutes in both games. The most impressive part of her display was that her performances improved as the competition got more challenging. Armenia posed the first real challenge and Susan responded with 35 points and 11 rebounds, and by the time Ireland faced their neighbours England in the final, Susan added 32 points and 12 rebounds. It was a display of complete dominance by Moran and Ireland as they showed that Promotions Cup level was beneath them.

Back at home in her last year of school, Susan started to get more and more recruiting attention with American schools looking for a commitment for the following year. St Joseph's of Philadelphia sent one of their assistant coaches, Reggie Grennan, who herself had Irish connections, to Tullamore. Moran was impressed, and after a visit to St Joe's, her mind was set. She wasn't entirely done in Ireland though, as she had one of her most memorable weekends at the club National Cup Finals in January. The biggest weekend of the year used to have an U19 competition with the semi-final on Saturday and the final on Sunday. Moran was playing for the Cyclones, who were effectively her school team with a different name. Susan had just turned eighteen the week before, and she marked the occasion by scoring 56 points in the semi-final game. She wrapped up the MVP award the next day when she added another 53 points in the final. As great as her exploits had been at school level years earlier, this was a different level again against higher-quality club players. Moran was taking a step to a level no Irish player had gone before.

Arriving in America, Susan had some initial doubts over whether she made the right choice in going to St Joe's. She voiced concerns to her coaches that maybe she should have gone to a Division-II school instead. Any doubts she did have were put to bed early in her freshman year. St Joe's had scheduled a challenging road game to the Thompson Boling Arena to face the three-time defending National Champions, Tennessee. The Tennessee Volunteers were coached by the incomparable Pat Summitt, who sadly died in 2016. Summitt is in every Hall of Fame possible, and the charismatic coach's résumé includes being a five-time National Coach of the Year, a multiple Olympic medallist, an eight-time NCAA Champion and a Presidential Medal of Freedom winner to top it all off. Her Volunteers squad was led by Tamika Catchings, who became one of the most iconic players ever in the women's game. Despite losing the game 82–59, Moran rose to the occasion and scored 16 points and grabbed 7 rebounds, while Catchings managed 15 points including a personal 9–0 run that blew the game open.

St Joe's hadn't won, but their young star had a 'welcome to the NCAA' moment, where she realised she could compete with even the country's best players. For Grennan, it was the start of a journey that solidified the hopes St Joe's had for Susan from the moment they started recruiting her. 'I remember watching her play in Ireland and thinking it's tough to tell who's she playing against. Nobody was even near to what she is. You're going, can she do it? Gerry Fitzpatrick says she's about six feet tall, and when she gets there, you're going, she's not six feet tall. But she was definitely an inside around the basket player; at that time she wasn't handling the ball much and she wasn't shooting at all from the outside. But she was one of the hardest-working players, and she improved so much. She just had a knack for rebounding, kind of like Charles Barkley, being so undersized, and for getting her shot off in close areas. Somehow she was able to get her shot off amongst the trees.'

That season the Hawks went on to win the A-10 title and Moran was named Rookie of the Year as she led the team in both scoring and rebounding. The title got St Joe's into the NCAA tournament, where they drew Tulane in the first round. In her first tournament game, Susan put up 21 points and 11 rebounds as St Joe's won 83–72. The first weekend of the tournament was hosted by a participating team each year. St Joe's' win earned them the right to play the host of their mini-tournament, the Duke Blue Devils, in Cameron Indoor Stadium. Duke eventually won 66–60, ending Moran's freshman year. That Duke team went on to reach the Championship game that year, upsetting the Tennessee Volunteers on the way to San Jose. Losing by just six points to the eventual runners up showed the level that St Joe's reached that season.

With a year at NCAA level under her belt, Susan returned to Ireland to lead the Senior Women's team in their European Qualification campaign. Averaging 15.5 points and 8.3 rebounds to lead the team in both categories, the nineteen-year-old had already established herself as Ireland's top talent. Heading back to Philadelphia, Susan left no doubt that she was continuing to develop as she led the university in both scoring and rebounding for a second straight year. Despite not winning the A-10 in their second year, St Joe's again earned a trip to the NCAA tournament, which turned out to be Susan's last trip to March Madness. In their first game, Susan and the Hawks faced Texas, and shut down the longhorn's offence on their way to a 69–48 win. Susan had 24 points and 13 rebounds and again showed what she was capable of on the national stage. Unfortunately, it was a second-round exit again, as Rutgers had too much for St Joe's in the second game in New Jersey. The following year St Joe's didn't make the NCAA tournament, but Susan did lead the team in scoring and rebounding for the third straight year.

Entering her senior year on the back of another summer leading Ireland, Susan was about to take her game to a new level again as she got the season off to a hot start. In just the second game of the year, she scored a career-high 30 against the number-eighteen ranked team Stanford, and a 19 point, 10 rebound double-double against number-twenty-four ranked Virginia. Another career-high matching 30 points secured a Kansas Classic title as Moran and the Hawks went to Lawrence and beat the Jayhawks. The season was up and down though, as St. Joe's had to rely on a lot of freshmen. Susan enjoyed more individual success than team success in that final year. That said, she did have lots of personal success, with the list of achievements incredible to read:

- Leading scorer and rebounder all four years at Saint Joseph's
- Leading scorer all-time in the school's history
- 2,340 career points
- Fourth all-time in rebounds
- Jersey retired at Saint Joseph's
- Philadelphia Big Five Hall of Fame 2009
- SJU Athletic Hall of Fame 2010
- Inaugural Atlantic 10's Legends Class 2013
- The third-leading scorer in America as a senior

Having finished up four years in Philadelphia, it was a question of what was next for Susan. The goal of the WNBA had become a real possibility during her senior year as scouts came to her games. In the 2002 draft, sixty-four picks were available but, disappointingly for Susan, she did not get selected. Her WNBA dream wasn't over though, as the New York Liberty called offering her a chance to come to their pre-season camp.

Moran later told of the surreal experience of staying with Therese Weatherspoon in a downtown Manhattan apartment and walking daily to practice in Madison Square Garden, one of the most iconic arenas in the world. Moran survived the tough camp and made the final roster, becoming the only Irish player ever to be on a WNBA squad.

Chances were limited, but Moran did get time in the pre-season, including scoring four points in one game in MSG. The moment was made sweeter by her parents being over for her college graduation and getting to share in the experience. The transition from Ann Ganley starting up a Sacred Heart team to this point is hard to fathom even on reflection years later. That season the Liberty had championship aspirations as Teresa Weatherspoon led them. The former Louisiana Tech guard became a Hall of Famer and was also named in the

WNBA's top fifteen players in the first fifteen seasons. They also had a young guard, Becky Hammon, who after an incredible on-court career, became just the second female assistant coach in NBA history and first full-time female assistant when she joined Greg Popovich's staff for the San Antonio Spurs. The Liberty were coached by Richie Adubato, a former NBA head coach who brought the Liberty to the WNBA Finals three out of the four years he coached. Unfortunately for Moran, Adubato preferred to keep a very short rotation, and he never put Susan into a regular-season game. Susan moved between the inactive injury reserve and the main squad throughout the year, but she never competed outside of exhibition games. The fact that Susan was an undersized forward helped her throughout her college career as she was quicker than all of the post players she faced, but at the WNBA level, it hurt her, as the athleticism and size were of a higher quality. Despite the lack of opportunities, Moran looks back at the season with fondness knowing she had a courtside seat all the way to the WNBA Finals and was able to practice with some of the best players on the planet. 'When we won the Eastern Conference Championship, just being in that moment, I wasn't playing in the games, but I was part of practice and doing all that stuff every day, I was the one with the camera. I had the camera under the chair, so when the confetti started coming down in Madison Square Garden I have footage of it all; I was that person on the court with the camera because I knew I wasn't getting in the game, I was on the Injury Reserve. I was so young, and I was just taking it all in. I didn't know the gravity of it, because I don't think the Liberty have got anywhere close since.'

The WNBA wasn't a full-time gig for players at that time as it was only a three-month season. So once the summer ended, players went to Europe for their second season. Susan was no different, and headed to Spain to play in the top league. The big development for her was that she started to move into the guard spots and played more as a three internationally than as a four like she had in college. Like her male counterparts, Susan quickly learned of the value of her passport: 'When I graduated, it helped me. At that point, more Americans were going over to Europe to play and, not jealousy, but people would say, "Oh man, you already command so much more money because you don't count in their international players".' After the season, Moran was invited back to the Liberty training camp with an opportunity to make the team. Disappointingly, she didn't graduate to the next stage, and her time in the WNBA was over. The Liberty were looking for a guard, and Moran was still transitioning from an undersized forward. Ultimately the move ended up being Susan's last WNBA interaction. Although her opportunities were limited, the incredible achievement of getting there and being part of a WNBA team can't be overlooked. With the Liberty contending for titles, a rookie's opportunity to get playing opportunities would be rare, particularly during such a short season. What could have been if a different team had been the ones to pick Susan up, we will never know.

At that point in her career, there was a desire to keep playing, but equally, the professional route was far less glamorous for women at the time. Unlike the opportunities for men, professional life wasn't always a simple choice for female players. It was at that time that Cindy Griffin asked Susan to join the Hawks staff as an assistant coach. The two struck up a deal that allowed Susan to coach during the year and then go to the southern hemisphere and play during the summer. It gave her the stability she desired but also the opportunity to play.

In her two seasons in the southern hemisphere, Moran had huge success. In the first year, she won the New Zealand Championship and was named the league MVP. In her second year, she headed to Australia in what turned out to be an eventful year. Her team had won just two games the year before, and they quickly topped that total with Susan in their ranks. However, a registration issue saw them lose a number of their key wins and they eventually missed out on the playoffs. Despite that, Moran won MVP again, showing the class that she had.

The travel and year-round schedule wasn't the life that Susan wanted at that time, and she retired from playing after just three professional seasons.

After a break from international basketball, Susan caught the playing bug again in 2008 after watching the Olympic Games, and she returned to action. Despite not playing basketball competitively for a number of years, Susan was clearly still elite and averaged a team-best 18.3 points and 6.8 rebounds. The Irish team at that time was a mix of young talent and experienced stars like Moran and Michelle Fahy. Sadly the campaign would be Ireland's last qualification one for more than a decade, with the team being cut due to funding issues within the organisation.

This meant that Susan's last game was an Irish win over the Netherlands in Dublin 67–62. Twelve years earlier in her debut tournament, the Netherlands game was the only game she hadn't played in, with Ireland losing 80–52. It was fitting that her final game showed the progress that Ireland had made during her era.

The strange ending for Ireland also provided Susan with an unexpected end to her career:'Some of it, in a weird way, was good, because I never had to deal with retiring. There was no sing-song about it, there was no, "alright, this is it, this is my last game". It happened, and I had no control over it, and it ended. As an athlete, coming to the end of your career can be a big thing mentally to wrap your arms around, but I didn't have to go around that too much, because it was just like, "right, it's over now, you're too old, OK!"'

In 2019, Susan's contributions to the game in Ireland were honoured as she joined Siobhan Caffrey as the first-ever female inductees to the Basketball Ireland Hall of Fame. A fitting tribute to someone who dominated the domestic game at youth level, broke records at the NCAA level, and led Ireland for so many years internationally.

Chapter 23: The Davidson Wildcats

For many basketball fans in America, college basketball was always the driving force of the game. While the NBA is great, for many the purity of the game truly lies in the 'amateur' game. The appeal of college basketball has been diluted somewhat in recent years with the prevalence of one-and-done superstars, who are only playing in college simply because they can't enter the NBA draft straight out of high school. Back in 2001 though, the NCAA was still king and college basketball was at the heart of the American sport.

If NCAA basketball in general was big around the USA overall, it was ALL that mattered in some states, including North Carolina. The Tar Heel State has long been the epicentre of the college basketball world, with the Atlantic Coast Conference considered by most the best basketball in the country. Within the ACC, the rivalries of some of the most storied universities and coaches tend to have links to Tobacco Road. Duke University with Mike Krzyzewski, and North Carolina with Dean Smith, and later Roy Williams, not only held one of the fiercest local rivalries in any sport, but often the NCAA championship was within arm's reach of one of the two schools each year. It was in this environment that Ireland's first ever NCAA export John O'Donnell from Cork had thrived for North Carolina, paving the way for future alumni including non other than Michael Jordan himself. The Dean Dome – home of North Carolina – was built in 1986. Named after John's legendary coach, Dean Smith, it remains one of the most iconic basketball arenas in the world today. The powder-blue floor markings are unmistakable, and there is something particularly magical about watching games there. In 2001, Chapel Hill was graced by two more Irishmen as they went against the North Carolina Tar Heels with their Davidson Wildcats team in front of 14,705 fans.

Going into that remarkable game, Davidson's Irish duo of Michael Bree and Conor Grace probably didn't have a huge amount of hope. The two men were at opposite ends of their college career. Bree was starting his senior season after what had been a very impressive three years to that point, while Grace was about to play just his second-ever NCAA game. Davidson had lost their season opener against Charlotte, so heading to Chapel Hill was likely low on the list of places Coach Bob McKillop wanted to go.

Davidson University is a small liberal arts university in North Carolina that has an excellent reputation as a mid-major basketball programme. Located just 128 miles away from the Dean Dome, Davidson travelled the two-hour trip knowing that history was against them. Since 1949, the two teams had played thirteen times, with Davidson only winning once back in a 1952 home game. The Wildcats had never travelled to Chapel Hill and won, and this was the task faced by a team led by a young Irish point guard from Sligo, Michael Bree. For their part, North Carolina were about to start a difficult period under Coach Matt Doherty. Doherty was a former teammate of Jordan's in North Carolina and had taken over the job in 2000. He was named the AP Coach of the Year in his first year with the Tar Heels as they claimed a share of the ACC regular-season title with Duke. The second season was off to a rocky start though, as they had lost their first game. It would ultimately prove to be the beginning of a negative slide over the following two seasons that saw Doherty eventually replaced by Roy Williams.

As the game tipped, Davidson's goal was just to mount pressure on the Tar Heels and stay in touching distance. Coach Bob McKillop decided to play a zone defence, which was very rare for Davidson, and it worked. Michael Bree was in the starting line-up, and he helped contribute three free throws and an assist in the early exchanges as Davidson went blow for blow with the Tar Heels. Grace meanwhile was still searching for his first-ever win and he checked in to the game for eleven first-half minutes. Both players did well as Davidson found themselves tied with the Tar Heels for large parts of the first half; things were going to plan.

In the second half, McKillop leaned on his starters very hard, with Bree playing all twenty minutes of the second half and Grace providing two of the three total bench minutes. With ninety seconds remaining, Davidson led 54–51, but a huge three-pointer by Jason Capel tied the game for the home team, and the game was now anyone's to win. With just twenty-nine seconds to go, Davison retook the lead, 56–54, through a Chris Pearson dunk assisted by none other than Michael Bree. A turnover by North Carolina and subsequent free throws sealed the deal as Davidson pulled off the huge upset and won in Chapel Hill for the first time. Bree helped lead the way with 6 points and 5 assists, while Conor Grace earned his first career win with 3 rebounds, an assist and a point. Bree's memory of a unique moment in time centred around the Tar Heel fans and a surreal moment for him as the crowd got behind the home team: 'I was walking the ball up the floor in the second half, there must have been four or five minutes to go, and the game was tight. The fans had stood up and were shouting because the game was close, and the floor was shaking. I was dribbling the ball up the floor with no pressure, and I could feel the floor rocking underneath me! In my head, I was just thinking, "this is awesome!"'

Davidson's coach Bob McKillop still smiles almost twenty years later as he recalls that game.

'We needed Conor to just start hitting people, and he did! I think he fouled out in thirteen minutes. He fouled out quickly anyway! He was an enforcer. I grew up in New York and was a Knicks fan, and my father was a Boston Celtics fan. My father would have me watch the NBA game of the week, and the Celtics were always on in the sixties with Bob Cousy, Tommy Heinson, Bill Russell, Casey Jones, John Havlicek. So I knew the Celtics. Conor Grace was a guy the Celtics would want. Michael Bree was a guy the Celtics would want. They were the Cousy and the Heinson – that's what they represented to me in our team. It came to fruition in that game against North Carolina. It required tremendous toughness, and that toughness was worn on the hearts of our team because it was worn on the hearts of Conor and Michael.'

The win's significance for Davidson couldn't be overstated by McKillop, who knew it played a large part in the future progress of his programme: 'You have to understand what the history of North Carolina vs Davidson was. Back in the sixties when Lefty Drissell was the great coach of Davidson, the school was Top 10, and North Carolina beat Davidson to get to the Final Four on two occasions. North Carolina had broken Davidson's heart twice. For the army of alumni who had gone to Davidson College, that memory is embedded in their brain. For us to get that victory, it got rid of a lot of the demons for a lot of the alumni. And of course, the stature that North Carolina has as a blue blood programme, a consistent powerhouse, and for us to beat them! That was eighteen years ago, when we were in the embryonic stages of development as a programme,as a culture, but that was a defining moment in our history.'

Indeed, to get to that moment and for both Irishmen to contribute in such a significant way is incredible. Understanding their journey, and where they came from before they went on to achieve that, is even more remarkable.

Sligo is a town on the west coast of Ireland that has approximately 20,000 people living there, one of whom, in the 1990s, was Michael Bree. Sligo has a rugged coastline that has become synonymous with surfing, while the local basketball club, Sligo All-Stars, has been a massive part of the community for many years. The club had early success at a national level in the 1970s and had many club members represent the country internationally. It wouldn't be until much later, though, that the Bree family helped drive the club forward again in the 1990s. Michael was the youngest of seven children. He was initially a keen soccer player, but soon found that he enjoyed the basketball people's company more, so stuck to that instead. By the time he was in his late teens, Bree was about to burst onto the scene, not only domestically playing for the All-Stars at National League level, but also internationally, representing Ireland.

The Irish underage team of players born in 1980 were in many ways the golden era for Ireland, particularly at underage level. Ireland has had successes at various levels over the years, but this Junior Men's team were the first to really have success and create a name for themselves. The team went further in European competition than any other group before them, and only one men's team since (before the restructuring of the European Championships). In the 1990s, the European Championships had yet to be split into an A and B division. Back then, there were three rounds of the tournament with a qualifying group, a challenge round and then the finals. Ireland had never made it past the qualifying group, and they faced a tough challenge this time too in Poland, Portugal, Spain, Sweden and Iceland. The Irish team was led by Bree, Neptune's Niall O'Reilly and Killester's big three of Jonathan Grennell, Paddy Kelly and big man Garry Dredge. Many of the team went on to either play in America or to star in the domestic leagues, but this was the beginning for the team coached by John O'Connor. Bree's self-confidence quickly stood out, and he was coming into his own as a top talent, although he believed it was already there before the tournament.

'I think I confirmed it there. I had the mindset prior to that. Playing against older guys, playing in Sligo at my own age group was fine, at 15/16 when I started to compete against older men and I was able to be the version of me against them, I got a lot of confidence from that. Then, coming back to your own age group, you saw it a bit differently. I had a different perspective going into those tournaments on who I was, and one of the best things for me during them was John O'Connor coming to me and saying, "Mike, I need you to score, I need you to shoot, I need you to be aggressive". He empowered me to be the best version of myself in that moment. It was what I needed to hear for me to express myself the way I knew I could, and things took off from there.'

Bree quickly established himself as a top player in the qualifying round as he averaged 22 points a game, good for fifth overall in the qualifiers. After splitting their opening two games, Ireland had to face Spain and their own golden generation led by Juan Carlos Navarro. Spain went on to win the European Championships and then claim the world title at U19 level in 1999, beating the USA. Fortunately for Ireland, big man Pau Gasol was missing for Spain for the Irish game, but Navarro was the team's real star as he was just months away from making his full debut for Barcelona in the ACB. Navarro won the duel with Bree (19 points to 15) as Spain went on to victory, but it was a clear indication that Bree could compete with the top talent in Europe.

'Afterwards you know who the names are. For me, playing against them I didn't care who Juan Carlos Navarro was or Andrei Kirilenko was in the next round. It didn't come across my consciousness in terms of who we were playing. My mindset was plain and simple: when I was playing in those tournaments, I wanted the other coach to pick me first. So, if he had a choice to pick someone on the floor at the end of the game, he would say, "Yeah, I would pick you first if I had a choice from all of these players". So that was kind of my motivation every time I stepped on the floor. I was going to defend them, I was going to attack them, and I was going to show them what I could do.'

Not to be put off by back-to-back losses, Ireland secured an incredible victory over Sweden by just three points (87–84). The win set up a do-or-die final game with Iceland. If Ireland won, they went through, and Bree led the way, scoring 29 points along with seven steals and three assists as Ireland created history by reaching the challenge round for the first time.

In the lead up to the Challenge Round, another opportunity awaited Michael, as he headed to Paris to take part in Nike's first-ever Euro Camp that highlighted the top European talent. After his showing in the qualifiers and at the camp, Coach Bob McKillop had heard enough from his sources, and he wanted to sign the young star. McKillop himself has strong Irish connections and had already been to Ireland to conduct coaching clinics courtesy of an invitation from Enda Byrt. He was immediately taken by the Irish attitude to basketball and was keen to experience more. For both Bree and Grace, Davidson was the ideal landing spot, as he had developed a reputation as a top coach for international players, albeit almost by accident. While coaching in a high school in Long Island, future NBA Champion Bill Wennington moved from Montreal and landed on McKillop's team. Suddenly, McKillop had a reputation for coaching international players as Augusto Binelli found his way to Long Island Lutheran to play for him, and it snowballed from there. By the time Michael Bree reached Davidson, he wouldn't be alone as an international player on the team.

Having competed in the challenge round where Ireland were outmatched by major European powerhouses like Russia, who featured future NBA and EuroLeague star Andrei Kirilenko, Bree moved to North Carolina. In truth, he wasn't entirely sure what he was about to get into. He would quickly learn though, and his debut was about as harsh a lesson as any college player could learn. Playing on a neutral court in the home of the Charlotte Hornets, Davidson went up against the Number 1 ranked Duke Blue Devils. Duke would go on to reach the National Championship game and finished the year with a record of 37–2. Elton Brand, Trajan Langdon, William Avery, Corey Maggette and Shane Battier all played on that team and went on to play in the NBA (Brand was the National Player of the Year and the Number 1 pick in the 1999 NBA draft).

'My first game playing college was against Duke in Charlotte Coliseum. I came on as a sub as our point guard picked up two quick fouls,' Bree reflected. 'I was forced into the game, and I drove the ball up to half court, William Avery was guarding me, Corey Magette run-and-jumped me and caught me over the corner in the trap zone of half-court. I put the ball above my head, and Magette just came in and took the ball right out of my hands and dunked. I had three turnovers in two to three minutes, and that was my introduction to college basketball.'

A 94–61 loss was respectable, but it was the start of a mixed year for Davidson as they finished 16–11 overall and did not make it to the NCAA tournament. Bree did appear in every game though and averaged 4 points.

In his sophomore and junior years, Bree had similar success individually, but Davidson was constantly around the .500 mark as a team. Two more tussles with future Number 1 pick Jay Williams and Duke in Cameron Indoor Stadium led to lopsided losses. That's why, despite Carolina's issues as they hosted Davidson at the start of that senior season, you could excuse Michael for not holding out much hope. Instead, the Carolina win kick-started a senior season that saw him average 10 points a game while Davidson had the most success of his four-year career. Winning their conference tournament, Davidson headed to March Madness for the first time in Bree's career. Sadly, an injury picked up in the conference final ruled him out for the NCAA tournament as Davidson lost narrowly to Ohio State in the first round. The absence of their key guard would make Davidson fans wonder if their first Cinderella run could have come years before Steph Curry, if their Irish point guard hadn't been hurt. Coach McKillop recognised that impact too:

'The great thing about our programme is, you have players that no matter whether they are scoring 20 points or putting a uniform on, they are a vital component of our team. Michael, in a sense, was a tremendous leader and really willed us to victory in that conference tournament. There was a boy named Peter Ander who came out of nowhere to get the MVP of that tournament to get the bid to the NCAA tournament, and that doesn't happen unless Michael is the leader of that process.'

Despite the disappointing end to his college career, Bree had an excellent overall career and clearly showed he could compete at the top level. For a player from Sligo to reach that level is something that few would ever have believed. Coach McKillop's words sum up the player: 'He went through a rocky road here from the standpoint of adjusting to the style of play, his role on the team, and he never quit – that was the remarkable thing. Frustrating him, even more, were injuries, he had a rash of injuries, and he fought through them. His toughness was extraordinary; he had a sensational basketball IQ and was a great teammate. Amidst the injuries and adjustment, he came and never quit. He was a pioneer.'

Despite his time in America coming to an end, Bree's career wasn't over, and it was time to begin his pro career which started in the French second division. He played several years in France, Poland and then Sweden before settling down there, where he now coaches. While playing pro, he also stepped up to serve the Irish team. He was one of only two home-developed players who regularly competed on the key Irish teams between 2003–07.

While in many ways, Michael Bree was the young Irish prodigy who was destined to make it in the NCAA, his teammate Conor Grace didn't follow that same path. In fact, while he was in Ireland, he wasn't even the best player on his club team growing up, let alone the national team. Grace came to the game late, playing club basketball for the first time when he was sixteen. He played some schools basketball for St Andrew's College – which at the time wasn't a major basketball school – but once he had shot up to 6'8, it was time to see what basketball could offer and he joined Marian BC.

After developing with Marian, Conor quickly made the Irish Junior Men's team. The team didn't have the same success as the age group above them, but they still had some excellent performances, and Grace certainly stood out. He averaged 13.6 points and 9.6 rebounds in the five European Championship games, incredible for someone with so little experience leading up to the tournament. A fifteen-point, sixteen-rebound effort against Belgium, and 21 points and 8 rebounds against Turkey showed what he was capable of and the future was bright for Conor. Unlike Bree before him though, he wasn't directly recruited by Davidson and instead, he went to America for a year of prep school before joining Bree in North Carolina. When McKillop became aware of Conor and saw him for the first time, his eyes lit up.

'I have this bias that Irish kids are tough as nails. Michael definitely demonstrated that, and Conor demonstrated that with seven more inches of height. So, when you get the toughness and heart of Michael Bree, and you add six or seven inches, my goodness gracious you have a heck of a tough player who was willing to play whatever role was asked of him! He seamlessly adjusted to the College game. I'm not sure if he was a starter at Bridgeton or not, but I remember watching him and saying, "I have to have this guy, he has to play for us"."

The NCAA tournament appearance capped that freshman year and Grace played in the loss to Ohio State, although he saw limited time. His freshman averages of 3.6 points and 2.6 rebounds were solid, and he had shown Coach Bob McKillop he was capable of more. More is exactly what he provided in his second season – his best statistical season in his four-year career at Davidson: 9.7 points and 8.6 rebounds, which are incredible numbers for a senior, let alone a sophomore. With a 17–9 record going into their conference tournament, there were hopes of another trip to the NCAA tournament but a first-round loss to a Virginia Military team – who had a 3–13 conference record – put an end to those dreams. Despite the high hopes of the sophomore year, Conor's averages fell in his junior and senior years, although they remained respectable. Overall, in his Davidson career, he averaged 6 points and 5.7 rebounds.

As he finished his time at Davidson, he was the ideal young player to play professionally and help the Irish senior team. A 6'9 hard-nosed big man who was happy to defend and rebound and had the ability to stretch the floor and hit a three is exactly what was looked for in a big European player. Thriving in an environment with former NBA players and top-level European talent, Conor learned how to be a pro. He started near the very top as he headed to Italy to play in the top league. In just under nineteen minutes a game in the Serie A, Grace averaged over 4 points and 4 rebounds a game in his rookie year. It looked like he would progress to EuroCup level, but unfortunately, it wasn't to be. Instead, he played across Europe in Sweden, France and Greece at a solid level, though not quite with Europe's top teams as the perfect situation never materialised for him.

On the international side, Conor played as a young apprentice to the senior Irish American players in the early campaigns from 2001 onwards, before becoming the team's leader and captain under Jay Larrañaga in 2009. Grace averaged 10 points and 7 rebounds a game in those qualifiers, but Ireland could not progress. Unfortunately for Grace and the young players around him, this was the last time that Ireland attempted qualification, as financial constraints hit the Federation and the Senior International teams were pulled from competitive action.

Despite a period in the Irish basketball wilderness, Conor had a late career revival as he arrived back to Ireland to do his master's degree. He joined forces with Templeogue BC and helped them to reach their first-ever National Cup Final in 2015. An innocuous incident just before the final ruled him out of the championship game with a freak hand injury, but Templeogue went on to win the game. After recovering from injury, Grace helped lead an Irish Select team to China to face the Chinese national team in a friendly four-team tournament in 2015. It was effectively the restarting of the Irish national team, and once again, Grace was at the heart of it. During the 2015–16 season, a unique experiment allowed Ireland to enter a combined club team into FIBA's EuroCup. Named the Hibernia team, they were led by Grace, who scored 10 points a game.

For a man with Irish heritage, Coach Bob McKillop played a central role in both Irish players competing at a high NCAA level and enjoying professional careers afterwards. McKillop maintains his Irish connections by supporting young Irish coaches and giving clinics in Ireland when he's in the country. Irish players also helped Davidson to build its strong reputation. That reputation skyrocketed just two years after Grace graduated when Steph Curry caught America's attention with some amazing displays in March Madness. McKillop has a sense of pride when he reflects on his two Irish players. 'The greatness of their individual careers became what our programme is built upon. We have a culture now. What Michael and Conor did to contribute to that culture is extraordinary. They were selfless. Sacrifice equals reward [is the team' motto], and they lived that in the way they played the game, practised the game and interacted with their teammates.'

Aside from the impact that Irish players have had on Davidson, Davidson players have also helped contribute to Irish basketball in recent years. Lawrence 'Puff' Summers was on the bench for that North Carolina win alongside Bree and Grace in 2001. In his Davidson career, he had a limited impact, but an opportunity to play in Ireland arose, and he has more than made the most of it. His biggest impact has come as a coach as he helps to grow the game around the country. He has also achieved a lot on the court, winning leagues and cups for Templeogue at the tail-end of his career. One of those cup wins came against a fellow Davidson alumnus, Dan Nelms. Dan – who arrived in Ireland to work rather than play – reached the National Cup Final with Swords

Thunder and played a starter's role. He also played for DCU Saints in the Super League and for UCD Marian at a local level. Dan's career coincided with Steph Curry, and the 6'9 big man has added an extra chapter to the Davidson–Ireland story.

Hopefully, there are more chapters to come in the Irish Davidson connection, but as Ireland strived to progress internationally with a new era of professional Irish Americans, two of their young stars had progressed up the ranks and were now ready to try and help them.

Chapter 24: The Breakthrough

As the 2000s began, Ireland were now almost twenty years into the Irish American journey that Byrt helped start back in 1980. Following on from the organisation's decision to part ways with Enda, Ireland looked to a familiar face to take over in a temporary capacity before recruiting for a freshly developed Head of Coaching role. Timmy McCarthy previously captained Ireland and had been a major force with the national team in the 1980s and early 'nineties. Interestingly, his international debut in European competition had also come courtesy of Byrt and Irish Americans in a roundabout way. As a nineteen-year-old, McCarthy was part of Danny Fulton's squad in the preparation games for the 1980 European qualifiers in Jersey. His place came with the understanding that he would not be part of the qualifiers' final ten. That was of course until FIBA ruled Ireland's initial American duo of Joe McGuire and Craig Lynch ineligible and McCarthy was suddenly on the main stage. From that point onwards, he never looked back. He was now back on the main stage again as temporary head coach, and he immediately provided an open door for some of the domestic stars who hadn't featured during the nineties for Ireland. Liam McHale and Stephen McCarthy were two of the initial targets Timmy wanted to get back into the squad. His support for the domestic game seemed in line with the organisation's direction at the time, as outlined in the announcement of Byrt's dismissal. In the *Evening Herald*, McCarthy responded to what was described as the 'thorny question' of foreign-born Irish Americans. 'I want to select the best ten players to represent Ireland, and until I see them all, I can't say. I've always believed we have Irish-based players who are good enough to play in Europe and I really believe we can get a good enough team together and qualify, that is why I took the job.[xlv]' He also recognised the importance of Irish Americans and today remains a major supporter of their value for Ireland. 'As a coach, my philosophy was, they can help us achieve. We have the opportunity to bring in people who qualify for Ireland, and Jack Charlton can do it, and hockey can do it, and rugby does it in the modern era, we should do it. There's no question we should do it because it gives us a chance to achieve.'

McCarthy's initial call for domestic talent was answered ahead of the preliminary round of the European Championships which were held in Denmark. Liam McHale was still absent, but Stephen McCarthy ended his long-term absence.

The six-team group included Ireland, Denmark, Cyprus, Luxembourg, Romania and Georgia with the top two teams automatically qualifying for the European Championships' semi-final round. The team's route to that achievement was a gruelling five games in five days, which started against Romania. The only comfort for the Irish was knowing they had beaten Denmark, Cyprus and Luxembourg in the recent past and had been just one basket away from beating Georgia. It was a tough group, but one Ireland had hopes of progressing from.

Timmy McCarthy's start was ideal as Ireland won a low scoring defensive battle with Romania 57–51. Ken Lacey shone through with an impressive double-double of 20 points and 12 rebounds in the win. In the second game, old foes Cyprus were on hand, and they clearly identified Lacey as the key man to slow down as he was limited to just 8 points on six shots. Stephen McCarthy showed Ireland what they had been missing with 14 points, but Cyprus thwarted Ireland again, narrowly winning 68–65. Ireland were yet again left to rue their performance at the free-throw line as they missed eleven of their thirty free throws in the loss.

In game three Michael Bree (who was still in college in Davidson), Gareth Maguire and Peder Madsen all contributed offensively as Ireland narrowly beat Luxembourg to set up a crucial game with Denmark. The home nation had already beaten Cyprus and Luxembourg, but the teams were well matched, and Ireland came into the game having had the better of the match-ups over the past five years. Ireland had beaten Denmark by 25 two years earlier but Dan Callahan who had 16 points and 16 rebounds that day wasn't here to help the team. Ireland led at the half, but a strong late surge by the hosts clinched the critical game 62–58, ending Ireland's hopes of automatic qualification. With the pool decided Ireland played out their final game against Georgia losing comfortably despite another big performance by Lacey who finished as the group's top rebounder (12.8) and joint top scorer (17.4). Disappointingly for Ireland, Ken's 27 points and 15 rebounds against Georgia were his last for the team, it being the final time he suited up for Ireland in qualification. Lacey instead followed Alan Tomidy in focusing on his club career in Europe, where he played at a high level in Italy.

On reflection, without Callahan the front line was too thin, and McCarthy knew it going into the tournament. He had pursued Pat Burke who was playing at Panathinaikos at the time, but the Greek playoffs were clashing with the preliminary round. FIBA rules dictated that players must be released for their national team and Timmy wanted to utilise the rule.'Pat Burke was playing in Panathinaikos, and I called for him to play for Ireland. The Greek Championships were on, and I said to (then CEO) Scott McCarthy we're calling him; he has to play. Pat didn't want to come because Panathinaikos obviously didn't want to release him. I said to Scott we need to enforce this, if we get Pat and Alan Tomidy we'll break through, and we'll get to the semi-final round. Long story short, Scott wouldn't do it, unfortunately.'

In a group that was so closely decided, having an extra body like Burke's would undoubtedly have made the difference. Burke himself admitted that he wasn't ready to play for Ireland at that stage of his career:'A lot of the managers would come up and be like, "Pat,

Ireland is bothering me to get you. Come on, what's Irish basketball? We're not releasing you, can you please make them go away." At that time FIBA had protected the ability for national teams to, let's say, recover their players to come and play for them. There was a little bit of a snooty, come on you are not Greece, you are not Spain, you're not Italy or Germany, we're talking about Irish basketball here. At the time, I listened to what they were saying because of the first experience I had with Irish basketball. I felt we are by ourselves right now, we are trying to climb this mountain, and it's very challenging and difficult. So, I took on this [mentality]: I don't want to get hurt I'm in my professional career, and I don't want some accident to happen to me at the time. It's funny because at that time in 2000 I don't know if there were any injuries going on in sport that you couldn't recover from at the time. It was more of a safety net that was unrealistic, and I look back at it now, and I wish I would have gone and been a part of it.'

Burke wasn't the only target, and McCarthy wanted to find a way to get Alan Tomidy back into the green jersey. Tomidy was playing for Benneton Treviso at the time and didn't want to risk his professional career. Treviso's general manager wanted to do everything

272

possible to keep his big man too. The CEO Scott McCarthy called him and had a bizarre conversation. 'I said, "Listen, I'm going to need [Alan] to play in this tournament,"and he said, "He can't, he has to play for us." I said he has to play and it's our right; we are going to invoke the rule if he doesn't play, he'll have to sit. He said, no! No, you can't! We're fighting back and forth, and finally, he calls me up and says we'll give the Irish Basketball Association something if you don't make him play. I said, what are you going to give us? He said 3,000 basketballs! What do you mean? He said we have this sponsorship deal with Spalding we can literally send you crates of basketballs; you can give them all over the country and make basketball a big thing.'

Four weeks later, new basketballs arrived in the National Basketball Arena, and Tomidy stayed in Italy. It was further proof that although the FIBA rule was there for countries to get their players released, the reality of the situation was far different, and Ireland had minimal sway when it came to trying to negotiate with Europe's major powers.

As Ireland returned home from Denmark, all was not lost as they still had another chance in the qualifying round, which would start just over a year later in 2001. But two major changes were on the way that would completely change the trajectory of the Irish team moving forward.

The first started with a phone call from the States to Scott McCarthy. Bill Dooley got in touch to find out what opportunities were available and how he could secure a job coaching in the Irish Super League. Dooley (who has Irish heritage) and his wife were about to come to Ireland, as his wife was tasked with overseeing a servicing function that her American company was setting up in Ireland. Bill had previously coached at Richmond and was now the Delaware Valley coach, but was about to be jobless as he followed his wife to Europe. As mentioned earlier, Timmy McCarthy was the Irish head coach in a temporary capacity, as Scott McCarthy was looking for a new role to be created. Scott's vision was that a new coaching role would support coaching nationally, and the successful candidate could also head up the Men's national team. Dooley's call couldn't have come at a better time, and he was quickly appointed as Ireland's first Director of Coaching. In the announcement of the role, it was highlighted that Dooley had extensive contacts within the American game.

These contacts would become a critical factor quickly. Following on from a court case in Europe, FIBA was set to lift the restrictions on passport holders playing for national teams. Suddenly, the players in Europe, thanks to the Bosman Rule back in 1995, were now qualified to play immediately for Ireland without waiting for eligibility (previously they had to wait a number of years to become eligible if they hadn't received their passport before turning nineteen). This instantly opened up a new pool of players for Ireland and presented an interesting challenge for the organisation. Ireland suddenly had to rethink how aggressively they wanted to pursue success at the international level. Would they continue with the Irish development mentioned over the previous year or try and make the most of this new opportunity?

Dooley knew the size of the opportunity, and Scott McCarthy was clear in his direction that he was to pursue it as Ireland aimed for the semi-final stage. McCarthy felt that a successful senior team would lead to a trickle-down in interest at the grassroots level. To Bill Dooley, the direction was clear;'The association wanted to up the level. They wanted to be more competitive with the larger Europeans. So, it was a matter of recruiting. I had so many contacts college-wise, that I just started making a lot of calls. I just recruited, really to find out who was going to be eligible. If any one of their grandparents were born in Ireland, they were good to go, and this can happen relatively quick.'

Dooley's contact list was extensive, and he was friends with key people like Jim Larrañaga who had met Enda Byrt years earlier at the 1996 Final Four. Securing Jay Larrañaga was the critical first piece for Dooley, as it gave him a well-respected professional who others could see was worth following. In Ireland's recent shortcomings, they missed out on a primary scoring threat, and Larrañaga looked like the answer Ireland needed. Dooley also dipped into his other Colonial Athletic Conference contacts and secured a 6'6 do-it-all wingman Jim Moran and a top-class defensive point guard in Billy Donlon. Tim Kennedy, who had briefly played for Star of the Sea in Belfast and was now in Portugal was also called up. Suddenly Ireland had three guards in Larrañaga, Moran and Kennedy who would all play EuroLeague basketball. The new-look team combined the recruits with experienced Irish Americans like John O'Connell and Dan Callahan who had been in the programme for years. Ironically, eighteen months earlier Ireland looked like it was stepping away from the Irish-American era, and yet, after Enda Byrt was sacked, the country was now about to go even further with the aid of overseas players.

Ireland's qualification path was straightforward. They were now in a four-team group featuring Iceland, Finland and the Swiss. The top team would make the semi-final stage and Ireland had to play all three teams both home and away in a new format that they hadn't done before. The first set of games took place in June 2001, while the return legs were later that same summer in August. Dooley had little European or international experience to draw on, and he couldn't rely on some of the squad's more experienced campaigners as Gareth Maguire and John O'Connell both missed out. O'Connell broke his hand during the season in Belgium and didn't want anybody to know, so had to ask Dooley not to call him up for the group. Maguire was all set to play until he picked up an injury at a Star of the Sea training session:'When Bill came in, I was so excited because there was something different coming in. The night before we went to our first tournament [where] I was captain of the team, I got an ankle injury at Star practice. I remember Bill telling me I was going to need to step back and get that ankle looked after. I was trying to work through it. And I remember crying so hard. I said, "Bill, I'm so sorry." I struggled to get back into the team because it was so strong.'

Despite the loss of his captain and O'Connell, the new influx of talent brought with it heightened expectations on the ground. Unfortunately, international experience is crucial, and the campaign stuttered before it ever got going with an opening loss on the road to Switzerland in Nyon. With just three returning players from the preliminary group (Mick Richardson, Adrian Fulton and Michael Bree) there was a lot of changes and a lot to be learned quickly for Ireland. The inside force of Alan Tomidy and Ken Lacey that had been there for the majority of the nineties was gone, and Ireland were smaller than they had been in many years. An injury to Dan Callahan complicated things even more for Ireland, as they ended up being outrebounded by the Swiss 33–24. Despite the talented recruits, Ireland's original height issues were coming back to haunt them. A slow first half saw the team trail by thirteen as the group tried to settle in and play a competitive game together for the first time. New point guard Billy Donlon was a tenacious guard and had enjoyed a stellar NCAA career playing for

UNC Willmington. Despite his impressive resume and undoubted skill, he had yet to play in Europe at this stage as he had immediately transitioned from playing into coaching. By his admission, he wasn't fully sharp, as he hadn't played competitively while he was coaching in St Peters. The combination of all these factors meant Ireland were 0–1 to start the group and were heading home for a must-win game against Finland.

Ireland returned to the National Basketball Arena in Dublin, knowing that a second loss in two games might end their qualification hopes before they even started. With Dan Callahan gone, Conor Grace was drafted into the squad to provide more height as the guard-heavy group would have to find a way to survive on the boards. Going into the game, Dooley didn't know much about the Finnish opposition. Still, he was comforted knowing that he had quality throughout his team. 'These guys know they are good players. A guy like Billy Donlon looks around and says we've got a pretty damn good team. I had a bit of an issue with the relativity of it because I didn't know the specifics of a lot of teams around Europe. I would understand their reputation, but we have a pretty damn good team here, so let's see how good we can be.'

Ireland, as expected, were outrebounded again but the Larrañaga brothers (Jay and his younger brother Jon who was playing at George Mason) both came up with 9 points and 8 rebounds to help Ireland survive. Former Star of the Sea player Tim Kennedy shot the ball well in his second game for Ireland with 14 points, while Billy Donlon had got rid of some rust and scored 16 to lead the team. The Finnish team led at half-time, but as it came down the stretch it was a tied game, and Ireland had the ball. Despite being early in his Irish tenure, Bill Dooley was already aware of some negativity from certain clubs about players he was or wasn't picking. One of those questioned was the 2001 Super League player of the year, Damien Sealy. Sealy was a hard-nosed prison guard who's dogged defensive ability and tough mentality made him an instant fit for Dooley. As this new era of Irish-American basketball was trying to take off, it was an amateur, who had come through the Junior Men's ranks with Enda Byrt, that stepped up and hit a massive shot with less than two seconds remaining to win the game. For Ireland, it was a big moment. For Dooley, it was both a relief and an early vindication of sorts. 'Because of the number of Irish Americans we had, you're going to have fewer true Irish guys. I had gone to some league games assessing everything. I think I took a little bit of heat when I kept Damien, but he fit with us. And he turned out to be pretty good.'

For players like Jim Moran and Jay Larrañaga who were coming in from very different basketball backgrounds than the Irish-born players, there was a level of respect both from a personal and basketball perspective instantly. Larrañaga was so happy that Damien Sealy was the guy to step up and hit the shot:'It was a really cool experience meeting Damien and Fulty and hearing their stories. Meeting Damien and hearing that he was a prison guard and then having him go from shaking my hand to having me in an armbar in a split second! I had a tremendous amount of respect for Damien physically first of all, and second of all as a basketball player through the training camp and everything. Damien was the Irish player of the year that year, and there's only one person who can do that in every league, so I had a lot of respect for him already and then when he hit that shot, it was just really exciting, we got a great win at home and the fact that Damien hit the shot was awesome.'

For Jim Moran, the moment brought home how unique the team situation was; 'You have this team, and everyone has roots to this same country. Then you have two or three guys who are from that country. We're supposed to be these EuroLeague guys, these seasoned vets, the cream-of-the-crop guys that are coming in. The one thing that always stood out to me was Adrian Fulty, Damien Sealy – these guys, they went to work! They went to work, and then they came to practice. I was sitting in a hotel all day counting down the hours until I could go to the gym. That always stood with me. I remember when [Sealy] hit that shot . . . this dude has a real life and does real stuff and then comes to play basketball. I get paid to play basketball. I just remember how excited we were.'

The magnitude of the win for Ireland couldn't be overstated, as a loss to Finland at home was likely going to extend the hard-luck qualification story. The importance for Finland was also quickly apparent post-game too. Ireland stayed in the Citywest Hotel during these home games and their opponents did as well. Bill Dooley was sitting in the bar reflecting on a job well done, and his first qualification win as the Irish head coach. While he was sitting there, his Finnish counterpart walked in, and Dooley offered to buy him a beer. 'Afterwards at the hotel and we're in the pub, our guys are mingling, and their coach comes down, and he's distraught. I said let me get you a beer it was a hell of a game.' The coach wasn't too happy, so Dooley added, 'Hey man, it's one game, we hit a shot, it's just one play at the end that's basketball. He said, "yeah yeah".' Dooley quickly learned that people in Finland had already been on to their coach to find out how they had lost to Ireland. A result like this was a catastrophe for them. Dooley was bemused by this as he talked with the coach .'I've got a pretty talented team, and the coach says yeah, I know, but they don't!'

Ireland were taking advantage of the new rulings and had quality in the team that was setting them up for an exciting push. Dooley already knew it, and the rest of Europe was just about to find out.

Three days later Ireland welcomed Iceland to the Arena. On the back of big nights from Tim Kennedy (19) and Jay Larrañaga (18), the Irish used a big fourth-quarter push to win the game 70–59 to finish out the first round of games 2–1. One thing that was evident for anyone close to the team was that a special bond was being formed quickly and the new players were buying into the programme from the outset. Billy Donlon personified that buy-in. He returned home from his first experience in Ireland to drop a bombshell on his parents. He had decided to quit his stable assistant-coach job at St Peter's to continue his Irish journey and to pursue a pro career in Europe. These guys had experienced a cause bigger than themselves, and they were determined to come back at the end of the summer even more prepared. Fortunately, they were also going to have reinforcements.

Ireland's lack of size in the first three games was addressed by the return of the always dependable Dan Callahan. Even with Dan coming back, Bill Dooley's recruiting continued, and some new faces entered the fray. Ken Kavanagh was a 6'9 big man who was playing in the top French league. Kavanagh had played college basketball at San Jose State in the WAC and later for Manhattan in the MAAC. Kavanagh's involvement with Ireland had included the World University Games in 1999, but his time with the senior team would be limited to just these three games. The other new addition was much more significant, Mike Mitchell. The former WAC Player of the Year had had an outstanding college career and was playing professionally in Germany. The majority of Mitchell's career had been spent in Australia, but he was spending the final few years in Europe. In many ways, Mitchell wasn't the type of player that had been envisioned back in the eighties and nineties coming and helping Ireland, as he was only eligible through marriage and was yet to visit the country before his first game. Despite that, he had jumped at the opportunity to play and was immediately a key cog for the team.

With the reinforcements in place, Ireland welcomed Switzerland to the Arena as they looked for revenge for the away defeat back in June. Dan Callahan was the rock that Ireland needed, and despite trailing by two going into the final quarter, a balanced scoring effort from the Irish-American core helped Ireland push home to win 69–62. The win set up a winner-takes-all game with Finland who were now much more aware of the threat that Ireland posed.

The game was on live TV in Finland, and they had sent for reinforcements of their own in Hanno Mottola. The 6'11 big man went to college in Utah and had become the 40th pick in the 2000 NBA Draft, becoming the first Finnish NBA player. He would play 155 games in the NBA for the Hawks (where he would share some time with future Irish international Cal Bowdler). Mottola had just finished his rookie year in the NBA as Ireland came to town, and his presence was a huge issue for the team. Dan Callahan had the thankless job of stopping the big man as he limited Mottola to 24 points on the night. It wasn't one-way traffic though, as Callahan had 15 points and 13 rebounds himself in a great battle that showed the quality and competitiveness of Callahan, who gave up considerable size in the match-up. Ireland's recruitment came very much to the fore as it was needed in a tough road game. Both Bill Dooley and the players had the mentality that they should be beating Finland. They weren't weighed down by any baggage or inferiority complexes as they went into the hostile environment. Dooley explained it simply: 'We wouldn't have had the weight of that mindset on anything that had happened before. OK, we're playing Finland, what does that mean? It didn't really mean as much to us except that we were going to try and go out and beat them'. Together the new group scored 82 of Ireland's 84 points, with Jay Larrañaga having possibly the best night of his Irish career. He scored 29 points including big shot after big shot down the stretch.

Adrian Fulton could feel the momentum moving into Ireland's hands with each passing minute:'They were really good, but we hung in. They made the mistake of running their stuff, but they got tight. We kept the game close, and when it got tight down the stretch, they kept throwing the ball to Mottola.'

As Finland ran out of ideas, Ireland scraped over the line. They had achieved what had been the goal for so long: qualification to the semi-final stage of the European Championships. As the game ended, the gravity of the moment hit Jay Larrañaga instantly. It was Gareth Maguire and Adrian Fulton who drove it home for him. 'Gareth hadn't played in the first round, so I got to meet Gareth in that second round. Just hearing him speak, he talked about how special his experience was. After we beat Finland, I can still picture him and Fulty just grabbing each other face to face. I can see the gym and where we were. I just felt that was really cool because they had put so much time into this. It made me regret that I hadn't been able to be in some of those previous battles with them.'

Without a doubt, the rule changes from FIBA and Bill Dooley's arrival had set Ireland up for a new level of basketball. Dooley recognised the importance of maintaining a homegrown connection to the team, and although the involvement of players like Gareth Maguire wasn't immediately apparent on the scoresheet, their presence was something the new coach didn't take for granted. 'Gareth's got a way with the word. Not every game, but several games including the Finland game, the night before I would have Gareth say a few words. I asked him a few times, and he asked me a few times to address the team and give them a perspective of the meaning of it. Words about trying to grow basketball in Ireland and what this means to players like this playing for Ireland. It was from the heart, and there's no question that it had an impact on everyone, myself included.'

Those words also stuck with Tim Kennedy who knew Gareth well from his brief spell with Star of the Sea. 'What stands out for me is I remember Gareth talking about it in the locker room just saying how big it was. I think he could feel that we didn't understand the depth of it and how important it was. He gave a passionate talk about it, and that still sticks with me that it was so big. I got a chance to stay with Gareth and work out with him when I was with Star of the Sea and see what kind of person he was and what he was about. So it was kind of cool that I knew what kind of person he was and how he threw himself into everything and to see the pride that he had for us being able to qualify, it was really cool.'

As the new milestone in Irish basketball was achieved, the country's philosophical debates would rage on. Dooley was aware of them, but yet he was also under direction to keep going with the hope that Ireland could create an interest in the national team that had never been there before.'You always had this segment of folks, and I understood it, well you're Irish Americans, we want our own guys. Alright, fair enough, but the Association had decided to follow this path to try to gain more attention and maybe let it trickle down. I hear what you're saying, and I can appreciate it, but what about the Irish soccer team, are they not mostly all from England? OK, what's the major difference here?'.

For Scott McCarthy, the path to success was clear: 'I was never in the camp that we should get ten Americans in, I thought we could maybe get 50/50 . . . We used to debate that a lot at board meetings; if we had the chance would we go to nine Americans? I think we had a loose rule that it would be six and four, with a good percentage of Irish guys. I always believed, and everyone has a different opinion on this, that your marquee product is what sells the thing. Our statistics when I left were staggeringly good in terms of participation. It was still quite invisible. We had a great schools programme and the weekends with the schools coming were unbelievable, but it was still very under profiled. For me, I thought the profile was really important. I thought that all the tides would rise. If we were going to the semi-final round people start to think we are a basketball country a bit more.'

Ireland was now in the semi-final round. Was this going to help the game's perception and visibility in Ireland, and whether or not we could now be considered a basketball country? It was clear, however, that Ireland was in a dramatic new era of the national team, and it was a far cry from having just eight players competing in Jersey at the European Qualifiers only twenty years earlier.

Chapter 25: The Women's Recruiting Drive

2001 was a major year for Irish teams in Europe as the Senior Men finally made their breakthrough to the semi-final stages courtesy of an Irish-American-dominated team. The women had stayed away from American-born players in the Europeans up to this point and in 1999 had come agonisingly close to qualification, losing out to Denmark by just one point. As the European Championships campaign started in May 2001, it was time that the women explored the Irish-American route themselves; a final push to see if they could get over the top and into the semi-final round. Gerry Fitzpatrick was the women's coach at the time, and he knew that the move they were making was necessary. The team were facing full-time professionals and needed help in any way they could find it:'At that point, we were just looking at how could we strengthen that team, knowing there was no Division A and B, so you were playing the Italys or Spains or whoever in your qualifying group. The chances were that you were playing against full-time professionals and you were trying to bridge that gap with seriously committed amateur players from Ireland, so maybe we were grasping at straws at times trying to bridge that gap.'

The men's recruitment route had effectively followed three different eras. Firstly, Ireland tried to use local connections to find Irish Americans capable of representing the national team. Secondly, an exhaustive campaign by Enda Byrt utilising both a network of contacts and some clever localised advertising in the States had found more talent. And then Bill Dooley arrived into the Irish job, bringing with him an even deeper pool of contacts that allowed him to target high-level professionals capable of playing for Ireland. Gerry Fitzpatrick and the women's team didn't have the same opportunities available to them. There had been no long-term recruiting in the States and the professional game in Europe was so underdeveloped (particularly financially) that many eligible players weren't even coming to Europe to play. Finding experienced players that could come in and make a big difference for Ireland was going to be a challenge and Gerry Fitzpatrick knew it. 'There wasn't an awareness at the time of the women going down that route. The biggest thing really, which maybe Enda was aware of, for a national team what you are looking for is older players playing in bigger leagues. For a college player in America, they were largely unavailable to a national team until it came to competition time.

The few little experiments we had in my latter years with the women's team where we did bring in a couple of Irish Americans who weren't in college, it wasn't a hugely significant thing because they weren't playing in leagues. The big difference, bottom line, was that the likes of Jay Larrañaga and Marty Conlon were playing in the Greek, Spanish or Italian leagues. College players in America were still very much in the development stage of their athletic development, and it wasn't really a feature at all.'

The 2001 qualifiers had a big build-up for Ireland because of how close they had come in 1999 and also they were back playing on home soil. The qualifiers were to be held in the University of Limerick, making it the third time the women's team hosted qualifiers. In Neptune in 1987 and Tralee in 1991, Ireland had been disappointed, and hopes were that this time round would finally be the breakthrough.

Ireland had a tough group with Italy who were overwhelming favourites, joined by Portugal, Belgium and neighbours England. The top two teams from the group would go through to the semi-finals. With Italy an almost certainty to progress it looked like four teams were competing for one spot. There was cause for optimism in the squad as they had a balance of veteran domestic players like Jillian Hayes, a young star in Susan Moran who was coming off her junior year at St Joe's, another budding star in the NCAA, Siobhan Kilkenny, and for the first time three Irish-American players.

Siobhan Kilkenny was making the step up to Senior European level for the first time. She played on underage teams alongside Susan Moran, but her career really took off when she went to the States to play for Manhattan in the MAAC. During her four years at Manhattan, she scored 959 points, had 232 assists and 201 steals. A 2003 MAAC title topped off her career as she helped guide the Jaspers to the NCAA tournament where they played Mississippi State. The Lady Jaspers lost in front of a sell-out crowd in New Mexico, and Kilkenny finished out her career with a thirteen-point seven-rebound effort in the tournament. Her contributions were valued so much that Manhattan inducted Siobhan into their Hall of Fame in 2015.

As the 2001 qualifiers were starting, Kilkenny had just finished her sophomore year, and more experience was needed. Given the connections to St Joe's and Fordham that Ireland had, it was no surprise that the first wave of Irish-American support came with ties to the two universities.

Amy Mallon came in as the most interesting prospect of the new group. She had played for Richmond University for three seasons in the late 1980s early '90s and had helped Richmond reach the NCAA tournament twice while being named to the All CAA team in both 1990 and '91. After three years in Richmond, she transferred for her final year, and it took her to St Joseph's before Susan Moran had arrived on campus. In her one year playing at St Joe's, Mallon became the Big 5 Player of the Year, an honourable mention All-American and first-team All Atlantic 10. Her brilliant college career opened up an opportunity to play professionally in Luxembourg, which she did before returning home as an assistant coach, first at Villanova and then St Joe's. After some time on the bench, Amy had another professional opportunity, this time in the USA as part of the short-lived American Basketball League. In her time there she played alongside the USA Basketball legend Dawn Staley and they reached the ABL Finals in their first year. After the league ended prematurely, Mallon went on to coach again at Episcopal Academy, when Ireland came calling. Later, after playing for

Ireland, she joined the Drexel University staff in Pennsylvania for sixteen years before becoming the school's head coach in 2020.

While coaching at St Joseph's in 1997, Mallon shared the bench with a familiar face in Regina Grennan. Regina, who had starred at Arizona as a point guard, was an assistant coach at Richmond while Mallon played there. She then helped bring Mallon to Pennsylvania when she moved to St Joe's as an assistant in 1991. Regina was also the coach sent to Tullamore on a recruiting mission to sign up Susan Moran, so her connections with the team were strong. Initially, she joined the Irish team in a coaching capacity but came out of retirement to play in 2001 due to necessity more than anything. Her playing career had ended in 1990 when she had graduated from Arizona as one of the programme's all-time leaders in minutes played. In her time in Tucson, she led the Wildcats in assists for all four seasons and also led them in steals and three-point field goals made for two seasons. Both of Grennan's parents were Irish, and a strong connection to Gerry Fitzpatrick led her to join the staff as a coach initially. Her goal was simple: 'Really, it was a chance to recruit when other coaches weren't allowed be out recruiting. The NCAA rule at the time was if you're working with a national team, you are allowed to go out to their tournaments. So, it gave me an opportunity to be at games that no other coaches could be at. We ended up getting a player from Moldova.'

But after coaching, things would end up changing, as Gerry Fitzpatrick was looking for help. 'It wasn't to play, it definitely wasn't to play, playing was so far off my radar. We went to France for a training camp for a week, and a couple of players went down with injuries. I had to play in practice, and Gerry had this great idea that maybe I should play. He said both of your parents are Irish right? I said yeah. He said, did you get your Irish passport? I said no; I had all the paperwork, but I hadn't got around to sending it in. He said, any chance of you sending it in and getting that passport?' Despite it not being on her radar initially, it was an opportunity she relished. And when she finally stepped on the court to play for Ireland in Limerick, it was something that hit her hard emotionally'For me, it was amazing the chance to play for Ireland since my parents were Irish . . . I even get choked up about it now. I guess it was when the national anthem played. It was really cool and totally unexpected. I had been there coaching them and then suddenly I was out there on the floor, and it was totally unexpected.'

The final piece to the team would not have a St Joe's connection. Kelly Fitzpatrick had been teammates with two Irish internationals, Emer Howard and Suzanne Maguire, at Fordham. In 1994, Fitzpatrick was the MVP of their conference tournament as Fordham reached the NCAA tournament. After graduating, she went on to play in England for a brief spell.

At the time, Susan Moran was Ireland's star. It was clear to her that recruiting would have quite a different approach than the men's tactics: 'I don't think we were trying to do similar. I think there was a disconnect. If you look at the two Americans there [in 2001], one was my coach, and one was best friends with my coach, and they happened to have Irish heritage. I don't think people went searching them out as much as it kind of just happened. There was no real comparison with the men at all. In fact, the men's and the women's [campaigns] were very separate; it's not like now where they'd know each other, we didn't really know who was on the men's team . . . I feel like the men's players now, in hindsight, were like game-changers. Even Reggie and Amy – they played but they were not like superstars.'

Ireland's route to qualification in Limerick was relatively straightforward. They would likely need to beat England in their opening game and then try and beat either Portugal or Belgium to qualify. Beating England was not straightforward though, as Ireland had struggled in qualifiers numerous times against their neighbours. The best chance at victory had come in 1987 in Neptune, but despite leading by 9 points with under five minutes to go, England dragged their way back into the game and won with a three-pointer with just six seconds remaining. This time in Limerick it was set to be even harder, as England had Andrea Congreaves in their ranks. Congreaves later coached Glanmire during the 2012–13 season, in which they had huge battles with a star-studded UL Huskies team. At this time, though, Congreaves was still at the height of her playing powers. She had played four years for Mercer in the NCAA and had led the country in scoring for both her junior and senior season. Following her college career, she went on to play in the WNBA for three seasons and then professionally in Europe. Limiting her was going to be a major challenge for Ireland.

Ireland got off to a slow start offensively and found themselves trailing by five after the first quarter (19–14). As the Irish settled in, they clawed their way back into the game, and by the end of the third quarter, they had a three-point lead, 51–48. Like previous years, closing the game out proved difficult as Ireland's offence ground to a halt with only 10 fourth-quarter points. England scored 18 in the final quarter and stole the game from Ireland, 66–61. The damage wasn't done by Congreaves but rather Shelly Boston, who was a 6'2 Australian who had recently qualified to represent England. She had 21 points and 10 rebounds and caused Ireland lots of trouble inside. A lack of outside shooting also doomed Ireland as they hit 1/9 from three, compared to England's 5/14. As Ireland was learning, these were the fine margins at the European level.

In the second game, Ireland lost heavily to a fully professional Italian team as expected. After a rest day, Ireland were back to face Portugal in a must-win game. The Portuguese had lost to Belgium and beaten England, so this was their final game. They knew they had to win and hoped that Ireland could beat Belgium in their last game. It was do or die for Ireland as they needed a minimum of two wins to be in contention. Ireland's offence struggled again as they managed just 62 points and Portugal won by 9 in the end. Moran scored 20, and Caitriona White added 17, but no other player made it into double digits. With one game left, Ireland's qualification dream was over. In the final game, Belgium won out 85–79 in a much higher-scoring game. Moran again had a double-double with 24 points and 10 rebounds and Jillian Hayes helped with 19 points.

At the end of the five-day tournament, Ireland had no wins and lots of battle wounds. Losses of 9, 6 and 5 points were all competitive games, but Ireland had lacked a guard to control the offence.

The American experiment had mixed results. Amy Mallon finished fourth on the team in scoring with 5.5 points, and third in rebounding with 3.5. Grennan led the team in assists with 1.8, but had almost twice as many turnovers as assists as she tried to adjust to competitive action again. Fitzpatrick played the fewest minutes of the group and had a solid if unspectacular impact.

It was clear that finding a female equivalent of a Jay Larrañaga or Jim Moran wasn't going to be possible, as the opportunities for female players just weren't there. Gerry Fitzpatrick reflected on the issue: 'We just didn't know, we couldn't locate or access people who were eligible to play for Ireland who were playing at a high level in Europe. Your best chance was finding a player in college who could declare, but even at that, it was really difficult because [playing in Europe] wasn't seen as a pathway for women as it was for men.'

For Regina Grennan, the disappointment of Limerick is something that still hurts.'I think we were hoping that that tournament was going to be a big step because we were so close in Athens. I remember just being deflated; it was so close, and we blew it – we just couldn't close it.' Grennan's journey to the team summed up the issue for Ireland. Graduating from Arizona a decade earlier, she was an ideal candidate to help Ireland, yet it was almost ten years later when she was a full-time coach that Ireland did get her.

The disappointment of the event led Ireland to a new crossroads. Gerry Fitzpatrick was finishing up his tenure, and a lot of the senior domestic talent were likely retiring too. The Irish-American route had been explored with less success than hoped, and the team was in a state of transition. As it turned out, FIBA was set to change their competitions' structures to stop countries like Italy beating Ireland in qualifiers again. A new configuration of an A and B division was aiming to have more parity between teams. What it unfortunately led to was a three-year break from European contest as Ireland had to wait 1,216 days to get back on the court in FIBA competition. The rate of change was so dramatic that Ireland would only have Susan Moran and Siobhan Kilkenny from the UL tournament playing in their first game back in 2004.

If Ireland wasn't going to get help from Irish America to lift them over the top, could they produce enough homegrown stars to deliver them to the newly formed A division? And even if they could develop them, would they be able to get them all together at the same time consistently? These were the questions facing the women's programme as the men started competing against some of Europe's top teams.

Chapter 26: The Semi-Finals

Ireland's Senior Men had finally reached the semi-final round, and the reality of the situation quickly set in as the group details emerged. Ireland was part of a six-team group that would play on a home and away basis. Unlike previous years when the games were played in one or two short bursts, this campaign would run from November 2001 until January 2003 in four windows. Aside from anything else, the format would put pressure on any domestic players hoping to be a part of the squad, as the time commitment away from work would be considerable.

The group draw brought up some familiar faces as Ireland faced Macedonia for the first time since 1995 and their old nemesis Cyprus yet again. Without a doubt, though, all eyes went to the top two names on the draw as Ireland were paired with Croatia and Germany, two international powerhouses. The idea that Germany was bringing their national team to compete in the National Basketball Arena was a surreal proposition for Irish basketball and one that seemed impossible only a decade earlier.

Coach Bill Dooley was back in the top seat, and ahead of the new campaign, he had been tirelessly working to find even more talent for Ireland to draw on. At the time, the organisation was doing well financially as the Celtic Tiger was at its peak, and the financial constraints that Enda Byrt felt limited by were less of a factor.

There was no time for Dooley and the team to ease themselves into this next level – Ireland's first game was away to Germany in November 2001. Despite the increased competition level, some things hadn't changed, and the constant battle with international clubs to get players released continued. The FIBA rules were seemingly there in name only, and the power remained with the clubs, who could make life difficult for any player that wanted to be released. Ireland was operating in a professional world that they weren't used to, and some of the top clubs were slow to want to deal with them.

Players like Alan Tomidy and Ken Lacey remained focused on their club careers, while Pat Burke was now in the NBA and wasn't available. For Bill Dooley, the most disappointing absence was one of his most trusted contributors, Dan Callahan. Callahan was already in Germany for the first game when he signed for a team in Italy. It was made clear to Dan as he signed a very lucrative contract that he had to immediately report to Italy, and it would cost Ireland his services for the first two games of the campaign. 'When you play in some of those teams in Italy, they are paying you a lot of money, and they don't want you to go and play somewhere else. There was a lot of fighting with agents talking to the teams. If you had two or three days off, they tried to control everything, they didn't want you getting hurt, and they fought you leaving. The national team took priority under the FIBA rules, and that was understood, but it was also understood that you would be penalised a little bit – maybe playing time getting cut or whatever it might be. It was pretty tough.' His loss was huge for Ireland, as he was the team's most experienced Irish American and one of the most prominent personalities.

Another big personality, John O'Connell, was back after missing Dooley's first campaign. As he joined the squad, John wondered whether this new group of recruits would match the original line-up and understand the importance of representing Ireland: '. . . Fortunately, the guys who I had played with had said nice things about me, so I felt a warm welcome right away, but I also immediately saw how much they loved playing for Ireland, that passion. I remember I was curious if they would. I had played with that other group for ten years before I met these guys and to play for Ireland meant the world to us. I remember being surprised by how equally passionate they were about it, and it meant the world to me: Jim Moran and the little maniac Billy Donlon and their passion to represent Ireland. Even in the locker room before the game, realising the historical opportunity that they had . . . I even tear up thinking about it, because we recruited the right guys who wanted to do it for the right reasons.' Not only were they high-character guys, but the level of play was something O'Connell hadn't seen with Ireland before: 'I knew I was not the man anymore. I remember Coach Dooley saying to me, "I hear Jimmy Moran plays a lot like you, you guys have a similar game." Then I saw Jimmy Moran play and I thought, I *wish* we played similar! They brought it up to a whole different level than where I was. They were the pros of pros; their bodies were better, their games were better, they took care of themselves on a different level, they were professionals. They had their fun, it's not like they were robots, but they were just different, it was a different professional level, it was apparent immediately.'

One thing that made Dan Callahan's absence slightly more palatable for Dooley was Marty Conlon's arrival into the squad. Conlon was a ten-year NBA veteran who had a decorated career across multiple teams in the league. The 6'10 big man had been there and done it all and was now in Europe playing out the end of his career. For Conlon, the fact that Ireland had reached the semi-final round was irrelevant, simply playing for Ireland was a big deal for him and his family. He had always intended to compete regardless of the level. Back in 1984, Enda Byrt recruited him for the Junior Men's team. Although he wanted to play, his commitment to Providence blocked him from doing so. Now at the other end of an incredible career, he was there for Ireland and ready to contribute.

In the opening game, Ireland got out to a slow start against the Germans who raced out to a big lead at the half 44–24. The level of play was a major jump for Ireland who had played at Promotions Cup level only seven years earlier. Adrian Fulton, one of the men who had been there all the way since the Promotions Cup in Wales in 1990, could do nothing but laugh at where the team suddenly found themselves:'I remember turning to Gareth Maguire inside the first five minutes on the bench and laughing. I said, what are we doing here, the level of play was so good, the jump was just, wow.' Ireland continued to battle throughout the second half. Mike Mitchell, who was based in Germany at the time, and Conlon both dazzled with 25 points each, as Ireland clawed their way back into the game trailing by just 5 points with five minutes remaining. Unfortunately, Mike Mitchell fouled out soon after and Ireland lost by 8 points, 85–77. For the German coach Henrik Dettman, Ireland posed a real threat, and players like Conlon and Larrañaga commanded respect from the Germans: 'Ireland had a good team, we really fully respected Ireland. It was not like, we are going to play Ireland, a small basketball country – we knew that you had good players and a good team, and we were very serious. I remember when we did the scouting, and we talked about the players, you had guys who played at a higher level in Europe. Also, the way your players were playing and behaving, they were good guys, that was a good basketball team.'

Dooley reflected in the media after the game, 'We played pretty well, and we're disappointed we lost in the end. Let's say we're disappointed but we are not discouraged'.

Returning to Dublin, things weren't going to get any easier for Ireland as they hosted Croatia in the National Basketball Arena. Croatia counted on 6'7 swingman Gordon Giricek, a second-round draft pick in 1999 who was currently playing for CSKA Moscow. Giricek was a familiar face for some of Ireland's players who had faced him in the World University Games almost a decade earlier. For Ireland, it was a top-class opposition coming to Dublin and a huge chance to make a moment that could boost the sport and blow the group wide open. In his programme notes, the Irish Basketball Association president Tony Colgan summed up both the magnitude of the occasion and how the sport saw it as a major opportunity for growth: 'Tonight, Irish Basketball embarks on a new and exciting adventure. After many years of near misses and a lot of heartbreak, our Men's national team has achieved qualification for the semi-final round of the 2003 European Championships. . . Without doubt the forthcoming games represent the highest quality basketball ever seen in this country. In the excitement of the success achieved during the qualifying round played last summer, it is easy to forget the promotional opportunities that are now available. A large international media presence is expected for each game. Spectators will experience the excitement and emotion that is unique to international basketball and young players will have the opportunity to see first-hand what it takes to compete at this level. These all have positive implications for the development of basketball in Ireland, and it is the intention of the IBA to take maximum advantage of these opportunities.'

The game was very balanced in the first half before a run by Ireland opened up what looked to be their most famous ever result. When Adrian Fulton found his former Star of the Sea teammate Tim Kennedy for a three on the wing, Ireland led by 12 with just over ten minutes to go. Croatia wasn't done though, and they ate away at Ireland's lead as tired legs meant the home team's offence ground to a halt. Marty Conlon fouled-out late on, and Croatia took full advantage, grabbing the lead in the final minute with a big score inside. The basket turned out to be all that they needed as they narrowly escaped Dublin with a two-point win 78–76. Jay Larrañaga led the way for Ireland with 21 points, but the loss is one that still sticks with him: 'I have a lot of regrets in that game. I had a three in transition during the fourth quarter that went in and out, and I felt it could have iced the game. I was guarding Gordon Giricek; I didn't do a good job guarding him. I should have either guarded him better or had the humility to let somebody else like Billy Donlon or Jim Moran guard him. He went off in the fourth quarter, and we didn't do a good job. We definitely should have won that game. We were better than them that day, but we didn't finish it off.'

Jim Moran remembered similar: 'I really remember feeling deflated. It was a what-if moment. At the time, you can't sit there and think about how much that game was going to impact everything else. You sit in the locker room and hope that someone will beat someone for you, and you cling on to hope. At the back of your mind, as an athlete, those what-ifs always creep in. The way we lost that game – it's one thing if we played bad – we just gave that game away. In professional sports you can't get rid of those ones, they stick with you, they always hang around, and they just pop back up. Gordon was a great player; he was in Europe for a long time and in the NBA. You lose a game like that, and you think of every possession.' For Moran it highlighted that Ireland was missing one thing and that was having a go-to star.'I think we felt they had the guy [Giricek] but we had the team. We didn't have the guy; we had a bunch of guys who could do stuff, but we didn't have the one guy who could take everything over.

That's what pissed us off. We felt we had won that game and their guy decided to win the game.'

For the whole team and Dooley, it was another in a long line of what-if moments for Irish basketball. Adrian Fulton wasn't sure whether international basketball was ready to see Ireland win games like that. A key missed call against Croatia's star man is one that still grates on Fulton 'No doubt about it we got screwed and Dooley thought it as well. No doubt about it, the refs thought the Irish guys are not supposed to beat these guys. We had them, maybe they were missing a couple of players but we had them that night.' Years later Dooley still wonders about what that win could have done for Irish basketball 'The game I'll never forget, unfortunately – you remember the ones that got away, Croatia in Dublin. We had them. Up 10 in the last quarter, missed free throws and a layup. Granted they made some plays, and they had some very good players including Gordon Giricek, who became an NBA player. We absolutely had them. I always felt that Croatia are so well-respected basketball-wise, if we had of got that game it would have done wonders, but it slipped away.'

Ireland was hurt on the inside on the night as Conlon tried to cover everything for Ireland, but he was doing so alone. The thought of how close a moment it was for Ireland makes you think of names like Pat Burke (Panathinaikos EuroLeague and A1 Greece), Alan Tomidy (Benneton Treviso EuroLeague and Serie A), Ken Lacey (Serie A) and Dan Callahan (Serie A) – four big bodies with Irish experience that could have been the difference between a what-if moment and a golden moment for the sport. Again, these are the fine margins at the international level.

The final contest of the first three-game stint for Ireland was a home game against Macedonia. When the teams met in 1995, Macedonia comprehensively beat Ireland, and it was time for Ireland to gain some revenge. It looked like there was a hangover from the Croatian game for Ireland as they trailed 38–22 at the half, in what could only be described as 'awful' by Coach Dooley. Mike Mitchell led a balanced effort with 17 points, as five Irish players scored in double digits and Ireland fought back with a huge second half to record their first-ever win at the semi-final stage, 75–68.

A break in the schedule meant Ireland would come back in January 2002 for the next group of games as they faced Cyprus and Bosnia and Herzegovina. Ireland first headed to Limassol in Cyprus. Adrian Fulton was the only holdover from the 1992 Promotions Cup trip there that saw Ireland receive death threats and coins thrown at them. This time the drama was again away from the court, as Ireland couldn't get Jim Moran (injured), Dan Callahan (club commitments) or Mike Mitchell (injured) to play in the games. Ireland did have a greater depth available to them and a new recruit, Glenn Sekunda, was a very welcome addition. The 6'9 big man had already played in Italy for several seasons and was now based in Spain. Having played in Syracuse and then Penn State, he had developed a reputation as a marksman, and he was the first real stretch four that Ireland would have since Frank Powell retired. Sekunda's quality shone through in his debut as he scored 31 points, but the game wasn't without drama as crowd trouble behind the Irish bench disrupted the game. Undeterred by the commotion, a huge basket from Jay Larrañaga helped seal the dramatic win for Ireland 74–67. Ireland was not the same young team who had come into Cyprus in 1992, and the professionals were capable of withstanding the distractions in the Arena. The incident did make it to the national papers the next day as Aidan O'Hara reported in the *Irish Independent*: 'Things turned ugly when up to 100 Irish fans were attacked by rival Cypriot supporters. As the Irish supporters became more vocal when Ireland started to pull away in the final quarter, about 20 home fans jumped over the barriers that separated the crowds. There were also some coins thrown onto the court which was protected by a Perspex shield. The Irish fans were given a police escort out of the Apollin Stadium before the end of the match, and when the final buzzer sounded, the Irish players and coach Bill Dooley moved swiftly to the dressing room.'[xlvi]

After consecutive wins for Ireland, Bosnia came to town on what was a very strange occasion for Adrian Fulton and Gareth Maguire. Ireland, unlike their professional counterparts, did not have domestic breaks for international play. As a result, the two Star of the Sea players played in the Cup semi-final in the National Basketball Arena on Friday night, and the next day at 3 p.m. lined out for Ireland in the European qualifier, all before the possibility of a Cup Final on Sunday. Less than ideal for any player, particularly amateurs, and again it highlighted the challenges that were now facing Ireland's non-professionals. The change in competition structure and the rise in the talent meant that it was almost impossible to have domestic players playing for Ireland. It's a testament to the commitment of both Fulton and Maguire that they had remained this long.

The Bosnia game had huge significance for the group as both teams had an equal record, so a win for Ireland could keep them in contention for a Finals spot heading into the second round of games. Unfortunately, they were outclassed by the Bosnians, led by their dynamic guard Mrsic Damir. The Fenerbahce guard scored 20 points, and the Bosnian's defence smothered Ireland on the way to a 74–59 win.

The Bosnian loss meant that Ireland now faced an uphill battle and things were about to get tougher. After three solid years in green, Billy Donlon retired from international basketball to get back to the coaching career that he had given up in 2000. Bill Dooley's time in Ireland was also over as he returned to the States with his wife. Gerry Fitzpatrick, who had previously served as the assistant to Dooley and as the Senior Women's head coach took over the reins heading into the November internationals.

Fitzpatrick's presence saw Stephen McCarthy return to the squad and it also saw Davidson graduate Michael Bree back in the team. The headline name joining the team for this set of games was Cal Bowdler, who had just started his career in Europe having played for the Atlanta Hawks for three years. Bowdler was the 17th pick in the 1999 NBA draft, and at 6'10 he would provide an incredible inside presence to go with Marty Conlon.

After being jaded by a tough NBA experience, the enthusiasm within European basketball had captured Cal's imagination. He had just moved from his first team, Bologna, to Siena, who would turn out to be a EuroLeague Final Four team. For Cal, it was a step in his planned return to the NBA, and the opportunity to go and play for Ireland during that time was one he relished.

In the lead up to the second round of games Ireland beat England in a warm-up game with Cal Bowdler and Glenn Sekunda partnering well, and spirits were high in the camp. One negative was the absence of Mike Mitchell, who picked up a hamstring injury while playing for his club. The injury severely impacted the veteran's international career, as he tried to prolong his professional club career by managing his body. Most disappointing was Jim Moran's absence, who was under pressure from Gran Canaria not to play.

Just one month before Ireland played Germany, the Germans finished third in the World Championships in Indianapolis. This German team was largely the same, except they were without their star Dirk Nowitzki. Their coach at the time felt that this was the peak of his team's powers: 'It was more or less the same team [as the bronze medal World Championship team in 2002], the only guy that was missing was Dirk. I think we played our best basketball at this time; we played really well. We gained self-confidence from EuroBasket 2001, and the team were young and hungry and playing good basketball.' Germany had stars like Ademola Okulaja, a 6'9 big man who played at North Carolina, and the team in general were well-respected veterans around Europe. A slow start again from Ireland saw them face a ten-point deficit, and despite their best efforts, they could never fully claw it back. Cal Bowdler was a standout though, as he showed what he was capable of by playing with a freedom that had escaped him during his time in the NBA. On the night he top-scored with an incredible 26 points. For Dan Callahan who was around Irish teams since 1993, to see Ireland progress to this level of competitiveness was amazing:'It was a sense of pride, and we were excited just to see how far we'd come in a short amount of time. We were playing one of the top teams in the world, and we were just this little country and some people didn't even think we had a league. Even the Ireland league: they are teachers and work in prisons, and they play a couple of times a week, and we are playing against teams that have won medals at the Olympics – it is impressive. We did pretty good, we held our own too.'

Three days later, Ireland had to play in Croatia as they tried in vain to keep their qualification hopes alive. Gordon Giricek was again the man as Croatia beat Ireland comfortably 87–69. The most dramatic moment came early in the game when one of the Croatians threw down a dunk so hard that it shattered the backboard, causing minor cuts to some of the Irish big men. Bowdler again top-scored with 25, while Glenn Sekunda added 18. Still, Ireland were outclassed on the night as a big Croatian third quarter (36–18) proved the difference.

Any mathematical hopes of staying in the group were ended just four days later as Ireland were outgunned by Macedonia, who hit thirteen three-pointers on the way to an 83–72 win. For Ireland, it ended any possibility of reaching the European Championships final round. Despite that, there were still two games to be played the following January as Ireland faced Cyprus in Cork and Bosnia and Herzegovina away.

Ahead of the Cyprus game, Gerry Fitzpatrick promised a show of pride by the Irish as they played in the Mardyke Arena in Cork. Speaking to the *Examiner*, Fitzpatrick said, 'this is a game everyone wants to win. This is a patriotic thing with the players. I mean they are probably the only team in the competition who don't get paid for playing for their country. I'd hate to tell you what the Germans get paid.' [xlvii]

Cork's disconnect with the national team had been an issue since the early 1990s when Enda Byrt had taken over. The Irish team were now coming into town with a team made up largely of Irish Americans with the hope of changing some perceptions. It was guaranteed to be a dramatic affair too, as it was old foes Cyprus coming to town. The memories of the crowd trouble a year earlier were still fresh in the minds of many.

The occasion was also to have even greater significance for Ireland for two reasons. Firstly, Adrian Fulton and Damien Sealy were set to retire from international basketball, and this was their last home game for the national team. For two incredible servants of the game, everybody wanted to send them out on a high. The second reason was a tragic one, and it was fitting that the game was being held in Cork. Emmett Neville, a former Junior Irish international, and one of Neptune's young stars in the Irish Super League, tragically died the day before the game after suffering an epileptic fit and heart attack. Neville was only twenty-two years old and was one of the country's brightest talents.

A minute's silence and a black band on the Irish jerseys marked Neville's passing as 1,200 people packed out the Mardyke Arena for a game that had no bearing on the standings, but had the potential to change the Irish public's perception of the national team. John McHale, writing for the *Evening Echo*, summed up the impact that seeing the top level of basketball had on the Cork public: 'For the virgin Cork public this was a unique experience. To see the players the calibre of Jay Larrañaga, Cal Bowdler, Marty Conlon and Glenn Sekunda in an Irish jersey was an eye-opening experience. For a public fed on a diet of Super League basketball, this was a feast from the top table, a real five-star experience and something they were not used to. Professional players strutting their stuff against a very talented and aggressive Cyprus side. And the gulf in standard compared to what the public usually see was as clear as the nose on your face. They played the game in the correct manner. No shouting, no screaming at officials. No tantrums when being taken off. No contesting calls by the referee. Just 100% effort to help their team win.' [xlviii]

The match itself provided huge drama as the game went into double overtime before Ireland came out victorious. Cyprus had the game won at the end of the first overtime when they secured a rebound leading 88–87 with just two seconds to go. Rather than be fouled, the Cypriot player threw the ball away in an attempt to run out the clock. Unfortunately for him, the ball hit out of bounds and Ireland got the ball back with a chance to win the game. Glenn Sekunda drew a foul and hit one of two free throws, sending the game into a second period of overtime. In the final period, Marty Conlon helped seal the win with four free throws as Ireland signed off an incredible night in Cork in style.

The win was important as it gave Gerry Fitzpatrick his first competitive win as Men's head coach. Critically it also helped convince people that the Irish Americans representing the country were doing so with a genuine desire to help the country. John McHale interviewed Jay Larrañaga before the game, and after speaking to Jay about his love for playing for Ireland and witnessing the game in the Mardyke, John wrote in his *Examiner* column: 'How many calories are there in humble pie? I hope there aren't too many because if there are my diet is in serious trouble, as I have just been forced to eat a very large amount of pie. For years I have been a fierce critic of the Irish Basketball Association and their policy of selecting the best overseas players to play for Ireland at the expense of the local players plying their trade in the ESB Super League. I was wrong.'[xlix]

Ireland hadn't qualified through to the final round of the European Championships. Still, they had won over some of their fiercest critics. They had also competed incredibly well against some of

Europe's elite teams, all while missing key players for different games. Ireland were now far beyond Promotions Cup level and had seemingly graduated to another level of European basketball. With two former NBA players in situ, the team's reputation had increased so much that the door looked like it would finally be open for Pat Burke to play at senior level. Of course, nothing is ever simple, and FIBA were about to move the goalposts again with a change in the competition format.

Chapter 27: The B Division

Fresh off a very positive semi-final round, the national team's future looked as bright as ever heading into 2004. The performances against established European powerhouses Germany and Croatia had given the team credibility, and the win over Cyprus in Cork had done wonders to change the public perception. People understood now that this was a professional team, and the calibre of players playing for Ireland was much higher than the available domestic amateur players. For the IBA, it was hoped that the progression would open more possibilities, particularly financially, as new CEO Debbie Massey outlined in her initial opportunities analysis back in 2001, when she took the job: 'Get behind the national teams. We need the success and consequent and related TV financial and profile bonuses.'

Ahead of the new campaign, FIBA had changed their European Competitions' structure to ensure that the top countries were playing against each other more regularly. Europe was now split into an A and a B division, with promotion and relegation between the two. This meant that Ireland had to play in the B division for both 2004 and 2005. There was a major reward on the line though, with the possibility of reaching

Europe's top tier of just sixteen teams if they could earn promotion. Achieving promotion would mean regular games against Europe's elite which, it was hoped, would open up huge opportunities for the sport both in terms of profile but also financially.

The major positive news ahead of the campaign was that Real Madrid's Pat Burke was finally going to make his senior debut for Ireland after several near misses. Burke had played alongside several fellow internationals at club level, with Jim Moran making a particularly big impact on him. 'Jim was the perfect situation for me. I played with Marty and then playing with Jim it kind of put some pieces together of who was on the Irish national team at the time . . . Just talking to him and kind of feeling out what the Irish national team is like . . . it was a lot of shared memories of good stuff . . . so I started to get into that, I missed that opportunity, I missed the fact that you were part of something bigger.' For Ireland, the signing was as big a coup as possible, and team manager Sean O'Reilly showed his delight to Aidan O'Hara in the *Independent*: 'To put it simply, Pat is our Roy Keane. He's recognised throughout Europe for his quality, he brings NBA experience from his time with Orlando Magic and has been a vital player for Real Madrid.'[1]

With Burke's arrival, Ireland suddenly had a squad with three players 6'10 and above, all with NBA experience. Thinking back to 1984 when Enda Byrt was told that Ireland needed to find the 'high player', they now certainly had the size they needed to compete, and their frontline was as imposing as any team in Europe. The fact that two of the three big men had their first connections to Irish basketball through Enda so many years earlier again showed the foresight and vision that Enda had.

Leading up to the qualifiers, Ireland had to shed some rust after a nineteen-month layoff from competitive play. Preparations started with a four-team tournament in Ireland that featured England, Denmark and Turkey. The field alone showed the stature that Ireland now held, with countries like Turkey willing to come to Ireland to play. Ireland lost to Denmark but went on to beat England and then claim one of its most impressive scalps ever by beating Turkey 66–61 in Dublin. The win was made even more impressive by the absence of Pat Burke, Jim Moran and Dan Callahan. The trio were not released from their clubs until just before the first competitive game more than a week later. In a big sign of Ireland's changing financial times, the team finished playing the home tournament and then went abroad for a training camp in Cyprus before flying to the first game in Malta. The level of preparation would have been unimaginable just a decade earlier when the senior team's budget for the Promotions Cup was initially only £3,000.

For Ireland, the start of life in Division B came with many changes in the squad. Adrian Fulton, Damien Sealy and Gareth Maguire had all retired from international basketball. It's hard to sum up what these men did for Ireland. Not only had they been on the entire journey since the junior men's teams of the 1980s, but they had also helped integrate multiple groups of Irish Americans. Their absence signalled a key turning point in Irish basketball history as the national team moved to a fully professional team. Part of the magic of what Ireland had tried to achieve in the past was the mix of high-level pros and Irish amateurs who were willing to give everything for the green jersey. That was now gone.

Without Sealy, Fulton and Maguire involved, the domestically developed talent in the Senior Men's squad was suddenly down to just two, the Davidson duo of Michael Bree and Conor Grace. Both had limited interactions with the senior team already but were now poised for bigger roles. For the established Irish Americans like Dan Callahan, finding a way to fill the void left by the domestic players was impossible: 'We definitely let the new guys on the team know how important it was. How much it meant to Gareth and Fulty, and even though he was gone, Enda. Because Enda was the one that started it all. You're representing a country. We always tried to stress you're not playing for Northeastern University or Boston University; you are playing for an entire country that's on your shirt, and it's important. I think you learn pretty quickly once you are around some of the guys.'

There were changes again on the Irish-American conveyor belt, as Ireland was about to start a new era. Glenn Sekunda, who led Ireland in scoring in the semi-final campaign, was no longer available and Ireland were also without two influential wing players, Tim Kennedy and Mike Mitchell. It wasn't all doom and gloom though, as several new and returning faces were added over the upcoming two years of qualification. Jon Larrañaga (Jay's younger brother) returned in 2005. Jon played for their dad Jim at George Mason and had gone on to play for Benneton Treviso in the Italian topflight. His impact in Europe would not be on the same level as Jay's, but he was another outside shooting threat that would replace some of Tim Kennedy's production. In 2004, Chris Bracey was the only domestically based player on the team. The American-born player played at West Texas A&M and later made a name for himself in the Irish league with the Tralee Tigers. After his stint in Ireland, Bracey went on to play in Switzerland and then to Greece.

Justen Naughton was another man with Super League experience, who also played in Switzerland, Japan, Spain and Austria. He was a mobile big-man that provided extra size for Ireland if needed, although with the star-studded frontline there already, he wasn't expected to make a big impact initially. The final addition was Billy Collins, who played three years at Boston University. The 6'7 forward averaged 10.3 points for his career there, while providing some floor spacing hitting over 40 per cent of his threes in his senior year.

For the first game in Malta, Ireland was led offensively by Chris Bracey as they completely outclassed a Maltese team that were the minnows of Division B basketball. The game saw Pat Burke make his competitive debut, although not much was asked of him or Ireland's other big stars like Jay Larrañaga or Marty Conlon in the easy win.

In what should have been a moment of pure joy for Ireland as Burke made his debut, the Maltese game instead provided a footnote in history signalling warning signs about the overall direction that the programme was going. The increased level of preparation and the requirements for players to be available for longer periods meant that having domestic amateur players on the team was now proving impossible. As Ireland played against Malta, the team was without squad members Michael Bree (injured) and Conor Grace (still in Davidson). For the first time in the programme's history, Ireland played games with no Irish-developed player on the team. Pat Burke was the only Irish-born player for the game, and he had left Ireland before he started primary school.

The movement to a more professional team was something people had seen gradually developing. The worry for most was not about the character or quality of the guys coming into the team but rather the increasing disconnect between the basketball community and the team. Even some of the players involved with the team in the past were uncomfortable with where the team was moving. Mark Keenan was one of the most capped players in Irish history. Having been through the Junior and Senior Men's programmes with Irish Americans, Mark wondered whether the connection was being lost. 'I retired in '97 and I think we maybe had four [Irish Americans then] and to me, that was the limit. It should never have gone beyond that number. When it went to ten, or ten out of twelve, I didn't quite agree with that way of going . . . , back when we had the four guys, and these guys had all played underage as well, like Tom Casey and Frank Powell, they had been around so people could probably identify with them a little bit more.'

The active players were also aware that the issue was there in the background, with Pat Burke knowing the connection couldn't be the same with the Irish public without homegrown players. How many Americans should or shouldn't play was not for the players to worry about though. Their focus was on having the best team possible and helping Ireland to progress.

In terms of domestic players, the other concern was that there wasn't a lot of young talent progressing to play professionally at any level. As a result, Irish players were unlikely to be able to balance work commitments at home while also playing internationally. The first Junior Men's team to qualify through to the semi-final round had players like Michael Bree, Paddy Kelly and Gary Dredge amongst its stars. Bree went on to play professionally, but injuries limited Dredge's career and Paddy Kelly focused on playing domestically despite having the talent to play abroad. The World University Games team of 1999 was similar in that Bree was the only player to have a strong professional career. In the 1990s, players like Alan Conlan and John Burke were able to go and play in Europe, and worryingly in 2004, this was happening less for homegrown players.

This all fed into the big question in the background – whether Ireland was losing sight of the original goal of short-term help from American-born players while Irish talent developed. That was an issue for the IBA to decide upon.

The team had more immediate concerns as a tough Swiss test lay ahead in Dublin. Fortunately, domestic talent was back on show as Michael Bree returned to the line-up and played twenty minutes. Jay Larrañaga led the way with five threes and 18 points, and Dan Callahan added a double-double of 16 points and 10 rebounds as Ireland won 79–68, helping the team build momentum ahead of a tough road game away to Slovakia.

Ireland struggled in this next tough test as Michael Bree again sat out, making Ireland's biggest weakness shine through. The team finally had a powerful front line, but they didn't have options at the guard spot. The team lacked a true point guard without Bree, and it cost them as they racked up 17 turnovers as a team (compared to 11 for Slovakia). Pat Burke had his first double-double with 14 and 12, and Dan Callahan chipped in another double-double. Still, it wasn't enough for Ireland as they lost out narrowly, 70–67, ending 2004 on a disappointing note. With a 2–1 record, Ireland still had a strong chance to get promoted heading into 2005. The team knew they would welcome Slovakia to Dublin in the final group game with a chance at revenge. All they had to do was win their other games to give themselves that opportunity.

The first game of 2005 saw a new addition in Australian-born Danny Mills, who took one of the more unusual routes to play for Ireland as he was born and raised in Australia. He played at the famed

Australia Institute of Sport before heading to America to play for Rivers Community College and then Oregon Tech in the NAIA. It was while Danny was in college that he ended up representing Ireland briefly and he retired soon after graduating. After some brief assistant coaching stints in Europe, he would eventually become a scout in the NBA for the Philadelphia 76ers. During his limited time playing for Ireland, it meant so much to the Mills family that Danny's dad flew from Australia to see his son in the green jersey.

Lorcan Precious, who was playing in the Irish league for UCD Marian, was drafted in as a back-up to Bree to ensure there was more point-guard balance for the second round of games. Notably, Conor Grace also came into the squad having graduated from Davidson just a few months earlier. The second round schedule was the same as the first, and Ireland handled Malta easily in Dublin, 98–49, to get the games started.

In the second game, Ireland travelled to Switzerland to face an improved Swiss team with a young star, Thabo Sefolosha. At this stage of his career, Sefolosha was still playing in Italy, but at the end of the following season, he would be drafted 13th overall by the Philadelphia

76ers. He showed exactly why scouts were excited about him in Switzerland on his way to 20 points and 10 rebounds, as the Swiss won 76–57. It was one of the poorest nights for Ireland in many years. Pat Burke was targeted by the Swiss defense with double and triple teams all night as he managed just 3 points in thirty-two minutes before fouling out. The team trailed by 16 at the half, 23 after three quarters and eventually lost by 19 in what was a forgettable night.

The loss left Ireland with a mammoth task as they came back to Dublin for the final game. Switzerland beat Slovakia by 17 and lost to them by 6. This meant that Ireland had to beat the Slovak's by 13 points or more to finish top of the group and earn a playoff spot. On the plus side for the Irish, for the first and only time, Ireland would have all three of their NBA players together for one game as Cal Bowdler rejoined the squad. With the possibility of a promotion playoff on the line, there was increased media coverage. The qualifier was shown live on television, the first time the national team had been on Irish TV since the 1994 Promotions Cup Final. For Pat Burke, the increased attention was something that reaffirmed his decision to play for Ireland: 'The build-up to the game was very exciting. There was a number of interviews. A number of people were coming up to us telling us that the game was going to be televised, which was unheard of. We were very excited. We're all going to die on this floor. We're going to go as hard as we could.'

Despite a huge early dunk by Burke, Ireland's task became even more ominous after a slow first quarter saw them trail by 5. A big second quarter gave the Irish a four-point lead at half-time, but even with the lead, things had to improve dramatically if they were to get to the important +13 number.

Fortunately, the third quarter was possibly the best quarter in Irish history, as they won it 28-10 to take control of the tie. Leading by 22, Ireland were now on course for a playoff, barring a disaster in the fourth quarter. Of course, the team wouldn't have been a true Irish team if there wasn't some drama, and the fourth quarter provided plenty of that. Ireland's offence came to a halt as Slovakia battled back to just 14 down with a minute to go. Both teams would miss open jumpers before Ireland turned the ball over with twenty-five seconds to go; their playoff hopes hanging in the balance. Fortunately, Slovakia missed twice on the last possession, and Ireland pulled out a huge win.

A visible outpouring of emotion post-game answered any questions of what playing and winning with Ireland meant to the team. Players hugged each other and celebrated with the Irish crowd in the National Basketball Arena in the brightest moment Ireland had experienced since 1994. This win was against even higher standard opposition, and it opened up a playoff against familiar foes Denmark, with a spot in Europe's A division on the line. Although there were questions about the long-term strategy, for this night at least, everyone was on the same page. The Irish nation was starting to get excited about the possibility of a seat at Europe's top table.

Chapter 28: The Playoff

For Ireland, this was the moment that everything had been building to. The dream had always been to have a competitive international team that could compete at a high level and get people interested in the sport. The semi-final stages in 2002 showed that when Ireland faced off against top teams like Germany and Croatia, they could compete. Now they wanted more.

A win over the two legs against the Danes would catapult Ireland into the top sixteen teams in Europe. With that would come regular visits from top-flight teams and the chance to build Ireland's basketball reputation both at home and abroad. The playoff also offered a unique opportunity to capitalise on the increased attention the team were getting. The national broadcaster was now showing games, and there was an interest in the team beyond the traditional basketball community. Although Ireland had captured the country's interest, they knew it was still precarious, and success against Denmark could solidify it.

Pat Burke's presence as an NBA player definitely helped drive that general interest in the team. With their three NBA players finally together, Ireland had momentum going into the playoff and were likely favourites heading into the tie. But things are never straightforward for Ireland.

Pat Burke had just signed with the Phoenix Suns and was about to start his second stint in the NBA. With his second (and likely last) opportunity in the American league, Burke was determined to do everything in his power to make the most of it. The challenge was that the playoff was two additional weeks' commitment in Ireland beyond what was originally planned. After discussing it with the team, the big man decided to return to the States, meaning he would miss the critical playoff series. It was a tough decision for Pat and an understandable one due to the opportunity available to him. At the same time, it was deflating for Ireland as they headed into their biggest potential break yet.

Despite the loss of Burke, Ireland had experience on their side. The core group of Callahan, Moran, Conlon, and Larrañaga had been through many big games for Ireland. There was still confidence that the team could beat a young Danish squad; they were even possibly favourites.

The first game was in the National Basketball Arena on the 17th September 2005. Ireland performed incredibly well with six players scoring double figures. Marty Conlon led the way with 14, but it was Michael Bree's performance that helped lay the foundation for the team. The Sligo native had 12 points, four assists and three steals as Ireland delighted the home crowd. Leading by 14 at the half, Ireland extended their lead to 23 points and looked destined for the top-flight. A poor fourth quarter from the home side gave the Danes some hope as they reduced the deficit by seven. Despite the late drop off, Ireland still had a sizeable fourteen-point lead by the end of the game.

One week later the two teams faced off for the second time in Aarhus. Denmark got off to the perfect start as they completely eradicated Ireland's lead inside five minutes and led 22–15 after ten. Ireland couldn't get going offensively as they managed just nine points in the second quarter as they lost it 17–9. After only twenty minutes, the aggregate score was suddenly against Ireland as they trailed by one overall going into the second half. The Danes 7'3 big man Chris Christofferson was having much more success in the second game, scoring 18 points. He also caused Ireland major foul trouble and fouled

Cal Bowdler out, with Cal only managing one shot in the game. At this point in his career, Cal was a shadow of the player who arrived in to score 26 in his debut against Germany just three years earlier. Constant injuries and personal issues away from the court had worn down the big man, and he was ready to retire from basketball. It was a testament to Cal's character that he had stayed to compete for Ireland despite already knowing his career was likely about to end.

In the second half, both teams turned the ball over, and the foul count was high as the players were now familiar with each other. Despite having their backs against the wall and missing their best player, Ireland showed incredible character to win the final quarter 22–20. The dogged performance earned them a trip to overtime as the scores were tied on aggregate. The gumption shown to battle back in tough conditions aside, Ireland lost overtime 12–10, and their promotion dreams were shattered in an instant.

What had been built up for so many years was suddenly over in the most dramatic of circumstances.What made the nightmare worse was the matter in which it happened. Denmark's Cristian Drejer had the performance of a lifetime in what would just be enough for Denmark to progress.

Drejer is a name many NCAA fans would know, as he played for the Florida Gators up to 2004. In the 2003–04 season, he was a key contributor to Billy Donovan's Gators, averaging 10 points a game before creating a major media storm in the US when he suddenly left the team mid-season in February to play professionally in Europe. Barcelona offered the Dane a two-year deal, and he accepted it, transferring to the Spanish giants before the NCAA season had finished. The 6'8 do-it-all forward went on to be the first Dane ever drafted in the NBA, picked upby the New Jersey Nets in 2004 in the second round. Although, he would never play in the NBA; in fact, his career ended up being very short in total. He played for Barcelona for two years without making a major impact and then spent three more seasons in Italy. In his final season with Bologna, the twenty-five-year-old only played six games before injuries that had started during his time in Florida ended his career prematurely.

In 2005 Drejer was still healthy and causing problems for Ireland. In the first leg in Dublin, he had been held to just seven points.

The performance bothered him as he felt the Danes weren't prepared to compete with Ireland. 'I remember the frustrations from the first game. We did not play well. I simply felt like nobody wanted to be there. The Irish team was good. But it was not about talent or strategy, but merely will, strength and team. I remember how they really outplayed and outhustled us in the first game.' The Danish game was completely different though, as Drejer managed to score an international career-high 39 points in the famous win. He added 8 rebounds, 3 steals and 3 assists in possibly the greatest display the B division has ever seen. 'The second game was different. It is so weird how you prepare yourselves for something more when you know you have to win by 15 points to qualify. And that we did. We came in with a completely different mentality and believed we could win. I think it was one of my best nights after I had had my injury.'

Ireland did feel hard done by, as Drejer shot 19 free throws and Denmark shot 30 free throws, ten more than the Irish. The refereeing on the night was a major issue for the Irish who felt that the referees were targeting them from the start. Michael Bree felt that something wasn't right from the first quarter:'I've been part of some match-fixing games, where we found out later that the referees were messing with the games we were playing. That happened in Sweden in 2003–04, there was a gambling scandal . . . So, I've been part of some games that were not above board with everything. All I remember in the first four minutes the game was tied; we were 14 points up coming into the game. Within four minutes the game was tied, they were at the free-throw line and getting layups. Granted they were going to come out with energy, but there was something fishy, there was something going on. After that, they let us play, but you never felt we had a legitimate chance to pull it through. I remember Jay Larrañaga at the end had a chance to score, and he got clotheslined and there was no call. He had a legitimate chance to win the game. Definitely, it was free throws . . .. We just didn't get the call, unfortunately. It was the one game in my life I felt it wasn't honest. It is what it is. It's how I felt, and today it's still how I feel.'

For Dan Callahan, who had been the bridge between so many Irish teams and had been there for so many heart-breaking moments in the past, this one topped the bill in terms of disappointment. 'That was the worst Irish loss for me ever. I remember I was so upset, I got the ball and kicked it to Jay, and he went down the middle of the lane, and I think he got fouled so badly and they didn't call it. I flipped out, and I actually think Fitzy yelled at me after the game for being too emotional. That never happened to me, I was always so in control, but I was so sad we had come so far and were maybe two free throws from getting to the next level . . . Jay almost got decapitated and they didn't call it, I feel a little robbed on that game and I'll never get over that.'

Jay Larrañaga himself remembers the play, but was also disappointed in how the team handled the situation at the time. 'I've regret for that game, I know I got a technical and a bunch of the guys got technicals. We should have been better than that. That was a game I felt we should have won. We shouldn't have allowed whatever was going on with the officiating to impact us. I still feel like we were the better team.'

Jim Moran had the feeling that Ireland had to be perfect to overcome the situation.'The officiating. It felt like everyone was doing everything they could, and we had no shot. We had to be perfect. You couldn't make any mistakes because any mistake would hurt you even more because you felt like you weren't getting a fair shake. In your

348

head you are like, man, is this really happening? And you keep it to yourself. And then you see everyone else's emotions pouring out, and you see Marty and Jay, and they are feeling what I'm feeling. So, this *is* happening, and I'm not crazy. It was just one of those things where you feel helpless and think, *come on*, give us a fair shake.' Moran was also reminded of Gordon Gircek years earlier for Croatia, being the star that Ireland couldn't match. Jim now coaches in the NBA and is familiar with stars parading to the free-throw line in the league. He jokes that the memory of Drejer heading to the line is something that still haunts him. 'It made you feel like they have a guy. Drejer is their guy, and we don't have that guy. I still feel some of those emotions as a coach on the NBA level. You're playing Houston, and James Harden is on the free-throw line every time he crosses over the halfway line, and I think I get PTSD and flashbacks to that Denmark game.'

For his part, Christian Drejer remembers the calls; 'I do recall a few calls by the ref that were in our favour towards the end of the game. I do not remember whether it was bad or wrong calls. But yes, at the end of a close game, the refs calls are important, and of course part of the result.'

Whether or not it was a foul on Larrañaga was something that Danish TV commentator Thomas Bilde, working the match, was unsure of. At the time the Danes felt the Irish team let their emotion take control of them and the lack of discipline closed the door on their promotion opportunity. 'I think it was a foul that could have been called, it could have gone either way; I'm not saying they were complaining without reason. I remember we were saying that Ireland just shot themselves in the foot, they lost their composure. They dropped the ball, I know it was their big chance, and the opportunity was there, but the way they took themselves out of the game with all of those technical fouls gave them no chance of coming back in it . . . I understand it, you're up 14, and you almost lost it, and then something like that goes against you, and they just complained, and one leads to another.'

The disappointment led to Ireland getting fined after the game, as Marty Conlon remonstrated too aggressively with the officials. When asked to describe his memories of the game, all he simply said was he was '€5,000 worth of mad!' In the changing room after the game, Conlon received a call from Pat Burke in Phoenix to find out what had

350

happened, and a crushed Burke found out that the dream had ended. It was something that, with the advantage of time, Burke looks back on with huge regret; 'When I look back now, I would not have gone to the Suns early. I was just this guy going in there trying to be a part of this special team, shit if I didn't show up early it wasn't going to change what happened with the Suns. So looking back I wish I had someone to lean on to ask that question, and they could be like, do you realise what you have right now in Irish basketball that may never occur again? The Suns have Amare and Shawn Marion and Steve and outside of you going in there and doing a couple of things, you aren't going to create a huge variable of change. So, I wish that I could go back and have played that Denmark stretch.'

Ireland had plenty of what-if moments over the years, and the Denmark playoff is undoubtedly the biggest of them all.

What if Pat Burke had been available?

What if the lead in Dublin had stayed out over 20 points?

What if the referees had given Larrañaga the two free throws?

All things, unfortunately for Irish basketball, that will never be known. In the past, each heart-breaking moment came with the hope that it was a stepping stone towards something bigger for Ireland. This felt different though. Ireland had got to where they wanted to be. A winnable game with the nation's eyes on them on live television. This was the moment to capitalise and make the entire vision a reality and allow Ireland to earn their place at Europe's top table.

Rather than looking forward to a new exciting adventure in the A division, Ireland now had to dust themselves off and try again over two more years to earn promotion.

With an ageing team, there was an ominous feeling that this could be a fatal blow to the national team vision, and it was something the players felt immediately.

'That loss was really deflating,' Jim Moran recounts. 'It felt like that was everything we were heading for. The importance of that game; after that I was just tired of arguing with my club team the whole time to get over there. I felt like if we had won that game, they would have taken our efforts more seriously. It felt like our wave was coming to an end. A lot of guys knew we were hitting the reset button and starting this over again.'

Dan Callahan feels similarly.'It was never the same. I think that was the conclusion. We were so close, and I don't want to sound like a cry-baby because I'm not that guy, but I feel we got robbed. Believe me, Jay Larrañaga would not have missed those free throws, put your life on it. We could have gone to the next level, and to have played all those years and to get that close and to feel that you got robbed was disappointing. That was probably the last true game of all of us.'

As Ireland headed into 2006, for the first time in many years there were more questions than answers and more doubt than optimism.

Had this been the final chance for Ireland?

Chapter 29: The Changing of the Guard

As the dust settled on the Denmark result, Ireland looked to have one more go at reaching the A division.

Pat Burke signed back up to return for 2006, and the veteran trio of Marty Conlon, Jay Larrañaga and Dan Callahan all decided to give it one last shot. At this stage, age wasn't on the group's side, particularly with Conlon and Callahan in their late thirties. Sadly, Jim Moran wasn't part of the squad this time as he focused on his professional career in Gran Canaria. Reinforcements were needed, and Ireland had to dip back into the Irish American pool to see what talent could be found. The main find heading into 2006 was Donnie McGrath. He had just finished an impressive career at Providence and was at the beginning of a pro career that eventually saw him play EuroLeague for top teams including Zalgiris from Lithuania. McGrath had been on Ireland's radar for several years as he played at Marty Conlon's alma mater. Gerry Fitzpatrick had tried signing him a year earlier, but his NCAA commitments meant it wasn't possible. It was hoped that he could be the first elite Irish American point guard since Billy Donlon left, three years earlier.

Two more Americans also joined: Mike Williams and Baker Dunleavy. Williams was a standout big man at Bryant University and helped the school reach the Division II NCAA Final in his senior year. With 987 career rebounds and the single-season record for blocks, Williams would be inducted into the Bryant Hall of Fame. He would also play professionally, initially in Switzerland and Italy, and later in the NBA D-League for the Maine Red Claws and Springfield Armor. As Williams started his Irish career in 2006, he had just finished his season in Switzerland where he averaged 11 rebounds a game.

The more eye-catching name was Baker Dunleavy. Baker was part of a basketball dynasty in America that included his father Mike Dunleavy Sr and his brother Mike Dunleavy Jr. Baker's dad played in the NBA for four different teams and then later became a head coach in the league. He was named the NBA's Coach of the Year in 1999, and he also led the LA Lakers with Magic Johnson to the NBA Finals in 1991. Mike Jr. followed in his dad's footsteps with an outstanding playing career that surpassed his father's. The 6'9 forward was a McDonald's All American in high school before committing to Duke University. During his Duke career, he became a second team All

American and won the 2001 National Championship. In 2002, the Golden State Warriors used the 3rd overall pick in the NBA draft on him. His NBA career lasted fifteen seasons up until 2017, and he played 986 games. Not just a journeyman, Mike averaged 11 points a game for his career including 19.1 a game for Indiana in the 2007–08 season. Ireland had aspirations of finding a way to get Mike Jr. to play for Ireland, but they were having little success. The prospect of getting someone of Mike's calibre was something not everyone was convinced of either. Dan Callahan was worried that players coming in might not fully appreciate what it meant to represent Ireland. 'I was scared if we got a Mike Dunleavy, he's a big NBA player making 10 million dollars, and we are just a bunch of guys bouncing around Europe doing what we could do. You don't know if they'd appreciate the history of Ireland or if they'd get it. I didn't want people just to play to get their passport to play in Europe. I was hoping they'd understand the history of Irish basketball and what we were trying to accomplish.'

In 2006, the opportunity arose to get Mike's younger brother Baker, who had just finished a career playing at Villanova. In his college career, Baker played sparingly, averaging less than a point a game in his senior season. In total, he appeared just twenty-eight times for the Wildcats. Despite the lack of college production, he arrived into the Irish squad in 2006 before heading to play in the Netherlands for part of a season. His pro career wouldn't last long though and he initially went into the banking sector before later becoming an assistant coach at Villanova under Jay Wright. Following in his father's footsteps on the sideline, Baker became a very good coach, and by 2017 he took over as head coach at Quinnipiac.

Overall the increased number of new faces was a concern for stalwarts like Callahan. 'In the 2000s I definitely missed the Fulty's and the Gareth's of the world. They were just the best guys, and it was fun having a mix. I definitely missed the regular Irish guys who played for us, but we tried to do our best. Some guys got their passports and came, but they weren't really from Irish American families. I grew up where all my relatives had a brogue and [was surrounded by] Irish music and festivals, so I was really aware of where I came from and to be proud. Maybe some of the other guys didn't know this, but I knew it, and I always appreciated it.'

The other major change heading into the qualifiers was at the head coaches' position, as Gerry Fitzpatrick stepped down after the Denmark playoff. Fitzpatrick had given incredible service to Ireland across the men's and women's national teams since the early 1990s and had to step back because of work commitments. His role in the Waterford Institute of Technology meant that the longer preparation periods that Ireland were now embarking on made it almost impossible for an amateur coach to balance a job and the national team role. It was another progression in the team's professionalism that now, not only could domestic players not meet the burden, but coaches couldn't either.

The Association replaced Gerry with their Australian technical director Greg Gurr, making Gurr just the fourth international coach Ireland ever had after Dan Doyle, Rich Connover and Bill Dooley. Gurr was appointed by Debbie Massey as the technical director in 2003 and worked in the Association ever since. Before coming to Ireland, Gurr had already developed an excellent CV having coached the Singapore and Thailand national teams as well as the Western Australia team. While Ireland went through the last campaign, Gurr worked in the background to improve the structures and now was stepping up to continue the work as the head coach.

The campaign kicked off away to familiar opposition, Switzerland, on 3 September 2006. Any hopes for a bounce-back campaign after 2005 were dealt a serious blow immediately when Ireland lost on the road to the Swiss in that first game. With Thabo Sefolosha now in the NBA, the Swiss were without a key player for the first leg, but Ireland couldn't punish them. Pat Burke led the way with 14 points, but no other player got into double digits as Ireland lost 59–57. Ireland shot just 20 per cent from the three-point line which doomed them in a close game. A glaringly obvious issue was that Ireland hadn't been able to find talent of the same calibre as they had lost. Jim Moran was a seasoned European veteran, and his minutes were replaced by Baker Dunleavy who had yet to start his professional career. Dunleavy missed all eight of his shots and had four fouls and three turnovers in a tough debut.

With the opening loss, the pressure was now on for Ireland as they came home to Dublin to face Romania. Another failure would potentially be catastrophic to the campaign. Any hopes that Ireland's backs being up against the wall and having home-court advantage were enough to get us by Romania were dashed early in this game. Romania were the more aggressive team, getting to the basket and the free-throw line regularly. Ireland trailed 24–12 after the first quarter and by half-time were down by 20. The game was killed off by the end of the third quarter, and although Ireland rallied late, they still lost by 19 points. The loss spelled the end for Ireland, as they now had to win the rest of their games (including a trip to Romania) and hope that the Romanians would drop another game.

The group had started as badly as possible. With one game left in 2006, Ireland welcomed their most familiar foe, Cyprus, to Dublin for another must-win game. Down 10 after the first quarter, Jay Larrañaga and Pat Burke dragged Ireland out of the hole and led them to a six-point win, 76–70. It was a positive result for Ireland, but many knew the writing was on the wall for the campaign and major changes were on the way.

All was not right in the camp. Pat Burke finished the Cyprus game with 20 points and 12 rebounds, but it was his last game in an Irish jersey. Burke's exit was joined by three of Ireland's most influential and senior players. Dan Callahan, who first played for Ireland in 1993 in the World University games and from 1995 onwards was Ireland's most dependable star, finished the era as the country's top rebounder. Marty Conlon was thirty-seven years old, and he also took a step back from the team after giving so much at the end of his career for Ireland. His arrival had started a new era for the team and given the programme so much respect from other professionals. He had given everything his body could, but the tank was unfortunately empty. Jay Larrañaga wouldn't return in 2007, although his time with Ireland wasn't over just yet as he returned in 2008.

The exodus partially came because there was a clear need for a new wave of talent, as qualification looked to be beyond Ireland already after the first round of games. The bigger issue was that the relationship between the new coach and experienced players could be generously described as strained.

For Pat Burke the feeling wasn't the same as when Gerry Fitzpatrick had been in charge, something was missing: 'There was a dramatic change in the team. Nobody wants to go out with a loss, but when Greg Gurr came in, we were all asking is this guy even a basketball coach? And that weighs on you. We're thinking we've gone further than we've ever gone, now we're coming back let's rally this, and I just remember it didn't feel like playing for Ireland anymore.'

For Marty Conlon, the introduction of the coach felt like an outsider coming in and the players weren't sure about him. 'It was kind of nutty. We didn't know who he was, I guess he had worked for Ireland Basketball prior, but I didn't know who he was.' Conlon tried to help bridge the gap, but things weren't right.

Callahan could see things moving backwards again for Ireland after so much progression. 'It started falling back off after '05, it came back down. I think they started losing some funding and I think that goes hand in hand because you are not going to get these big-time players if it's a mickey mouse show over there.'

Jay Larrañaga struggled with the group as he went from team captain to being out of favour with the new coach. For his part, Larrañaga could understand the issue of a new coach coming in and trying to establish themselves with a group of veteran players: 'I thought Greg was a good coach, and he wanted to establish his programme and culture. That's tough, especially when you're dealing with a group of older guys, especially when they've had some level of success and had a level of comfort with the way Bill Dooley or Gerry Fitzpatrick did things. I don't envy anyone who has to coach a group of thirty-year-olds, they are much less coachable than a group of twenty-year olds.'

These players had been used to Enda Byrt, Bill Dooley and Gerry Fitzpatrick who all epitomised a player-first attitude, and the new regime didn't quite fit with the group. Mark Keenan, who was now working in an assistant coach role, could see the friction and would often be the middle man during some tense conversations. 'Greg was maybe a bit too abrupt at times and didn't realise how professional these guys were. There were a few times I was stepping in the middle to calm things down.'

Ireland was heading into an uncertain transition period; they were no longer knocking at the door for qualification for the A division. Equally, they weren't yet back at the Promotions Cup level either. With Burke and Callahan stepping away, the final connection to the Enda Byrt era, the 1993 World University Games squad was now gone completely from the Irish team. The big Irish-American question facing into the future now was whether Ireland could recruit enough quality

replacements to fill the void.

Chapter 30: The Rebuild

As the Irish team assembled for the second half of the 2007 qualifying campaign, it was clear that it wasn't the same team that had been there, not only in 2006, but essentially since the turn of the decade. The big NBA names of Marty Conlon and Pat Burke were gone, and so too were the team's heart and soul for many years, Jay Larrañaga and Dan Callahan. Ireland was almost certainly out of contention after a disastrous 2006, so the timing for a rebuild was right.

Greg Gurr's time as the head coach has a lot of negativity associated with it. Still, it was under his stewardship that several young Irish players made their debut. Part of it was out of necessity, as the Davidson duo of Conor Grace and Michael Bree were now the most experienced players available to him. Despite that, a new wave of talent was coming into the team to support them.

One of the main criticisms of the late 1990s and early 2000s was the disconnect between the Senior and Junior Men's teams. That was about to change, as for the first time since the late 1980s, a group of talented Irish players were breaking into the squad together. Timing had so often been an enemy of Ireland's national team, yet this rebuild's timing couldn't have been better. The country's finances were starting to fall off, and the money required to support high-level Irish Americans wasn't there anymore. Additionally, the calibre of Irish Americans had plummeted too. Without Enda Byrt's tireless pursuit in America or Bill Dooley's extensive connections, Ireland was suddenly struggling to find suitable players. The time was right for new players to get an opportunity and fortunately it coincided with the development of one of Ireland's best ever junior teams.

Within Irish basketball, the name Joey Boylan is synonymous with the game. His impact has been felt at senior Irish level as an assistant coach, at national level with St Vincent's and perhaps most at underage level with the Junior Men. Back in 2001, as Ireland was making strides at senior level, Joey was developing his best junior team. The squad of players born in 1984 reached the semi-final round of the Junior Men's tournament, matching the achievement that Michael Bree's age group had been the only ones to achieve previously.

The team's talent was apparent from the beginning with two future stars leading the way, Colin O'Reilly and Paul Cummins. The two ended up having very different careers and journeys, although both made a significant impact wherever they went.

Colin O'Reilly was part of a basketball dynasty in Cork, with his brother Niall part of the first successful Junior Men's team alongside Bree, and his younger twin sisters Sinead and Orla both representing Ireland and playing college basketball in the States. Colin was a rangy 6'6 forward who developed a reputation for his basketball IQ and scoring ability. Colin went to America to Teikyo Post where Irish players like Mick Richardson, Peder Madsen and Gray Dredge had gone before him. Similarly to Ken Lacey years before him, O'Reilly saw America as a stepping-stone to his pro career rather than an end destination in itself. As a result, he only lasted two years in college before returning to Europe to play. He went on to have an impressive professional career in Ireland, Germany and England. During his time in Ireland, he was dominant both as a player and then again as a player-coach. In fact, in his second year as player-coach, his Blue Demons team had a perfect season, going unbeaten in all competitions. Colin's reward for it was to become Ireland's second-ever player-coach behind Jay Larrañaga.

Paul Cummins didn't come from a big basketball family, nor did he come from a big basketball stronghold like Cork or Dublin. Raised in Kildare, just north of Dublin, he developed into a very talented young player who got a chance to go to America for school. On the recommendation of Bill Dooley, he initially went to high school and then the following year attended Kent Prep. One of Paul's teammates at Kent Prep was Dorrell Wright who went straight to the NBA after that season. There were also five more NCAA Division I scholarship recipients on the team, including Paul. Cummins followed in the footsteps of John Brennan and committed to Lafayette. Playing under Fran O'Hanlon, he developed into an elite perimeter threat in the Patriot League. Over his four-year career, he scored an impressive 649 points, and his career highlights included 14 points against NCAA Champions Louisville. After graduating, Paul continued to play while furthering his education. He played well in both Scotland and Ireland although he never really pursued the professional life in the same was as others around him would. Chronic knee injuries limited him considerably, and although he later picked up trophies in Ireland, he did so as a less mobile version of the young player he was in college.

The duo of O'Reilly and Cummins developed together, as they led Ireland in their Junior Men's qualification group in Portugal. In the team's first game they came up against the future 7th pick in the 2004 NBA draft Luol Deng. Deng played for Duke before becoming a two-time NBA all-star for the Chicago Bulls. In England's first game Deng scored 50 against Turkey, so Ireland considered it a good job limiting the star to just 42 points on 15/18 shooting, as he added 18 rebounds and five assists in a 97–76 win. In wasn't all one-way traffic though as Colin O'Reilly gave plenty back, ending with a double-double of 32 points and 13 rebounds, while Cummins added 16. After losing to England, Ireland lost heavily to Turkey, meaning they had to win their final two games to progress to the semi-final round. In the first game against the Netherlands, O'Reilly scored 24 as Ireland won 77–75, setting up a crunch game with the hosts Portugal, a place in the semi-final round on the line. Portugal had beaten the Netherlands and only narrowly lost to England so were heavy favourites coming into the game, especially at home. Cummins scored 20 before fouling out, and Colin managed an unbelievable 31 points and 12 rebounds, as Ireland forced overtime and won out 87–85 to progress to the next stage. Later that year, in the semi-final round, Ireland managed to go even further than Bree's team when they won a game in the second round. In the historic win over Bulgaria, O'Reilly again showed himself as a generational talent with an incredible stat line of 34 points and 18 rebounds.

As Ireland moved back to a more homegrown team, Cummins and O'Reilly headlined the new recruits. There was more help from around their age group too, as an exciting batch of new players were all about to enter the senior setup. Ian O'Boyle was a prolific shooter who had spent time in the States with NJIT before returning home. Jason Killeen was a 6'10 big man who had spent time at Winthrop and Augusta State and would play professionally in Malaysia, France and Ireland. Eleven years after his father played in European Qualifiers, Isaac Westbrooks followed in Jerome's footsteps and played for the senior team. Isaac's career was also in its infancy, and he would go on to play professionally in both Iceland and England before an excellent career at home.

On top of the Irish talent, there was also some new international talent too. Liam Farrell was a Canadian sharpshooter who had played in the Irish league for Limerick, winning Bosman of the Year in 2003. He was added alongside David Mitchell, an Australian-born big man who had played at Adams State University. As the new signings joined the team, it was hard to shake the idea that the original purpose of recruiting passport players had been lost. Ireland was no longer getting top Americans with strong Irish heritage. Instead, they were getting lower tier professionals, and it was understandable when people began to question whether the players were there to help Ireland or simply help themselves.

The first campaign was tough for the newcomers as the veteran leadership had been almost exclusively wiped away overnight. Switzerland came to Dublin and had Thabo Sefolosha back in their ranks as they won 86–58. The result quickly highlighted the clear gulf between where Ireland had been and where they now found themselves. Ireland went on to lose against both Romania and Cyprus and finished the group in third place with a 1–5 record. The team's main bright spot was the progress of captain Conor Grace who averaged 14.6 points across the three games.

As the year ended Greg Gurr lost his position as head coach. The Gurr era had left a feeling of doom and gloom around the national team as the glory years were over. A youth revolution was starting, but Ireland weren't yet ready to compete with the top European teams.

At the same time as the men were starting again with their youth movement, Ireland's women's team were closing in on their peak. The 2005 campaign had seen them come second in their group behind Sweden despite playing more than half of the campaign without Susan Moran. Susan was now retired from the game, and Michelle Aspelle was also unavailable to Mark Scannell. There was new talent waiting to break through though, with one of Ireland's greatest athletes, Lindsay Peat, amongst them. Peat was a multi-sport star who over the course of her career has represented Ireland in football, basketball and rugby as well as playing Gaelic football for Dublin. As a basketballer, she was a tenacious guard, and opposing teams struggled with her direct style and athleticism. Also coming in to the ranks were two exciting young talents with NCAA experience. Rachel Clancy had enjoyed a very good career at Duquense followed by Cal Poly and was another guard capable of causing problems. Perhaps the biggest hope was for Orla

O'Reilly. Orla was only seventeen and a half as herself and her twin sister Sinead were called up to the senior squad. Both went on to play at Binghampton, where Orla starred,averaging 11.7 points a game as a senior. She was six foot, but with the skills to do-it-all guard and she went on to have a successful pro career in Spain and then Australia. Even at this stage in 2007, people knew a very bright future was ahead for her.

In that qualification group, Ireland ended up winning just one of their six games. A five-point win over Norway was the highlight, with Niamh Dwyer top-scoring on 18 points. Dwyer at that stage was just twenty-five years old and was coming off a season playing in the EuroLeague in 2006, the only Irish player ever to do so. Niamh developed in Thurles before going on to America playing at junior college and then four years at Division I level for Monmouth University. After graduating she went on to play professionally in Lithuania, Latvia and later in England, as well as having a glittering domestic career mostly alongside her younger sister Grainne in Glanmire.

Despite the losses, there were positives to take for the squad, especially with Lindsay Peat's development, who averaged 10.5 points a game, good for second on the team behind Michelle Fahy. If Ireland could find one or two extra pieces to go alongside Fahy, Dwyer and Peat, there was hope that the Irish women could have their brightest days ahead of them.

Chapter 31: The Last Dance

2008 saw a major positive change that would reignite interest in the Men's national team with Jay Larrañaga returning to the fold as Ireland's first-ever player-coach. Jay understood the need for full investment in youth and in rebuilding the culture around the national team. In his first move as coach, he reached out to Mark Keenan and Pat Price, two of the country's leading coaches and asked them to join his staff. From the outset, Keenan realised that Jay trusted both of his coaches: 'Jay just becoming a coach at that time, he was very happy to lean on myself and Pat, and everything was really inclusive, deciding what's what. It was a great experience.' Price is an American who had come to Ireland and had enjoyed a lot of club success before joining the staff. At this point, he was at the start of a journey that would see him become an integral part of the youth development movement at the national level for the country. Pat was immediately taken by Larrañaga's approach, and the mutual respect was obvious. 'His humility. He's a guy steeped in tradition from a basketball family. He was a ten- or twelve-year pro, and he came in and just handles himself the right way. He's a wonderful man-manager, he gets that connection piece. He respected guys, and would give you respect rather than making people earn it. When you start off by giving a guy respect, you probably go further. He was wonderful with Mark, and he was wonderful with me.'

The focus on youth was something that was a clear discussion point at the time, and as Pat remembers, Larrañaga drove that. 'I think it was acknowledged at that stage. And most importantly acknowledged at the decision-making stage that the long-term benefit was going to be to provide an aspiration for these guys . . . . what's the pathway for an Irish domestic kid if we are really trying to develop the game? . . . That stuff was being discussed actively, and I think the guy that helped foster that was Jay . . . He even went to the extent, when he put that team together, it was half and half. We would actively try and encourage some of the up-and-coming Irish guys. We would have brought Cian Nihill to training camp, Kyle Hosford to training camp. Colin O'Reilly was hitting his stride at that stage, so he was getting a big role. But there was a segway into, let's make sure we have a proper representation here, that creates goodwill on the ground.'

The issue of goodwill on the ground was something Price was well aware of in Cork and was something that he struggled to comprehend at times. 'The longer I was here, the more people open up to you, and you hear the side rumblings, "sure he's not Irish at all", but back then I was like, you were pretty cool with the whole Jack Charlton era weren't you? . . . You would hear that talk. You would. When you're doing it, you're not taking in that kind of stuff. It's the same as the guys saying Irish first when they are wearing Man United jerseys, how do you even unwrap that?'

Ireland faced a tough group with Sweden, Georgia, Luxembourg and Slovakia, and critically, resources were becoming increasingly difficult for the team. Gone were the preparations that were possible in 2004 and 2005. Larrañaga was now facing the same issues Enda Byrt did as he fought for increased funding to give the team a chance at competing. The wider economy was starting to play a factor in 2008 too. In the middle of the first group of games, the Lehman Brothers Bank went bankrupt in one of the first major moves that triggered a significant economic recession that would devastate Ireland as the Celtic Tiger era came to an abrupt end.

At the time, of course, that wasn't the focus for the squad. There was some excitement around the team as Donnie McGrath was now progressing professionally in Europe, and he came in to take control of the offence. Another Australian big man Damian Matacz, who had played for Cork's Blue Demons in the Irish Super League also came into the squad. In the opening game, Chris Bracey top-scored on 18, but Ireland couldn't match Sweden away from home. The game was notable in the rise of young Swede Jonas Jerebko. Jerebko had 16 points and 10 rebounds against Ireland that day. The twenty-one-year-old played in Italy at the time but went on to play in the NBA for ten seasons including for the Celtics under Jay Larrañaga.

Things didn't get any easier in the second game as Georgia arrived in Dublin with a tough, experienced squad. They had seven-foot Nikoloz Tskitishvili who had played in the Arena with Georgia ten years earlier and had considerable NBA experience. He would play this time and score 8 points while Zaza Pachulia, who was with the Atlanta Hawks, led the team with 16 points and 9 rebounds. Donnie McGrath had his best game for Ireland with 32 points, but the gulf in class was apparent as Ireland lost convincingly. It wasn't all doom and gloom for

Ireland though, as they easily beat Luxembourg in their next game with McGrath, Larrañaga and Bracey combining for 43. In the final match of 2008, Ireland hosted Slovakia and lost an overtime heartbreaker. Trailing by nine going into the fourth quarter the team rallied and forced overtime. Unfortunately, the rally used up the last of their energy as they'd lose 95–88. Conor Grace was impressed again with 20 points and 15 rebounds while the reliable Chris Bracey added 22 in his last game for Ireland having started back in 2004.

2009 saw the young Irish revolution continue with another one of Jerome Westbrook's sons, Aaron, making the team. It also saw that Paddy Kelly, a teammate on Michael Bree's underage Irish team, finally got his opportunity at the European Qualifiers level. Kelly was the generation's best domestic player and to finally have him play for Ireland was something the public were happy to see.

Two more imports would also arrive into the team with Bryan Mullins debuting and Michael Williams returning. Mullins was a standout point guard for Southern Illinois and was in to run the team as Donnie McGrath was unavailable.

Mullins had only entered the country for the first time just weeks before he'd debut for the squad and it was a baptism of fire for him. Ireland had a disastrous start against Sweden scoring only 2 points in the opening quarter and never recovered, losing by 16. The team struggled to generate good shots as they shot 3/20 from long range and managed just 50 points at home. Bryan Mullins improved a lot in his second game as he scored 18 and Colin O'Reilly added a double-double. Still, Ireland was again heavily beaten by Georgia. On the 22 August 2009, Ireland hosted Luxembourg and won convincingly in what would turn out to be the last home European Qualification game of the era for Ireland. Colin O'Reilly scored 25, and Ian O'Boyle added 23 as Ireland showed they were still clearly above the countries competing at the Promotions Cup level.

Ireland finished out the 2009 campaign in the Slovak Republic . The team was linked to so much of the history that had come before them, but they were also distinctly different. Links to the early 1990s were there through the Westbrooks brothers and assistant coach Mark Keenan. The breakthrough era was represented by player-coach Jay Larrañaga, who had helped Ireland reach new heights and was now ushering in the new generation. The big difference compared to just years earlier was the reliance on home-developed talent. Only three of the team who played were not raised in Ireland and of those Justen Naughton only played two minutes. The Senior Men's team were finally getting to a point where they mirrored the Senior Women's squad with a mix of domestic talent and players with NCAA experience. Of the group in Slovakia that day, seven of the Irish players were twenty-eight or younger. The main push of the Irish-American era Senior Men's squad had ended in the playoff in Denmark in 2005, but now a new wave of domestic players were coming up to try and create their own chapter.

Larrañaga, in many ways, faced the same challenges as Enda Byrt originally faced in the early 1990s, with height and money being two major constraints. Even with those limitations, he saw plenty of talent, particularly in Colin O'Reilly, and there was still hope moving forward: 'I was always very impressed with Colin O'Reilly who could play in pro leagues throughout Europe. I think a big part of the success I was able to enjoy as a player was because of the Dan Callahan's, Marty Conlon's and Pat Burke's – that size – and even Alan Tomidy who I didn't get to play with but was on the team when they were younger, that level of big centers and power forwards who could play in the NBA and at a high level in Europe allowed us to compete. With our group, we had Jason Killeen, Mike Williams and Justen Naughton but getting a surplus of big guys was probably our biggest challenge.'

After the 2007 campaign, the women's team knew that they needed reinforcements if they were going to compete. Fortunately, they were on the way with Susan Moran leading the charge as she returned to the squad for the first time since 2004. After seeing the Olympics on TV in 2008, the bug was back for Ireland's biggest star, and she wanted to compete again. It was music to Coach Mark Scannell's ears as he was assembling his squad for the qualifiers. It was now ten years since the women's team had a one-point loss to Denmark that cost them qualification to the semi-finals. The team now had the ambition and the personnel to go further and make a big push for promotion. Hope was there again for Ireland, particularly because they had finally pieced together as close to a full-strength squad as possible. There was the inside duo of Michelle Fahy and Susan Moran, two of Ireland's best-ever players side by side and with games that complimented each other.

There was scoring punch from the perimeter with Niamh Dwyer and stability at the point guard spot with the experienced Michelle Aspelle back alongside the tenacious Lindsay Peat.

Ireland also added in their most effective Irish American ever as Mary Fox joined the team. Fox had a very strong career at Iowa State and had come to Ireland to play for head coach (and Irish assistant coach) Mark Ingle at DCU Mercy. Mary was player of the year in her first year for Mercy, and she utilised her Irish grandparents to play for the national team.

In Division B, there was a six-team group, which Ireland was in alongside Montenegro, and a four-team group that Sweden was in. For Ireland to get to the A division, they had to top their group, which involved ten games over two years. Scheduling didn't help as Ireland had to travel to the favourites Montenegro for the first game.

By the time the first quarter was over the game was effectively gone as Ireland failed to get out of the traps and trailed 24–10 after just ten minutes. Ireland won the rest of the game by two points, but the damage had been done in the early exchanges. Susan Moran proved she still had it, as she came out of retirement with a big performance of 19 points. Unfortunately, no other Irish player scored in double digits and the home team got 12 additional free throw attempts which helped seal the deal.

Just three days later the Slovenian's arrived into Limerick. Susan Moran led the way again with 22 points, but it was a masterclass from Michelle Aspelle with 20 points and 10 rebounds that saw Ireland claw back a six-point half-time deficit with a huge third quarter (21–7) and earn their first win of the campaign. Ireland then went on the road to Switzerland and picked up their second win three days later as they beat the Swiss 79-65. Any fears of repeating the poor start from the last away game were gone in the first quarter as Ireland scored 31 to lead by 9. Michelle Aspelle was inspirational as she continued her amazing form with 25 points, Moran had 19 and Dwyer and Fox's shooting combined for 25. Ireland were suddenly riding high and had two more games to close out 2008.

First up was Iceland, who had beaten Ireland in previous groups. A balanced attack including 10 points from Rachel Clancy saw Ireland win 68–59 in the National Basketball Arena. Ireland then travelled to the Netherlands for their final game of the year. The Netherlands had also won all of their games except for the Montenegro game, which they had lost by just 2 points away from home. Ireland had to do without Susan Moran, who had to return to the States for work, and her absence left too much to do. The Netherlands overcame 23 points and 12 rebounds from Mary Fox; no other Irish player made it into double digits. Ireland also had 24 turnovers to the Dutch team's 16. Although Ireland led by 4 points going into the fourth quarter, they couldn't close it out without Moran, and they lost 77–65.

Despite the Dutch disappointment it was still all to play for in 2009, and Ireland knew they were growing into the campaign. Promotion to the A division remained a realistic goal.

The year started with a rematch against Montenegro in Dublin on the 15 August. Ireland stormed out of the gates and led by 6 points after one quarter. The second and third quarters were back and forth, but Ireland extended their lead in both quarters, and at the end of three quarters they led 55–47. They were ten minutes from blowing the group wide open as Montenegro had yet to lose. Ireland's lack of experience in closing out big games came to haunt them – their offence ground to a halt in crunch time as they were held to just 12 fourth-quarter points.

Montenegro scored 23 as they escaped from Dublin with a hard-fought three-point win that had echos of the men's loss to Croatia in 2002.

All wasn't yet lost for Ireland though; they knew that they would earn a promotion playoff with Sweden if they could finish ahead of the Dutch. Ireland bounced back from the loss to Montenegro with back-to-back wins over the Slovenians and Swiss.

Two games remained: Iceland away and the Dutch at home. Nothing less than two wins would do, and Ireland also had to beat the Dutch by 12 to equal the teams' first-round result. No road game in Europe is easy though, and Ireland may have had one eye on the last game with the Netherlands as they lost to Iceland by 9 having trailed by 18 after three quarters. It was a bitterly disappointing day for Ireland as it ruled out a playoff with one game to go. For Susan Moran, the game was one that always stands out in her memory. 'I had a horrific game; I played so bad. I distinctly remember that. The ball would not go in the basket, which didn't happen very often, and I knew it was a really significant game.'

With nothing to play for Ireland still came back to Dublin and finished the campaign out on a high beating the Dutch by 5 in Dublin.

Aspelle led the way with 18, while Moran and Peat both had 13. The Iceland disappointment possibly overshadowed the progress that was being made. Still, Ireland was in touching distance of the promotion spots. Aside from Aspelle, no player was in their thirties, and the idea that the best was yet to come for this team was certainly possible.

Sadly, as the players left the court on the 29 August 2009, it was the last time any of them would play in a European Championship qualifier.

Away from the court, financial issues had engulfed Basketball Ireland. As a result, the senior national teams were completely stopped as the organisation found itself in massive debt. It was a gut punch for the country's top players as matters out of their control had ended their international dreams.

Chapter 32: The Reaction

'Basketball Ireland has taken the decision to deactivate both the senior men's and women's international teams due to the effects of a financial crisis within the organisation.' *RTE.ie*, Wednesday, 24 February 2010

Just like that, it was over.

One hundred and seventy-nine days after the Senior Women's team left the floor for the last time, the Irish national teams were disbanded.

As it transpired, Ireland was €1.2 million in debt due to various issues at Federation level. At the time, Paul Meany, who had been one of the domestic leaders in creating the National League, was forced to step in in a voluntary capacity to try and fix a difficult situation. 'This is a financial rather than a philosophical decision. We have had to cut back on every possible way, or we face the scenario of Basketball Ireland collapsing. This time last year we had twenty-seven staff. Now we have eleven. I am here in a voluntary capacity. FIBA have been very understanding about this and have given us a measure of support. We have always had a hand-to-mouth existence here, but a combination of bad financial information and maybe trying to develop the sport more quickly than was feasible has left us with no choice but to make these decisions.'

There was disbelief at the female players' situation, particularly as the team were homegrown and willing to do whatever they could to keep it all going, as Susan Moran explained; 'I never thought it would really end like that. My memories are of playing terrible in Iceland and hurting our chances of getting to A but being really excited about the group that we had and thinking, man, we had got that close. Yeah, we were getting older, but we still had a good group of players left on the team. The ripples of it not happening came out – I just couldn't believe it to be honest. I knew there were financial issues, and I knew there was stuff going on, but I'm a little removed . . . I didn't realise the extent of it and that it could shut the whole association down . . . I really thought the team would go ahead. I knew the finances were bad, but I thought maybe we'd make a go of it ourselves. I feel like everyone on that team were willing to fundraise or find money or pay. People wanted to play, but that wasn't even an option for us, so that made me sad . . . There's a big sense of incomplete. Not personally but as a team, that group of players who were pretty damn talented. We were all Irish, we weren't importing players or getting superstars from America, these were players who had gone to America, done the time, put in the work and came home. We had a good group so to not ever see what that group could have achieved is hard to reconcile, it's unfinished business.'

Niamh Dwyer shared those feelings back in 2012: 'To come so close to qualification and then have no team at all was just very frustrating . . . That team had grown up together, and we felt we were the right age – mid to late twenties. So it was disappointing. For us, the decision came out of the blue. I don't know how long the organisation thought about it. I don't have any of the details, and I don't really want to know. But from our perspective, the whole thing happened in the space of a month, so it was very hard to put in a protest or anything. It came as a shock. I went to the AGM, and they did say they hoped to get up and running in the next couple of years, but as of now, it is in limbo. I am twenty-nine this year and it would have been great to have had those couple of years. But we have lost out on two years of quality competition and it is going to take a lot of training and effort to build that up again. Things like that don't just happen. Susan Moran was there a couple of years ahead of me. It was over two and three years playing together and coming up through the ranks so it is going to be very hard to replicate that. It was an exceptionally committed group. A lot of players had gone abroad and improved their game. It seems easy for me to say, how can they not see that? But there were other factors involved in the decision that we were not privy to.'[li]

On the men's side, Pat Price was shocked not only by the news but the way that he heard it. 'I got a text from Francis O'Sullivan, I was literally lying in bed with the swine flu, I'll never forget it. I was laid up in bed, and it was something like, "did you get the *Indo*?". . . and that's how I found out, I literally read it in the paper, and of course, my initial reaction was unprintable. It's rearview mirror now, but it was tragic at the time.'

Conor Grace was also disappointed, but even at the time, there was a realisation that the women's team were impacted more than the men. 'The players were told we could email in our thoughts. It was bad for us and even worse for the women. The women weren't bringing in as many Americans as we were, they had played their way to that level.[lii]' The women's team manager at the time, Ann Diffney, highlighted the disappointment for the team: 'There was a late entry date of 16 January, which we begged Basketball Ireland to go for. If we ended up not entering, the fine would have been €2,500. But if you are €1.4m in debt, what difference does that make? And we would have been prepared to pay the fine anyway. We felt FIBA would have looked favourably on our case because we are a small nation, we did well in the last competition, and there were only nine countries in our division: we would have balanced it up. But we were not given the option of raising the money, so we were out in the cold. The Dutch team, which Ireland was in direct competition with to claim second spot in their division, has an annual budget of €1m. Ireland's budget, by comparison, was only €48,000. Disappointingly the journey for both teams ended at this point with more question marks than answers. For years it had been feared that overspending with the national team could cause problems for the rest of the game. Although the teams did have sizeable budgets (the men in particular), the issues that brought down the teams were primarily caused elsewhere in the organisation. Back in 1996, Enda Byrt was interviewed by Cliona Foley in the *Independent* about the possibility of Ireland making a breakthrough internationally. He gave a prophetic answer: 'Yeah, if we qualify, and it's a big if, then great, regular internationals here, but if the IBA don't get the organisational structure in place early to deal with such a massive commitment, that could be very embarrassing. So, there's a lot of work to be done on their side too.'[liii]

Chapter 33: The Aftermath

The anger and devastation that existed as the national teams were scrapped eventually subsided and were replaced by acceptance and an emptiness at the top of the sport. The highs that had been enjoyed over the previous twenty years were being followed by the lowest low the sport will hopefully ever face.

As people came to terms with the situation in the game, questions began to be asked regarding who was really to blame. For some people, the men's national team and the cost of the Irish American imports was an easy route to follow. Those who had been vocal opponents of the influx of Irish Americans now had their proof that they were right all along. Of course, there are two sides to every coin, and it is something that will divide opinion indefinitely . . .Still, with the benefit of time, it's worth looking back and assessing the path that Ireland, and particularly the men, went down.

When Enda Byrt first took over the goal was clear, Ireland needed some big bodies to supplement the Irish talent he already had. Without a doubt, he followed that and had great success in building a competitive international team. Throughout his tenure, he would clash with Noel Keating and others as he fought for the team to be better resourced, but at the time, during the early 1990s, the sport was hamstrung by a new national basketball arena, and the IBA struggled to back the national teams while keeping the game growing domestically.

During Byrt's time, the Bosman rule had opened the door to potential recruits, and had he not initiated the process almost fifteen years earlier, it almost certainly would have come in the mid-nineties regardless. Shortly after Enda was replaced as head coach, FIBA made a dramatic change in the regulations that suddenly made a whole wave of Irish American's available. The timing couldn't have been better for Ireland and the then CEO Scott McCarthy. A new American coach with amazing connections had just fallen into his lap, and the financial situation of the sport was excellent. During the Celtic Tiger, basketball was thriving but still was under-profiled in McCarthy's opinion. A decision was made to further explore the Irish-American route with the goal of securing a greater media profile and new revenue streams, including television income. When Debbie Massey took over Basketball Ireland, her initial SWOT analysis of the sport contained the point, 'get behind the national teams. We need the success and consequent and related TV financial and profile bonuses'.

As Ireland progressed through to the semi-final round and throughout the 2005 campaign, the sport's profile did improve. The media was drawn in by names like Pat Burke and Marty Conlon and Ireland's competitive team. The 2005 playoff with Denmark was perhaps the biggest what-if moment the sport may ever have. If Ireland had won the playoff and made it into the A division, it could have done wonders for the sport's profile. Yet those rewards weren't a foregone conclusion either. Ireland had an ageing squad who would have needed considerable support to compete – it could have been even more catastrophic for Ireland by 2010 if the Irish had beaten Denmark.

Another question worth examining was whether or not the financial impact of getting to the A division was everything the governing body had hoped for. Denmark is a similar-sized country to Ireland in basketball terms, although they have a more developed professional league. They progressed to the A division, so what impact did it have and were Ireland right in thinking that there was huge potential financially in progression?

In short, it didn't have a major impact. Thomas Bilde worked on Danish TV for the Irish playoff, and he points to the advancement to the A division being more important for the people already established within the sport. It didn't bring in huge new levels of participation. It did however boost the confidence of their domestic players who were suddenly getting opportunities to go abroad and play professionally. An Irish win likely wouldn't have had a similar impact, due to the disconnect between the team and the rest of the sport. Financially it didn't do much either, according to Bilde. There was a television deal that came with the A division, but it wasn't game-changing: 'Not an amount that you would say, this is a good deal. A lot of the money that we put both into the Danish league and the federation . . .you had to earmark, you had to spend it back on promoting the league and developing the league. They were making some money, there was a TV deal with some money, but it was not a big number.'

Denmark's situation highlighted how Ireland's thinking was likely flawed as they tried to use the national team as a way to bring more people and money into the game. The Denmark situation raises concerns about the economics of a national team ever progressing to a higher level than they can currently achieve. In a way, Ireland was forced to try new routes because the Irish government wasn't supporting them. The CEO at the time that Ireland increased the American presence, Scott McCarthy, later went on to work in British judo, where £6 million of his £8 million budget came from government support. The case wasn't the same in Ireland. 'I think the Sports Council gave us £130,000 out of our £1 million turnover. They weren't a big part of our budget back then. I remember thinking the Irish government were way behind, the most we saw from the Irish Sports Council at the time was around £145,000, so we were always looking for ways to generate more income through TV and all kinds of stuff.' Sadly, for basketball, elite sports funding can often be split into two categories; the GAA and potential podium sports. In 2021, after a decision by the Irish government to provide grants of equal value for both male and female inter county GAA players, 67 per cent of the total elite funding available goes to the GAA.

Medals are often the barometer for the rest of the high-performance funding. As a result, lots of funding can go into minor sports with an individual medal chance rather than mass participation sports requiring numerous funding cycles to develop into a contender. This issue came up in Britain when basketball was compared to some of the minority winter sports that received ample financing. Lisa Wainright, the CEO of British basketball, highlighted the issue in an article in the *Independent*: 'But I have to ask – what is the purpose of a medal? I say that in relation to inspiring a nation. Policy could be different. For kids between the ages of eleven and fifteen, basketball is the second largest team sport in the country after football. The reach that this has in terms of inspiring kids in hard-to-reach areas of society is huge.' [liv]

As long as medals are the main priority for governments, it is hard to see a point where GB or indeed Ireland will ever get significant high-performance investment, despite the potential for impact in other ways.

So how can a sport ever progress without government support? The obvious answer is commercial support. In Ireland, that environment is challenging as the big three sports of rugby, GAA and football dominate that space. One of the restrictions that affects the commercial ability of smaller sports is the crowd capacity and the reduced or lack of ability to do corporate hospitality. The National Basketball Arena can take less than 2,000 people and has no corporate hospitality options. It means that basketball's ability to generate match-day income anywhere close to the twelve million that the FAI reported in 2018 is impossible. One option is to move beyond the National Arena and take a risk with a much bigger venue. This brings major risks for the sport and is likely impossible unless underwritten with government funding. In 2019, Irish hockey took a risk like this for their Olympic Qualifiers. Their match with Canada was a famous moment in Irish sport as they booked their place in the Olympics, courtesy of a dramatic penalty shootout. The risk still left the Hockey Federation with an €80,000 financial hole, putting the sport under significant financial pressure.

It's worth remembering the words in a 1999 edition of the *Irish Basketball Magazine*: 'It will eventually come down to money and commitment. On the financial front, international basketball is a bit like an intergalactic black hole that sucks up funds and shows little in return. From a commitment perspective, the basketball community, at all levels, must decide how important international success is. The two are closely linked.'[lv]

Outside of the finances, enough time has passed to look objectively back at the Irish-American era and judge what happened. Enda's initial recruitment drive undoubtedly set Ireland up to be a competitive middle-tier European country. That he did so on a shoestring budget made it more impressive. Although some disagreed with Ireland's route, it can't be argued that the policies to bring in players helped develop Ireland rapidly into a very competitive team. Had Ireland been able to have their top players consistently, they would almost certainly have reached the top sixteen of Europe and could have stayed there for a time.

Even during that time of winning, a disconnect existed, and everybody was aware of it. Gerry Fitzpatrick was involved in the semi-final round and the 2005 campaign. He knew that it was happening too much in isolation as people couldn't associate with the players.'When the team was winning, and the crowds were big, and there was the excitement of maybe going to Division A, there was a lot of publicity and interest around the team, but aside from that it pretty much existed

404

in a vacuum. Generally, people had no clue that we had two Irish players who play for Reggio Calabria; who are they, where are they from, and what do they do?'

John O'Connell was one of the die-hard early Irish Americans, and he was with the programme from the early nineties into the transition into an almost fully Irish-American team. In later years he was worried about some of the recruits maybe not understanding the Irish heritage as much as himself, Dan Callahan and the other early pre-Bosman-rulerecruits. The idea had always been to be a stop-gap, and O'Connell always thought that way: 'I remember as we moved on with my group that they didn't want to move on with more Americans. They never wanted more than five on a team, and it seemed reasonable. How are you going to build the game if you have nothing but American-born players on it . . . What's your goal? Are we helping to advance the game in Ireland? That ultimately should be the goal whatever we are doing . . . raising interest in the game back home. I thought that was always Enda's point – we are going to use you stallions here to make kids see how exciting the game could be for them. I think Enda's view was always a temporary goal;to use the guys to try and bring some excitement into the game and then get Irish kids interested.'

Pat Burke did help to raise that interest, and his presence helped do that more than any other. Still, he also knew that the team was missing homegrown success stories; the public couldn't fully buy into an Irish-American squad. Pat and many of the Americans experienced that same attitude away from the court, and it was not always an easy experience to be American-raised players coming in to represent Ireland. Guys were regularly questioned in hotel gyms or bars about who the real Irish team were. Eventually Pat and the guys gave up trying to explain their Irish connections and why they wanted to represent the country. 'If we went out for a pint, it was the people of Ireland who were telling us that. You're not Irish. I remember I was in a pub in Dublin, and I was almost being surrounded by some guys who wanted to kick my ass, and I'm just not going into what we are doing here anymore, I just stopped talking about it. You'd meet a header, and they'd be sitting there saying you're not Irish, and you'd just be like, OK fine. What am I going to do, start talking about my passport and my story? It's nothing. A lot of similar stories were coming back in the locker room to us, and we just knew no matter what we did, it was never going to be the dream vision of Irish basketball getting there and how they got there.

'Justen Naughton is a huge historian. We were in a pub having a get-together, and he would sit there talking about the situation. Justen would talk about the millions of people who emigrated to the US and this, that and the other, and I said, "Jesus, Naughty, why are you even trying to convince anybody you know what I tell them? I fart shamrocks, F off!"'

Justen Naughton came in at an interesting point – in his first game, Ireland played with no Irish players. Yet, just four years later, he was surrounded by young Irish talent. His perspective changed dramatically during that time too. 'I kind of had that awakening after being there a couple of years. The coaching staff were totally behind the idea of having these American almost All-Stars, NBA players and from the top leagues in Europe. I wasn't that level, I was hoping to be that level, I was ambitious, but I didn't have the idea there was something off about this because of how supportive Basketball Ireland was towards those guys. At the time, when I first got to the team, I was one of many Irish Americans, and I felt that that was a good thing because I felt Basketball Ireland understood basketball is not a big sport in Ireland, and it can be promoted more. And what better way to promote it than to bring back Americans with Irish connections to uplift the sport. At the same time, after being there for a couple of years, and especially when the turn happened and all of those guys left, I started to understand that they had gone too far in support of the top American players and they had neglected the Irish born-and-raised players. I saw that the guys who came up through the Irish system, they were really good players and they were passionate about Irish basketball, but they didn't gain anything from having a team full of Irish Americans for a decade. The sport in Ireland didn't really gain what it seemed like they would have wanted to. I think Basketball Ireland had the right intentions bringing all those guys, myself included, but I don't know if it worked out the way they hoped.'

The biggest negative that can be attributed to the Irish team during the era is that it operated within a vacuum and didn't benefit the rest of the sport. There were good intentions to use the team to create a trickle-down effect to help the game grow, yet it often lacked the additional follow-up tactics on how to truly do that. Some of the Irish Americans lamented how during their time they didn't do any clinics or community work, and were never even asked. With that isolation from the rest of the sport came a lack of connectivity to the youth national teams. In many ways, it is no wonder that so few Irish players progressed through to make an impact in the early 2000s. Peter O'Hehir's piece in '85 said, 'it must be decided whether we want to become competitive in the short-term or to work for long-term improvement and development. Priorities will be tested'. Priorities were tested, and short-term competitiveness was definitely valued over long-term development.

Whether the whole approach was right or wrong is easy for a hurler on the ditch to decide. But the real discussion is perhaps best had by someone like Adrian Fulton. Adrian grew up in a household under a former Irish senior coach, and he then played in those Enda Byrt years and throughout the Bill Dooley years. He is now an assistant coach with the Senior Men's team himself. When he looks back at the era, you can see how difficult it is to assess:

'You're always going to want as a coach to have some homegrown players. My dad and I would have had a different perspective. He was very much of the opinion at the time, even though he supported us and supported me, that there's too many Irish American's on the team. . . If you can't compete at the level that you're trying to compete at, cut it down and try and compete at the level of four countries or smaller nations, try and compete with a couple of guys. My view was very simple: "Dad, I don't care who's on the team as long as I am." I never really thought of them as Irish Americans. I knew them, and when you know their perspective and their views, there were very few guys that would have only been there because they felt obligated. The rest wanted to be there and appreciated their heritage and wanted to do their best and help us.

'In (2002), I was older and maybe more balanced in my perspective. I was coaching at school and looking for player pathways and thinking maybe we are going a little bit too much in this direction. It's a fine line. If I was putting myself in the position of the coach, I would probably pick the best team I could get my hands on – that might not be the right thing to do, but I probably would have gone down the same road. Maybe it's a case of trying to get the balance. But nobody seemed to have a problem with Jackie Charlton selecting John Aldridge or Ray Houghton or these guys. That was widely celebrated. Why? Because they got to the World Cup and they had some great success. They got to the World Cup quarter-final and so on, so they didn't care who was in the team. It's a tough one. You're always going to have to come down on one side or the other. There's always going to be a big divide there.'

Fulton's final point about the Irish football team was a commonly used one by people involved in the programme, and it holds merit.

In 2020, Ireland played a competitive football match for the first time since 1975 where all eleven starting players were born in Ireland. Better yet, in one of Ireland's proudest sporting moments, the penalty shootout to reach the quarter-final of Italia '90, all of Ireland's penalty takers were born in the UK.

It's not just football either; Ireland's famous rugby win over the All Blacks in Chicago included a try by South-African born CJ Stander. Ireland's famous World Cup cricket win against Pakistan was helped with the final runs by Trent Johnston from Australia. The examples are endless.

Judging our basketball history purely by results doesn't make sense. Had Ireland beaten Denmark, would the Irish people think differently of Jay Larrañaga or Dan Callahan?

Maybe.

Regardless of the end results, Ireland did become more competitive for many years and brought a lot of joy to basketball people. It's important to remember that the team went from a complete afterthought to a well-respected European team. They did so with a group of players who mainly had the purest of reasons; to help Ireland progress.

To Irish people, they were these big European stars, and yet for many they are NBA or NCAA coaches, police officers, financial advisors and even a movie producer.

It may not have ended perfectly, but both the Irish and Irish Americans who represented Ireland during our golden era on the floor, deserve the credit and thanks for doing so.

Epilogue

'There is a lot of excitement regarding the EuroBasket draw. This is a big step for Irish basketball overall – to be on the cusp of competing at the highest level of basketball in Europe is something that has been a long time in the works. So many leaders in the game, players and coaches throughout the country, have worked hard to get us to this point. Looking forward to seeing us test our mettle and to have the opportunity to show what we're capable of at a high level.' Dr Tim Rice, Chairman of Basketball Ireland's Elite Performance Committee, *www.ireland.basketball*, August 2021

They say timing is everything. When I started writing this book as Covid started taking a grip of Ireland back in April 2020, I had no idea what it was about to become in my life. It made me reflect on my own basketball journey a huge amount, and probably raised some regrets in terms of my own involvement with the national team. For a variety of reasons, I never got to represent Ireland in a full senior international, something that will always be an unscratched itch. Equally, what I didn't know as I started to look back at an era of progression and EuroBasket qualifiers was just how close Ireland was to a return to the big stage.

The return to the limelight has been a gradual one, that really started back in 2014 as Irish Select teams began being assembled to compete internationally. I was hugely fortunate to be a part of the strangest and most exciting journeys Ireland has ever been on. In 2015, an Irish Select team featuring eleven Irish-born players, including Colin O'Reilly (as player-coach) and Conor Grace, went to China to play in the Sino-European Games. The team competed with an Italian U23 team, a Russian universities team and the Chinese national team, featuring Yi Jianlian, the seven-foot, former 6th pick in the NBA draft. The Chinese game was broadcast on state television in China as a group of Irish amateurs played in front of an audience unlike any Irish team has ever played in front of before. I was lucky enough to start that game, and it will forever go down as my moment in the green jersey I'll always cherish, despite it not being a full cap.

The real return of the national teams started back in 2016, as Ireland returned to Small Countries level (the new name of the Promotions Cup). Both teams currently compete under FIBA's stricter new rules that allow only one player that didn't have their citizenship before their sixteenth birthday per team. These new rules mean that even if Ireland wanted to return to the Irish-American recruiting plan, it wouldn't be possible. That said, Irish Americans have continued to have an impact on Irish teams. Brian Fitzpatrick was Ireland's leading scorer in the 2016 Small Countries, and Fiona O'Dwyer, who grew up playing Gaelic football in the States, has been a regular contributor for Ireland's women in both 5x5 and 3x3 competitions.

The return to competition saw the Irish women continue their near misses as they claimed silver in both 2016 and 2021. The 2018 version was another familiar story, as they hosted a tournament but didn't get quite what they hoped, finishing fifth overall. The men's journey was also a struggle initially as many key players were missing in both 2016 and 2018. The 2016 team finished fifth while the 2018 group finished with a respectable bronze under American coach Pete Strickland (one of the early American pioneers in Irish basketball).

In 2021 though, there was an air of destiny around the men's team as they hosted the tournament for the first time since the famous Promotions Cup win in 1994. The tournament was due to be held in Limerick in 2020, but due to the Covid-19 pandemic, the games were moved into August 2021 and back to the National Basketball Arena. For anyone looking for parallels to the '94 team, you wouldn't have to look far, as the captain of that team, Mark Keenan, was now the head coach of the 2021 squad. Adrian Fulton, another one of Ireland's international heroes, who was Mark's backup in 1994, was now backing him up as an assistant coach. What made the moment even more special for the Fulton family was that Adrian's son CJ had graduated to become the team's starting point guard, despite being just eighteen years of age. Elsewhere on the squad, Jason Killeen was the only holdover from the previous EuroBasket journey in 2009 and fortunately, he was able to captain the team.

Despite there being no spectators allowed at the games, the Irish fans at home would quickly see that the modern squad was everything that they had always hoped for. The starting five for the duration of the tournament featured CJ Fulton, who had already starred domestically, winning a Super League at just seventeen years of age, and was about to start his career in Lafayette (following in the footsteps of John Brennan and Paul Cummins). Joining him in the backcourt was Sean Flood, who was coming off a successful professional season in Germany. Sean was another that had made a breakthrough at a young age into successful Super League teams and had then gone over to America to college. Lorcan Murphy, the most athletic domestic player

Ireland has ever seen, had dominated the Irish leagues for over six years and he was getting his chance to show just how good he was. And then on the inside, there was the young dynamic duo of Jordan Blount and John Carroll. Blount was from a family steeped in Irish basketball tradition and had long been on the radar of Irish fans. Having been dominant at a young age in Neptune, Blount went to England and then Gran Canaria before eventually ending up playing college basketball at UIC in Chicago. Jordan was a do-it-all forward who was coming into the tournament off a successful year in Spain's third division. John Carroll beside him had a similar journey having left Ireland at age sixteen to follow his dream in the States. Some injuries had halted his progress at times but Carroll had enjoyed an amazing Division I college career at Hartford where he averaged 15 points a game as a junior (14 as a senior) and ended up ranking 9th overall in Hartford's Division I scorers. After an injury cut short his debut season professionally, Carroll had also excelled in Spain during a Covid-impacted season.

The excitement around the team was borne from the idea that there was a young core of Irish developed players who were easily recognisable and ready to contribute. Will Hanley from Connecticut was the lone Irish American on the team and in reality, he was surplus to requirements as Ireland rampaged through the tournament. That said, Hanley, whose grandmother came from Cork originally, fit into the team seamlessly and added a veteran presence that had played professionally at the highest levels including the ACB in Spain.

As the tournament played out, Ireland was never seriously tested and were able to win convincingly. As much as the moment was savoured by Irish fans, it was clear to everybody involved that this was, just like '94, a graduation moment for the country.

At the time of writing (October 2021), Ireland has now re-entered the EuroBasket qualifiers for the first time since 2009. It is a return to the main stage of European basketball, where Irish people feel they truly belong. Undoubtedly the excitement and build-up is there on both sides. The men's team have the young core who have already delivered gold, and there is the possibility of more as players like Aidan Igiehon (Grand Canyon University, formerly of Louisville) were born and raised in Ireland and seemingly have a desire to play for the national team. It's in no way a stretch to believe Ireland could have a team full of professional players internationally who are supplemented by the top talents at home.

The women's team is no different, as a youth infusion has already happened. In 2017, Ireland won silver in the FIBA U18 European Championships and got promoted to the A Division. It was the first time an Irish team had ever been promoted and they did it in front of a packed National Basketball Arena in Dublin. That team were led by a golden generation of Claire Melia, Rachel Huidjsens, Sorcha Tiernan, Bronagh Power-Cassidy and Dayna Finn. That core would also win bronze and get promoted again at U20 level and Finn also spearheaded Ireland's first-ever win at A level in the U18 Championships in 2018. With that core alone, there are reasons to be optimistic, but there are also signs of more talent coming through that could mean Ireland become very competitive again internationally within the decade.

The other noticeable positive is off the floor: as of 2021, Basketball Ireland has cleared its debt of €1.2 million and is primed to support the growth of the game for the coming years.

What unfortunately hasn't changed is the financial support that the international teams receive. Irish national basketball is currently still on a self-funding model, where the players and their families have to fundraise to cover the majority of their costs. In an era where multiple inter-county Gaelic football and hurling teams have budgets over €1 million per year, one of Ireland's biggest participation sports can't even have its players funded to go to the European Championships. Ireland has lost lots of talented players in the past, and the worry remains that many more players will be lost in the future if they are not supported financially.

The overall sentiment for now though is one of hope as Ireland re-enter EuroBasket. Hopefully, for Irish fans, the new journey won't be plagued with the near misses and what-ifs of years gone by. With so many bright young stars, there's no reason that the next chapter won't be more positive.

The other hope is that the Irish teams get the support they deserve. The absence of the teams for many years have shown people just how much they are missed when they aren't there. Now that a new generation of Irish-developed talent is there to take it forward, hopefully, the public will get behind the team in a way they have never fully done before.

Regardless of any reflections on past generations, successes or misgivings, I'm certain of one thing, if the next generation of Irish talent care half as much about representing Ireland as the majority of Irish Americans who came before them did, Ireland will have a national team to be proud of.

References

[i] Foley, C. Goodbye to Burgerland and Blarney. Sunday Independent, 18 March 1990, p.31.

[ii] Whelan, J. Byrt puts it on the line. *Irish Independent,* 12 December, 1989. P.9.

[iii] Whelan, J. 1989. Byrt puts it on the line. *Irish Independent,* 12 December 2020.P.9.

[iv] Gorman, L. The Byrt File, *Irish basketball Magazine,* 1989/90 Season, No. 13, P.14

[v] Spillane, N. 1989, Cork official lashes basketball set-up. *Evening Echo,* November 7th 1989. P.16

[vi] Basketball win likely for Ireland. *Irish Independent,* May 24th, 1958, P.16

[vii] Kelly, L. 1977, Understrength Irish face tough test. *Irish Press,* April 6th, 1977, P.11

=[viii] Stokes, J. 1980, Giant sized task for the Irish, *Belfast Telegraph,* January 3rd, 1980, P.31

[ix] Neptune line up top teams, *Irish Press,* March 20th, 1981, P.13

[x] Spillane, N. Ireland name Demons pair, *Irish Examiner,* March 26th, 1981

[xi] Byrt, E. European Basketball Championships, *Basketball Ireland Magazine,* Vol.1 No. 3, Summer 1981, P.15

[xii] Basketball seeking out the Irish-American connection, *Evening Echo,* January 14th, 1983, P.14

[xiii] Shannon. K, Hanging from the Rafters, 2009. P.393.

[xiv] Spillane, N. Two Cork Players in International Squad, *Evening Echo,* April 17th, 1982, P.12

[xv] Hehir, P. Budweiser Tour 1983, *Basketball Ireland Magazine,* Vol 4, No 1. Winter 1983/84 P.18

[xvi] The astonishing demise of the Irish coach who promoted boxing's richest fight…and world peace. The 42.ie, Jan 28th, 2019

[xvii] American Producing Too Many Apples, *Western People,* November 23rd, 1983, P.4

[xviii] Hehir, P. Worthy Displays by Irish, *Irish Press,* April 23rd, 1984, P.14

[xix] Hehir, P. Squad chosen for Senior Four-Countries Championships, *Basketball Ireland Magazine,* March 1985 P.3.

[xx] Reid, P. Tough task for Juniors, *Irish Press,* March 26th, 1986, P.14

[xxi] Keating, N. *Basketball Ireland Magazine,* Vol.1, No.1, November 1980, P.4

[xxii] McGee, T. *Irish Basketball Magazine,* ICS Cup Final Programme, No.11, 1988/89 season, P.5

[xxiii] O'Hehir, P. Kenny is Malta bound, *Irish Press,* December 6th, 1988, P.37

422

xxiv Whelan, J. US Stars to knock stripes off opposition in Sheffield, *Irish Independent*, April 6th, 1990, P.16

xxv Curtis, R. This one is strictly for the Byrts, *The Star*, November 8th, 1989

xxvi Whelan, J. Top two out in the cold for US Tour, *Irish Independent*, November 3rd, 1989, P.14

xxvii American trio boost Ireland's cup hopes, *Irish Press*, December 12th, 1990, P. 59

xxviii *IBBA Basketball Magazine*, September 1991, No.19, P.4

xxix Baneham, M. *Basketball Ireland Magazine*, 1981, Vol 2. No.1 Autumn

xxx Hartigan, L. *Basketball Ireland Magazine*, 1981

xxxi Ten off to Cuba, *Irish Indepenent*, April 10th, 1984, P.13

xxxii Hehir, P. Concern for squad named by Hartigan, *Irish Free Press*, March 15th, 1991, P.79

xxxiii Post World University Games CUSAI Report, 1993

xxxiv Foley, C. Resign shock for Irish Seniors, *Irish Independent*, May 24th, 1994, P.13

xxxv Judge Y, 'Coach' IBA Official Basketball Magazine, Number 28, November, P.12 1994

xxxvi Foley, C. Mark: We did it for Enda, *Irish Independent*, June 9th, 1994, P78

xxxvii Mooney, B. IBA open door for Byrt, *Irish Examiner*, January 17th, 1995, P.17

xxxviii Post World University Games CUSAI Report 1995

xxxix Post World University Games CUSAI Report 1995

xl Shannon, K. Blow to Byrt as McCarthy ruled out of squad, *Irish Examiner*, May 15th, 1996, P.14

xli Irish cry foul as Cyprus win, *Irish Independent*, May 23d, 1996, P.47

xlii Shannon, K. Coaches must stress outside shooting, *Irish Examiner*, May 27th, 1997, P.57

xliii Foley, C. New sports body gets real clout. *Irish Independent*, June 24th, 1999, P.18

xliv Foley, C. Irish Coach Byrt gets sack, *Irish Independent*, November 19th, 1999, P.10

xlv Foley, C. New boss calls for cream of the crop. *Evening Herald*, February 17th, 2000, P.80

xlvi O'Hara, A. Crowd trouble mars Irish win. *Irish Independent*, January 24th, 2002, P.23

xlvii Mooney, B. Coach hopes Ireland can end on a high note. *Irish Examiner*, January 15th, 2003, P.24

xlviii McHale, J. A feast from the top table, *Evening Echo*, January 23rd, 2003, P.46

xlix McHale, J. Jay proud to wear green, *Evening Echo*, January 22nd, 2003, P.41

l O'Hara, A. Burke boost for Ireland, *Irish Independent*, September 2nd 2004, P. 26

li Duggan, K. Jumping through hoops for the cause, *Irish Times*, January 14th, 2012, Onli

lii Jump shots: The long road with Conor Grace, *Pundit Arena Website*, March 12, 2013 liii Foley, C. Burke and Tomidy honoured in the U.S., *Irish Basketball Magazine,* April 1996, P.5.

liv How the British Basketball funding crisis was brought to the fore by UK Sport's Winter Olympic outlay, *Independent.co.uk,* February 28th, 2018

lv 'Basketball Ireland Magazine, 'Getting there but still much to do', No.4 January 1999, P.18

Printed in Great Britain
by Amazon